BABYLONIAN INSCRIPTIONS

IN THE COLLECTION OF
JAMES B. NIES

VOLUME I

BABYLONIAN INSCRIPTIONS IN THE COLLECTION OF JAMES B. NIES—VOL. I

LETTERS AND CONTRACTS FROM ERECH WRITTEN IN THE NEO-BABYLONIAN PERIOD

BY
CLARENCE ELWOOD KEISER, PH. D.
MEMBER OF THE YALE BABYLONIAN SEMINARY

NEW HAVEN: YALE UNIVERSITY PRESS
LONDON: HUMPHREY MILFORD
OXFORD UNIVERSITY PRESS
MDCCCCXVIII

CONTENTS.

Page

Introductory Remarks 7

Name Indices
- Masculine Names 11
- Feminine Names 33
- Names of Scribes 33
- Names of Deities 33
- Names of Temples 34
- Names of Places 35
- Names of Canals 36
- Names of Gates 36

Catalogue 37

Autographed Texts .... Plates I–LX

LETTERS AND CONTRACTS FROM ERECH WRITTEN IN THE NEO-BABYLONIAN PERIOD

INTRODUCTORY REMARKS.

The one hundred and seventy-seven texts here published belong to the private collection of the Rev. Dr. James B. Nies of Brooklyn, New York. The collection, consisting of cylinders, vases, seals, objects in copper and bronze, tablets, etc., contains texts of nearly all the important periods of Babylonian history, from the Archaic to the Seleucid era. By far the larger number belong to the time of the Ur Dynasty; while the First Dynasty, Neo-Babylonian, and Persian periods are well represented. In a general way the material consists of important historical and votive inscriptions, hymns and prayers, letters, contracts and various other legal documents, exercise tablets, temple administrative records, etc.

The present texts consist of letters, Nos. 1–94; legal documents, Nos. 95, 97–130, 133; and temple administrative records, Nos. 96, 131, 132, 134–177. Their provenance is Erech, as is evident from the mention of this city, or otherwise from the contents. No. 126, however, is dated at Babylon; while Nos. 116, 123 are dated at the city Kar-^{d}Nanâ; No. 97 at the city Bît ^{m}Shabaḫi-ilu; and Nos. 98, 99, 102, 103, 115, 117, 125 at places in the district belonging to the ^{d}Bêlit of Erech.

Most of the letters are unbaked, and many, as the autographed texts show, are egible only in part. On the other hand the contracts are, as a whole, well preserved.

The texts belong to the Neo-Babylonian period (625–539 B. C.), and the first two reigns (539–522 B. C.) of the Persian. Thus in the legal and administrative texts are represented the reigns of Nabopolassar, Nebuchadrezzar, Evil-Merodach, Neriglissar, Nabonidus, and the two Persian kings Cyrus and Cambyses. Two belong to the period immediately before Nabopolassar's time: No. 134 is dated in the reign of the Assyrian king Gishshar-shum-ukîn (668–648 B. C.), formerly read Shamash-shum-ukîn; and No. 159 in the reign of his successor Kandalanu (648–625 B. C.). The letters, as is commonly the case, are undated; but for paleographic reasons, as well as from the personal names mentioned, they must be assigned to this period. Nos. 3 and 17, however, can be placed more definitely as they mention the 15th and 14th years of Nabonidus respectively. No. 93 is addressed to "the king of countries," which no doubt refers to one of the Persian kings, as in the contracts these bear the title "king of Babylon, king of countries." The writer is Bêl-nâdin-aplu, a name occurring on texts dated in the reign of Cyrus, thus indicating this ruler as the probable addressee.

With few exceptions the letters relate to matters of a purely administrative character; a number (see catalogue) being addressed to temple officials. For example, No. 13 is apparently a reply to a letter from the addressee. In No. 67 a request is made that wine be sent for the sacrifices to the sun-god Shamash; so in No. 77 that wool be given to the messenger sent by the writer. A number refer to transactions in money: No. 5 in which two individuals are asked to bring with them, when coming to Larsa, twenty mine of silver for the writer; No. 47 in which the writer specifies the disposition to be made of the fifteen shekels of silver that he sends; or No. 71 requesting the cancelling of a loan of five mine of silver, as it had been paid at a specified time.

A few give information about the grain sent by an individual for a stated purpose (e. g. No. 7); or concerning grain in Barsip^{ki} (No. 59). In Nos 2, 26, etc., the writer asks his readers not to be negligent in their guarding of the temple Eanna. In Nos. 18, 34, 62, 93 reference is made to a common oriental custom, convenanting with salt. No. 93 is a report made to the king, presumably by one of his officials. So also No. 94 is a report made by a subordinate to temple officials concerning a certain field. In these last two is to be noted the absence of the salutation so common in the letters.

The letters are of special interest to the student of history or civilization in so far as they add to our knowledge of the temple administration, refer to special phases of the daily life of the people, or mention such details, for example, as new personal names. The chief value, however, is to be found in the philological material that they offer Assyriologists.

The character of the other texts, i. e. the contracts and the lists, is indicated in the catalogue. The primary object of this series being to present only the texts with indices to scholars, attention is simply called to a few facts of value which these texts offer.

The relation, or rank, of the many temple officials is often a difficult matter to determine. In the letters the *šatammu*, *bêl-piqitti*, and *qîpu* are frequently mentioned. Nos. 108 and 126 are important in this respect. In 108:14–15 the *bêl-piqitti* is shown to be subordinate to the *qîpu*, while in 126:9–10 he is subordinate to the *šatammu*.

In the published texts, and in a number belonging to the Yale Babylonian Collection (in course of preparation for publication by a member of the Yale Babylonian Seminary) reference is made to a class of temple servants called *širqu*. The interesting fact about these *širaqu* is the mark they bear, and with which perhaps they were branded. This mark was also made upon animals. Only two of our texts, Nos. 120 and 169, mention this group, but from 120:4 it seems evident that the mark upon them was a star; as here the phrase, in the other places written phonetically *kak-kab-tu,* is written ideographically, namely *MUL,* the ideogram for star.

No. 167 is of interest as suggestive of the observance of a day something like the Hebrew Sabbath. See similar texts and discussion by Clay, *Miscellaneous Inscriptions, Yale Oriental Series, Babylonian Texts,* Vol. I, Nos. 46–51, and p. 75 ff.

It is with much pleasure that I express to Dr. Nies my sincere thanks for the opportunity of copying his texts and for making possible their publication; also my grateful appreciation and deep obligation to my teacher, Professor Clay, the editor of this series, for his numerous critical and helpful suggestions.

C. E. KEISER.

New Haven, Conn.

NAME INDICES.

Personal Names.

Abbreviations: b., brother; *cf.*, confer; d., daughter; f., father; gf., grandfather; gs., grandson; h., husband; m., mother; pl., plural; s., son; w., wife; NBC, Nies Babylonian Collection.

Determinatives: *âl*, city; *amêl*, homo; *d*, deus, dea; *f*, feminine; *ki*, place; *m*, masculine; *meš*, plural; *nâr*, canal.

Masculine Names.

A-bi-ri-ilu, f. *Nabû-zêr-ukîn*, 177:33.
Ab-di-iá, 13:1.
Abi-iá, f. *Ṣillâ*, 43:20.
Abi-ul-îdi, s. *Bulluṭu*, 171:8.
^{amêl}*addupu*, gf. *Bêl-iddin*.
Ag-ga-a, f. . . ., 25:44.
^{amêl}*agâru*, gf. *Nabû-bâni-aḫi*.
A-ḫu-dan-^{d}*Ištar*, (^{d}*Innina*),
1. s. *Ḫûnsû*, f. *Gimillu*, 99:16; 102:17; 119:15.
2. f. *Gimillu*, 19:19.
Aḫ-êreš(-eš), (*êreš*),
1. f. *Bibêa*, 177:3.
2. 175:61.
Aḫ-ḫu-tu,
1. ^{amêl}*dup-sar ša-ṭir u-il*[*-tim*], s. *Nabû-uṣalla*, 114:17.
2. 175:13.
Aḫ-iddin, s. *Tarbarušu*, 116:5.
Aḫ-iddin-^{d}*Marduk*,
1. s. *Nabû-ušallim*, 127:12, 19.
2. 149:5.
Aḫ-'-u-tu, gf. *Nabû-bêlšunu*.
Aḫê$^{\text{pl.}}$*-e-a*,
1. f. *Šum-ukîn*, 152:16.
2. 152:1.
Aḫê^{meš}*-ša-a*, *Aḫê*^{meš}*-ša-'*,
1. ^{amêl}[ ], 141:11.
2. s. *Nanâ-karâbi*, 159:44.
3. s. *Zêr-iddina*, 159:9.
4. f. *Eanna-šum-ibni*, 100:13.
Aḫê^{meš}*-šu*,
1. s. *Bal* (*?*). . ., 177:12.
2. 175:17.
Aḫu-lûmur, s. *Nabû-aḫ-êreš*, 46:6; 108:17.
Âlu-lu-mur,
1. f. *Nabû-šum-êreš*, 139:5.
2. 23:14, 27; 175:44(?).
A-mat-ilu, f. *Mušallim*, 127:9.
A-mat-su-uṣur, in ^{âl}*Ša* ^{m}*A-mat-su-uṣur*, 166:7.
Am-ma-nu, f. *Nanâ-iddin*, 125:5.
^{d}*Amar-zêr-iddin*, ^{amêl}*ràb li-mi-ti*, 24:5.
Amêl-^{d}*Ea*,
1. gf. *Mušêzib-Bêl*.
2. gf. *Mušêzib-Marduk*.
3. gf. *Nabû-bêlšunu*.
4. gf. *Nabû-nâdin-šum*.
Amêl-^{d}*Marduk*, *šar Bâbili*^{ki}, 136:11; 143:24.
Amêl-^{d}*Na-na-a*,
1. ^{amêl}*ša-qu-u*, 155:4.
2. s. *Iddin-Nergal*, 155:12.
3. s. *Nabû-šum-ibni*, 157:16.

4. s. *Nabû-zêr-ibni*, 142:18.
5. f. *Aplâ*, 142:3.
6. f. *Ardîa*, 155:15.
7. f. *Nabû-šum-ibni*, 151:17, 23.
8. 155:11; 156:6, 15; 175:25.

Amêl-^{d}Nabû,
1. s. *Balâṭsu*, 159:36.
2. s. *Nabû-uṣalla*, 157:18.
3. in *Bît ^{m}Amêl-^{d}Nabû*, 25:49.

^{d}Amurru-aḫê^{meš}-iddin,
1. s. *Bêl-šum-iškun*, 126:5.
2. 77:1.

^{d}Amurru-bêl-uṣur, s. *Kinâ*, 126:18.

^{d}Amurru-ḫa-ḫu,
1. ^{amêl}*SU*, 121:6.
2. f. *Bêl-iddina*, 121:3.

^{d}Amurru-lu-šal-lim, 28:8, 11.

^{d}Amurru-râmi-šarri, 16:18.

^{d}Amurru-šamši, 142:25, 26.

^{d}Amurru-zêr-ibni, 21:3.

^{d}A-nu-um-mukîn-aplu, s. *Ardi-Innin*, gs. ^{amêl}*šangû-parakki*, 101:3.

^{d}A-num-aḫ-iddin, 175:52.

^{d}A-num-iq-ṣur, 102:6.

^{d}A-num-upaḫḫir(?), 175:2.

^{d}A-nu-zêr-ušabši(-ši), s. *Šadûnu*, gs.^{amêl}[ ], 118:7.

^{d}Anu-aḫ-iddin,
1. s. *Bêl-aḫê-êriba*, 168:21.
2. f. *Bânîa*, 168:25.

Ap-la-a, Apla-a,
1. s. *Amêl-Nanâ*, 142:3.
2. s. *Iddinâ*, gs. *Ekur-zâkir*, 123:11.
3. s. *Nabû-ušêzib*, 159:35.
4. s...., 157:34.
5. f. *Dumuq*, 110:5.
6. f. *Kuddîa*, 126:5.
7. f. *Nabû-êṭir*, 174:7.
8. f. *Nabû-nâ'id*, 177:39.
9. f. *Nâdin*, 170:11.
10. f. *Silim-Bêl*, 112:3.
11. 19:10; 73:13; 90:1.

A-qar-aplu, 175:41.

A-qar..., f. *Nergal-nâṣir*, 108:10.

Ar-ra-bi, Ár-rab,
1. s. *Šulâ*, 119:2; 168:14.
2. f. *Nanâ-aḫ-iddin*, 162:19.
3. in *Bît ^{m}Ár-rab*, 119:11.
4. 158:20.

Ár-rab-tum, gf. *Nabû-zêr-ukîn*.

Ardi-ia, Ardi-iá, Ardi-a,
1. ^{amêl}*šu-ša-nu*, 131:8.
2. s. *Amêl-Nanâ*, 155:15.
3. s. *Innina-šum-êreš(?)*, 168:10.
4. s. *Nabû-bâni-aḫi*, gs. *Rîmût-^{d}Ea*, 98:3; 102:4; 103:5; 105:4; 110:4; 111:4; 115:3; 116:3; 117:1; 119:4; 125:3; 128:3; 129:3; 168:3.
5. s. *Nabû-šar-ilâni*, 108:18.
6. s. *Nabû-ušallim*, 156:14.
7. s. *Šâkin-šum*, 170:16.
8. s. *Šâkin-zêr*, f. *Nidinti*, 174:9.
9. s. *Šarru-êṭir*, 123:6.
10. f. *Dannîa*, 163:3.
11. f. *Gimillu*, 174:38.
12. f. *Nabû-nâṣir*, 163:11.
13. f. *Šamaš-aḫ-iddin*, 157:41.
14. f. *Šulâ*, 151:2.
15. 8:20; 117:9, 19; 125:11, 15.

Ardi-^{d}Bêl,
1. s. *Egibi*, f. *Lâbâši-Marduk*, 118:18.
2. s. ..., f. *Nabû-êṭir-napšâti^{meš}*, 120:6.
3. f. *Bêl-ittanni*, 174:62.

Ardi-^{d}Ea, s. *Êribšu*, 103:3.

Ardi-^{d}Gu-la, 158:19.

Ardi-^{d}In-nin,
1. s. ^{amêl}*šangû-parakki*, f. *Anûm-mukîn-aplu*, 101:3.
2. s. *Kinenâi*, 164:1.
3. s. ..., 147:3.
4. f. *Bêl-êṭir*, 93:17.
5. f. *Nabû-iddin*, 164:2.
6. f. *Nanâ-iddin*, 174:44.
7. 93:11; 164:7.

Ardi-^{d}Innina(-na),
1. s. *Nabû-šum-ibni*, 157:10.
2. s. *Nabû-zêr-ukîn*, 142:21.

Ardi-^{d}Marduk,
1. ^{amêl}*ràb-bânî*, s. *Zêrîa*, gs. *Egibi*, 169:3.
2. s. *Nabû-mušêtiq-urra*, gs. *Nûr-Sin*, 120:22.
3. s. *Zêrîa*, gs. *Egibi*, 118:17.

Ardi-^{d}Na-na-a,
1. ^{amêl}*aškapu*, 151:19.
2. f. *Guzanu*, 174:20.

Ardi-^{d}Nabû,
1. s. ^{amêl}..*gi-na*, f. *Nabû-bâni-aḫi*, 124:6.
2. f. *Mušallim-Marduk*, 65:7; 174:11.
3. 52:1; 95:26; 152:6, 16, 18, 22.

^{amêl}*ašlaku*,
1. gf. *Babâ*,
2. gf. *Ibni-Innina*.

At-kal-ana-^{d}Bêl, 38:16.

A..., f. *Nabû-šum-ukîn*, 157:36.

Ba-ba-a, s. *Iddin-Ellil*, f. *Balâṭu*, 127:31.

Ba-bi-ia, 50:23.

Ba-bu-u-tu, gf. *Šamaš-mukîn-aplu*.

Ba-di-ilu, 175:58.

^{amêl}*bâ'iru*,
1. gf. *Bêl-iqîša*.
2. gf. *Ea-bâni-zêr*.
3. gf. ..., 116:13.

Ba-la-ṭi, f. *Suqâi*, 174:65.

Ba-la-ṭu, *Balâṭu*,
1. ^{amêl}*bêl-piqitti ša* ^{amêl}*bêl-paḫâti*, 54:18.
2. ^{amêl}*ràb-bânî*, s. *Tabnêa*, 153:2.
3. s. *Babâ*, gs. *Iddin-Ellil*, 127:31.
4. s. *Ḫânbi*, f. *Rîmût*, 107:7.
5. s. *Kiribti*, 174:45.
6. s. *Miṣirai*, f. *Marduk-šâpik-zêr*, 103:15.
7. s. *Mušêzib-Bêl*, 3:8; 71:9.
8. s. *Nabû-bêlšunu*, 174:73.
9. s. *Nabû-zêr-iqîša*, 41:15.
10. s. *Ṣillâ*, 117:1.
11. s. *Zâkir*, 174:37.
12. f. *Nabû-aḫê-ušallim*, 97:11.
13. f. *Nabû-bêlšunu*, 170:7.
14. f. *Nabû-kâṣir(?)*, 117:5.
15. f. *Nergal-uballiṭ*, 108:12.
16. f. *Širiqtum-^{d}AZAG-SUD*, 169:24.
17. gf. *Zêrîa*.
18. 3:11; 5:2; 16:3; 57:5; 58:19; 64:3; 73:1; 117:10, 17; 153:8; 154:29(?).

Ba-laṭ-su, *Balâṭ-su*,
1. s. *Amêl-Ea*, f. *Mušêzib-Bêl*, 98:13; 110:14; 169:7.
2. s. *Bânitu-šu*, 159:32.
3. s. *Bêl*..., 177:10.
4. s. *Da'iqu*, f. *Mušêtiq-urra*, 101:2.
5. s. *Kinâ*, 175:23.
6. s. *Kuddîa*, 94:36; 108:16; 148:6.
7. s. *Nabû-nâṣir*, 154:8.
8. s. *Nabû-zêr-iddin*, 108:5.
9. s. *Nanâ-êreš*, 142:9.
10. s. *Šulâ*, gs. *Nabâi*, 133:17.
11. s. *Ṣillâ*, 157:24.
12. f. *Amêl-Nabû*, 159:36.
13. f. *Kudurru*, 159:40.
14. f. *Mušêzib-Bêl*, 174:13.
15. f. *Nabû-dannu*, 156:25.
16. f. *Šullumu*, 159:12.
17. 2:3; 14:2; 33:3; 38:2; 66:2; **74:1**; 82:2; 139:7; 158:21; 175:6.

Balâṭ-su-ilu,
1. s. *Nabû-ušêzib*, 156:9.
2. 156:30.

Bal-ṭi-iá, s. *Innina-zêr-ušabši*, 102:6.

Bal(?)..., f. *Aḫêšu*, 177:12.

Ba-ni-ia, *Ba-ni-iá*, *Bâni-ia*, *Bâni-iá*, *Bâni-a*,
1. ^{amêl}*bâ'iru*, f. ..., 116:13.
2. s. *Anu-aḫ-iddin*, 168:25.
3. s. ^{amêl}*bâ'iru*, f. *Bêl-iqîša*, 102:19; 103:17; 119:16; 129:15.
4. s. *Bi(?)-it-tab-ši(?)*, 151:3.
5. s. *Kalbâ*, 113:4, 9.
6. s. *Manna-kî-ummu*, 177:32.
7. s. *Naḫû-balâṭsu-iqbi*, gs. *Sin-lîq-unnînni*, 120:28.
8. s. *Nergal-ušallim*, 166:21.
9. f. *Ḫâmbaqu*, 115:5.
10. f. *Nabû-êṭir-napšâti*^{meš}, 126:17.
11. f. *Nanâ-êreš*, 177:13.
12. f. *Ša-Innina-taklak*, 151:24.
13. f. *Šamaš-mukîn-aplu*, 109:15.
14. f. *Šêlibi*, 174:8.
15. f. *Zêrîa*, 73:11.
16. 131:15; 156:42; 170:6, 20.

Bânitu(KAK-tu)-šu,
1. f. *Balâṭsu*, 159:32.
2. f. ...*iš* (or *mil*), 121:9.

Bânitu(KAK-tu)-šu-lîšir(GIŠ), f. *Nabû-nâdin-šum*, 140:3.

Ba-si-ia, gf. *Šum-ukîn*.

^{d}*Bau-iddin*, 154:11.
^{d}*Bêl-aḫ-iddin*,
1. f. *Iddin-Marduk*, 127:39.
2. f. *Nabû-êṭir*, 157:13.
3. f. *Šum-ukîna*, 127:34.
4. 155:9; 175:32.

^{d}*Bêl-aḫ-šub-ši*, in *Bît* ^{md}*Bêl-aḫ-šub-ši*, 166:27.
^{d}*Bêl-aḫ-u-šub-ši*, s. *Amêl-Ea*, f. *Nabû-bêl-šunu*, 169:6.
^{d}*Bêl-aḫ-ušabši(-ši)*, s. *Bêl-šum-iškun*, 151:21.
^{d}*Bêl-aḫê*^{meš}*-êriba*,
1. s. . . ., 157:29.
2. f. *Anu-aḫ-iddin*, 168:22.
3. f. *Isinnâi*, 142:19.
4. 13:17; 56:3; 175:22.

^{d}*Bêl-aḫê*^{meš}*-iddin*,
1. s. *Kuddîa*, 151:9.
2. s. *Nabû-zêr-ibni*, 127:13, 17, 24, 43.
3. s. *Tarbi*, f. *Balâṭsu*, 101:21.
4. s. *Zêr-iddina*, 159:42.
5. s. . . ., 122:14.
6. f. *Innin-šum-uṣur*, 127:41.

^{d}*Bêl-aḫê*^{meš}*-iqîša(-ša)*,
1. s. *Egibi*, f. *Nâdinu*, 118:20; 120:27.
2. s. *Mušêzib-Marduk*, gs. *Egibi*, 133:16.
3. s. *Mušêzib-Marduk*, gs. *Sin-ibni*, 133:20.

^{d}*Bêl-aḫê*^{meš}*-ušallim*, f. *Nanâ-êpuš*, 141:6.
^{d}*Bêl-apal-uṣur*,
1. f. *Dajân-Marduk*, 145:6.
2. gf. *Bêl-iddin*.
3. gf. *Bêl-supê-muḫur*.
4. gf. *Suqâi*.

^{d}*Bêl-êpuš(-uš)*,
1. s. *Erîši*, 159:38.
2. f. *Nergal-êṭir*, 157:22.
3. f. *Šulâ*, 122:4.
4. f. *Zabâbâ-nâdin-šum*, 122:4.

^{d}*Bêl-êreš*,
1. f. *Zabidâ*, 157:25.
2. 14:9, 16; 82:19.

^{d}*Bêl-êriba*,
1. f. *Nabû-ušallim*, 157:15.
2. f. . . .*iqbi*, 123:13.

^{d}*Bêl-êṭir*,
1. *ša eli qûppi*, 174:30.
2. s. *Ardi-Innin*, 93:16.
3. s. *Nabû-bâni-aḫi*, 103:2.
4. s. *Šullumu*, 157:38.
5. f. *Iddin-Marduk*, 159:37.
6. in *bâb* ^{nâr}*pît-qa ša* ^{md}*Bêl-êṭir*, 99:2.
7. in ^{nâr}*pît-qa ša* ^{md}*Bêl-êṭir*, 98:16; 105:19; 115:17.
8. 102:20; 103:19; 117:25; 125:21.

^{d}*Bêl-ib-ni*, (*ibni*(*KAK*)),
1. s. *Kinâ*, 171:4.
2. s. *Nadnâ*, 177:26.
3. s. ^{amêl}*šangû* ^{al}*Šallat*, f. *Lišuri*, 122:12(?).
4. s. *Šâpik*, 159:26.
5. f. *Bêl-iddin*, 177:23, 37.

^{d}*Bêl-iddin*, (*iddina*(*-na*)),
1. s. *Amurru-ḫaḫu*, 121:2.
2. s. *Bêl-ibni*, 177:23, 37.
3. s. *Marduk-zêr-ibni*, gs. *Bêl-apal-uṣur*, 124:15.
4. s. *Munnabitti*, gs.^{amêl}*addupu*, 107:11.
5. s. *Munnabittu*, 121:7.
6. s. *Nergal-iddin*, gs. *Kunâ*, 110:13.
7. s. *Zêria*, 33:12.
8. s. . . ., 117:23.
9. f. *Šamaš-êriba*, 107:3.
10. 27:31; 31:5, 8, 11, 18, 26; 52:1; 156:34; 174:60, 69, 72.

^{d}*Bêl-iq-bi*, s. *Ḫanap*, f. *Innina-zêr-ibni*, 169:8.
^{d}*Bêl-iqîša(-ša)*,
1. s. *Bânîa*, gs.^{amêl}*bâ'iru*, 103:16; 119:16; 128:12(?).
2. f. *Šulâ*, 121:10.
3. f. *Šûzubu*, 127:7.
4. f. . . .*mukîn-zêr*, 142:11.

^{d}*Bêl-it(?)-tan-ni*, s. *Ardi-Bêl*, 174:62.
^{d}*Bêl-ka-ṣir*, (*kâṣir*(*KAD*)),
1. ^{amêl}*apal-šipri* ^{d}*Nabû-šum-iškun*, 9:7.
2. s. *Marduk*, gs. *Kidin-Marduk*, 101:16.
3. 30:18.

^{d}*Bêl-li-mur*, s. *Egibi*, f. *Nâdinu*, 104:14.
^{d}*Bêl-li'u*,
1. s. *Sin-lîq-unnînni*, f. *Nâdinu*, 104:14.
2. f. *Nabû-êṭir-napšâti*^{meš}, 108:9.
3. f. *Nergal-uballiṭ*, 133:2, 11.

^{d}*Bêl-na-din-aplu*, 21:3; 57:3; 93:1.

^{d}*Bêl-nâdin-šum*, 175:8.
^{d}*Bêl-nâ'id*, 11:5; 12:6, 10, 18.
^{d}*Bêl-nâṣir*, 68:18.
^{d}*Bêl-ri-ba*, s. *Lâbâši*, 159:5.
^{d}*Bêl-ri-man-ni*,
 1. s. *Kibi-Bêl*, 126:19.
 2. 71:2.
^{d}*Bêl-su-pi-e-mu-ḫur*, s. *Itti-Šamaš-balâṭu*, gs. *Bêl-apal-uṣur*, 113:18.
Bêl-šu-nu,
 1. s. *Gimillu*, gs. *Dannêa*, 174:57.
 2. s. *Kalbâ*, 174:64.
 3. s. *Nabû-aḫê-iddin*, gs. *Egibi*, 124:14.
 4. s. *Nabû-zêr-ukîn*, 157:6.
 5. f. *Marduk-šum-uṣur*, 142:1.
 6. 57:3; 82:25; 85:3; 170:8.
^{d}*Bêl-šum-iškun(-un)*,
 1. s. *Dabibi*, f. *Marduk-êṭir*, 130:36.
 2. s. *Dabibi*, f. *Nabû-nâdin-šum*, 121:12; 130:28.
 3. s. *Kalumu*, 159:14, 41.
 4. s. *Nabû-iddin*, 159:23.
 5. s. *Šulâ*, 159:11.
 6. f. *Amurru-aḫê-iddin*, 126:5.
 7. f. *Bêl-aḫ-ušabši*, 151:21.
 8. f. *Marduk-êṭir*, 96:8; 108:4; 144:4.
 9. f. *Marduk-nâṣir*, 159:22.
 10. f. *Zêrîa*, 148:2.
^{d}*Bêl-tab(?) -ni-uṣur(?)*, 175:64.
^{d}*Bêl-uballiṭ (-iṭ)*,
 1. s. *Bûṣu*, f. *Marduk-nâdin-aḫu*, 169:4.
 2. s.^{amêl}*ša ṭâbti*^{zun}*-šu*, f. *Nabû-apal-iddin*, 113:20.
 3. f. *Gimillu*, 139:4.
 4. f. *Nabû-zêr-ukîn*, 93:19.
 5. f. *Rîmût*, 157:39.
 6. 66:5; 170:17.
^{d}*Bêl-upaḫḫir(-ir)*,
 1. s. *Dajân-Marduk*, 153:4.
 2. f. *Ibni-Innina*, 160:2.
^{d}*Bêl-u-sa-tu*, *(u-sat, u-sat-ti)*,
 1. s. ^{amêl}*KIM-A*, f. *Nergal-nâṣir*, 141:2.
 2. s. ^{amêl}*KIM-A*, f. *Rîmût*, 141:2.
 3. s. *Bêl-usat*, gs. ..., 116:14.
 4. s. *Ekur-zâkir*, gs. ..., 130:30.
 5. f. *Nabû-zêr-ukîn*, 159:31.
 6. gf. *Marduk-šum-lîšir*.
^{d}*Bêl-ušallim*,
 1. s. *Nabû-nâṣir*, gs. *Nûr-Sin*, 107:9.
 2. s. *Nabû-šum-êreš*, 142:7.
 3. s. *Šamaš-iddin*, gs. *Šu'atu*, 101:18.
 4. s. *Zabâbâ-êriba*, 126:16.
 5. f. *Ibni-Innina*, 112:14.
 6. f. *Nabû-zêr-ušabši*, 161:3.
 7. 163:8.
Bêl-zêr,
 1. s. *Basîa*, f. *Šum-ukîn*, 97:3.
 2. f. *Iqîšâ*, 142:8.
 3. f. *Nergal-êpuš*, 159: 13.
^{d}*Bêl-zêr*, f. *Itti-Eanna-GID-DI-iá*, 164:5.
^{d}*Bêl...*, f. *Balâṭsu*, 177:10.
Bêli-ia,
 1. s. *Šigûa*, f. *Mušêzib-Marduk*, 100:12.
 2. 170:12.
Bi-bi-e-a,
 1. ^{amêl}*GIG-BA*, 140:4.
 2. s. *Aḫ-êreš*, 177:3.
 3. 175:18.
Bi(?)-it-tab-ši(?), f. *Bânîá*, 151:3.
Bîti-a, ^{amêl}*nangaru*, 174:59.
Bul-luṭ, *Bul-lu-ṭu*,
 1. s. *Balâṭu*, f. *Zêrîa*, 133:14.
 2. f. *Abi-ul-îdi*, 171:9.
 3. 60:12; 175:4.
Bul-luṭ-a,
 1. s. *Nanâ-ibni*, 112:4; 157:1.
 2. s. *Nûḫḫuki*, 156:13.
 3. f. *Innina-zêr-ibni*, 154:17.
 4. f. *Nabû-êriba*, 108:19.
 5. 156:28; 175:55.
Bu-na-a, s. ^{amêl}*ušparu*, f. *Nâdin*, 146:3.
Bu-u-ṣu,
 1. f. *Marduk-nâdin-aḫu*, 153:3.
 2. gf. *Marduk-nâdin-aḫu*.
Da-bi-bi,
 1. f. *Marduk-êṭir*, 107:13.
 2. gf. *Nabû-mukîn-aplu*.
 3. gf. *Nabû-nâdin-šum*.
Da-'-i-qu, gf. *Nabû-mušêtiq-urra*.
^{d}*Dajân-aḫê*^{meš}*-iddin*,
 1. s. *Gimillu*, 135:12.
 2. s. *Gimillu*, gs. ..., 120:25.
Dajân-^{d}*Marduk*,
 1. ^{amêl}*ràb-bânî*, 140:7.

2. s. *Bêl-apal-uṣur*, 145:5.
3. f. *Bêl-upaḫḫir*, 153:4.
4. 2:3.

Dan-ni-e-a, gf. *Bêlšunu*.
Dan-ni-iá, s. *Ardia*, 163:3.
^{d}*Dan-nu-aḫê*$^{\text{pl.}}$*-šu-ibni*, ^{amêl}*pu-ṣa-a-a*, 165:10; 174:32.
Dan-nu-^{d}*Nergal*, 157:44.
Di-na-a,
1. f. *Iqîšâ*, 156:5.
2. 64:3.

Du-ba-a, (Perhaps to be read *Gub-ba-a; cf. Gu-ub-ba-a, BE, X* 61:2), in ^{nâr}*ḫar-ri ša* ^{m}*Du-ba-a*, 101:8; 166:20.
Du-muq,
1. s. *Aplâ*, 110:5.
2. 158:4.

Du-um-mu-qu, s. *E-sag*[*-gil*]*-a*, f. *Tukulti-Marduk*, 120:23.
^{amêl}*DU-ZU*, gf. *Etillu*.
^{d}*Ea-a-na-bîti-šu*, 47:9.
^{d}*Ea-bâni-zêr*, s. *Tabnêa*, gs. ^{amêl}*bâ'iru*, 133:18.
^{d}*Ea-êpuš(-uš)*,
1. f. *Nabû-šum-uṣur*, 157:5.
2. 156:17, 29.

^{d}*E-a-ibni*, 175:21.
^{d}*Ea-ilu-tu-ibni*, gf. *Nabû-bêlšunu*.
^{d}*E-a-kur-ban-ni*,
1. ^{amêl}*pa-qu-du ša Uruk*^{ki}, s. *Nabû-êṭir-napšâti*^{meš}, gs. *Ea-kurbanni*, 169:12.
2. gf. *Ea-kurbanni*.

^{d}*Ea-zêr-iddin*, s. *Nabû-bêl-uṣur*, 119:5.
E-an-na-ibni, f. *Marduk-êriba*, 157:42.
E-an-na-mutîr, ^{amêl}*nâš-paṭri*, 155:17.
E-an-na-nâdin-šum, s. *Babûtu*, f. *Šamaš-mukîn-aplu*, 103:18; 116:15; 119:17; 128:14.
E-an-na-šarru, 175:57.
E-an-na-šum-ibni, 166:4.
E-an-na-šum-lîšir,
1. s. ^{amêl}*DU-ZU*, f. *Etillu*, 106:10.
2. f. *Innina-aḫ-iddin*, 174:41.

E-gi-bi,
1. f. *Iqîšâ*, 177:9(?).
2. gf. *Ardi-Marduk*.
3. gf. *Bêl-aḫê-iqîša*.
4. gf. *Bêlšunu*.
5. gf. *Gimil-Šamaš*.
6. gf. *Lâbâši-Marduk*.
7. gf. *Nâdinu*.

E-kur-za-kir,
1. f. *Bêl-usat*, gf. ..., 130:30.
2. gf. *Aplâ*.
3. gf. *Nabû-bâni-aḫi*.

^{d}*Enurta-šar-uṣur*,
1. ^{amêl}*qîpi*, 144:6.
2. 22:1; 38:1; 40:1; 81:1.

Êpeš(-eš)-ilu, gf. *Mušêzib-Bêl*.
Er-ba-a-a, 27:31.
E-ri-ši, s. *Bêl-êpuš*, 159:38.
E-rib-šu,
1. ^{amêl}*ušparu*, 161:8.
2. s. *Mušêzib-Bêl*, 174:25.
3. s. *Nanâ-iddin*, 165:3.
4. s. *Ṭâb-Uruk*^{ki}, 174:18.
5. f. *Ardi-Ea*, 103:4.

E-sag[*-gil*]*-a*, gf. *Tukulti-Marduk*.
Eš-gur(?)-ru, 156:37.
E-til-lu, s. *Eanna-šum-lîšir*, gs. ^{amêl}*DU-ZU*, 106:9.
E-ṭe-ru, gf. *Ili'-Marduk*.
E-ṭir, f. *Šama'gunu*, 177:25.
Êṭir-^{d}*Šamaš*, s. *Nabû-aḫ-iddin*, 174:67.
E-zi-da-šum-ukîn, s. *Marduk-abu-šu*, f. *Nabû-aḫê-iddin*, 109:14.
Ga-šu-ra, gf. *Nabû-šum-ukîn dupsar*.
Gi-lu-u-a, s. *Šum-ukîna*, 159:16.
Gi-mil-lu, Gimillu,
1. s. *Aḫu-dân-Ištar*, gs. *Ḫûnsû*, 19:18; 99:16; 102:16; 117:22(?); 119:14.
2. s. *Ardia*, 174:38.
3. s. *Bêl-uballiṭ*, 139:3.
4. s. *Dannêa*, f. *Bêlšunu*, 174:57.
5. s. *Innin-zêr-iddin*, 165:7.
6. s. *Marduk-nâṣir*, 174:58.
7. s. *Šûzubu*, 127:35.
8. s. *Zêrîa*, gs. *Šigûa*, 124:13(?); 133:15.
9. s. ...*di*, f. *Kalbâ*, 100:11.
10. s. ..., f. *Dajân-aḫê*^{meš}*-iddin*, 120:25.
11. s. ..., 99:4.
12. f. *Dajân-aḫê-iddin*, 135:12.

13. f. *Ištar-šum-êreš*, 142:16.
14. f. *Nanâ-iddin*, 157:26.
15. f. *Šulâ*, 168:8.
16. 19:11; 33:9, 14; 63:2; 154:7; 170:17.

Gimil-^{d}Na-na-a,
1. s. *Nergal-uballiṭ*, gs. ^{amêl}*šangû-parakki*, 101:5.
2. gf. *Anûm-mukîn-aplu*.

Gimil-^{d}Šamaš, s. *Nabû-êṭir-napšâti^{meš}*, gs. *Egibi*, 113:21.
Giššar[1]*-šum-ukîn*, *šar Bâbili^{ki}*, 134:18.
Gu-bar-ru, ^{amêl}*piḫâtu Bâbili^{ki}*, 169:22.
Gu-za-nu,
1. s. *Ardi-Nanâ*, 174:20.
2. s. *Silim-Bêl*, 174:52.
3. 174:71.

Ḫa-aḫ-ḫu-ru, f. *Nidinti*, 174:56.
Ḫa-am-ba-qu, s. *Bânîa*, 115:5.
Ḫa-am-mi-du-u, 175:31.
Ḫa-an-bi, gf. *Rîmût*.
Ḫa-ar-ma-ṣu, f. *Nanâ-iddin*, 24:10.
Ḫa-ba-aš-tum, 117:7.
Ḫa-nap, gf. *Innina-zêr-ibni*.
Ḫa-pir-ku, f. *Nabû-bâni-aḫi*, 51:6.
Ḫar (or *Mur*)..., s. *Nâdina-aḫu*, 142:22.
Ḫi-ma-ri-iá, ^{amêl}*irrišu Nergal-uballiṭ*, 44:11.
Ḫu-un-su-u, *Ḫu-un-su-'*,
1. gf. *Gimillu*.
2. gf. *Marduk-nâdin-aḫu*.
3. gf. *Nergal-nâdin-šum*.
4. gf. *Nûrea*.
5. gf. *Šâpik*.
6. gf. ..., 116:12.

'I-bad, f. *Nabû-aḫê-iddin*, 175:11.
Ia-ḫu, f. *Nabû-nâdin-aḫu*, 97:12.
Ia-qa-bu-u, 23:18.
I-ba-a,
1. f. *Kinâ*, 168:26.
2. f. *Šamaš-zêr-iqîša*, 149:8.

Ib-na-a, s. *Ekur-zâkir*, f. *Nabû-bâni-aḫi*, 133:19.
Ibni-ilu, f. *Sin-êreš*, gf. ..., 117:22.
Ibni-^{d}Innina, (*Ib-ni*, *^{d}Ištar*),
1. ^{amêl}*sattukkû*, 131:6.
2. s. ^{amêl}*agâru*, f. *Nabû-bâni-aḫi*, 101:18.
3. s. ^{amêl}*ašlaku*, f. *Babâ*, 120:29.
4. s. *Bêl-upaḫḫir*, 160:2.
5. s. *Bêl-ušallim*, 112:14.
6. s. *Kurî*, f. *Nabû-êṭir-napšâti^{meš}*, 106:17.
7. s. *Nabû-šum-ibni*, 154:21.
8. s. *Nabû-zêr-ukîn*, gs. ^{amêl}*ašlaku*, 133:22.
9. s. *Šamaš-uballiṭ*, 174:70.
10. f. [*Innina*]*-zêr-ušabši*, 168:18.
11. f. *Zuzuzu*, 174:6.
12. 28:42; 43:1; 53:2, 37; 154:23, 31; 158:3.

Ibni..., f. *Nabû-bâni-aḫi*, 112:15.
Id-di-ia, s. *Nabû-uṣalli*, 177:5.
Iddina(*-na*)*-a*, *Iddina*,
1. s. *Ekur-zâkir*, f. *Aplâ*, 123:11.
2. f. *Nabû-ušabši*, 156:15.
3. 4:12; 19:4; 29:8; 175:30.

Iddin-^{d}Bêl, ^{amêl}*nuḫatimmu bît-ḫi-ri*, 174:16.
Iddin-^{d}Ellil, gf. *Balâṭu*.
Iddin-^{d}Marduk,
1. s. *Bêl-âḫ-iddin*, 127:39.
2. s. *Bêl-êṭir*, 159:37.
3. 175:39.

Iddin-^{d}Nabû,
1. s. *Kidin-Marduk*, f. *Innin-nâdin-aḫu*, 104:10.
2. 154:9, 10.

Iddin-^{d}Nergal,
1. f. *Amêl-Nanâ*, 155:12.
2. f. *Nabû-zêr-ibni*, 177:19.
3. f. *Nâdina-aplu*, 177:22.
4. f. ..., 130:34(?).

Iddin-nu-nu, s. *Šulâ*, 174:21.
Iddin-^{d}Papsukal, gf. *Nâdin-aplu*.
Iddin-^{d}Šam-šu, 1:2.
Il-ta-as-su, *Il-ta-su*.., 176:7, 10.
^{d}Il-ta-meš-id-ri-', 1:1.
Ili'-^{d}Marduk, s. *Nabû-šum-ukîn*, gs. *Êṭeru*, 98:5.
Ilu-na-dan-nu, f. *Itti-ilîa*, 100:1, 7.

[1] For this reading see Clay, *Business Transactions of the First Millennium B. C.*, *Part I Babylonian Records in the Morgan Library*, p. 11.

Ĭm-bi-ia,
1. s. *Kuri*, f. *Šamaš-rê'ušunu*, 125:18.
2. s ..., gs *Kidin-Marduk*, 128:11.
3. 38:7, 11.
I-ni-ilu, f. *Marduk-êriba*, 177:31.
ᵈIn-nin-aḫê^meš-iddin, 29:1.
ᵈIn-nin-ina-eši-êṭir, s. *Nabû-šum-iškun*, 127:38.
ᵈIn-nin-li..., *^amêl bâ'iru*, 54:15.
ᵈIn-nin-nâdin-aḫu,
1. s. *Iddin-Nabû*, gs. *Kidin-Marduk*, 104:9.
2. s. *Nanâ-iddin*, 109:8.
3. s. *Nergal-ušallim*, gs. *Sin-lîq-unnînni*, 124:16.
4. 70:2; 170:15.
ᵈIn-nin-šar-uṣur, 54:1.
ᵈIn-nin-šum-iškun(-un), s. *Nergal-ibni*, gs. *^amêl šangû-ᵈAdad*, 106:15.
ᵈIn-nin-šum-ušabši(-ši), 73:2.
ᵈIn-nin-zêr-ibni, s. *Nabû-aḫê-ušallim*, 118:5.
ᵈIn-nin-zêr-iddin,
1. f. *Gimillu*, 165:7.
2. f. *Gimillu dup-sar*, 106:18.
ᵈIn-nin-zêr-iqîša(-ša), s. *Nergal-uballiṭ*, 49:7.
ᵈIn-nin-zêr-ušabši(-ši), (*TIL*),
1. *^amêl âtû*, 174:19.
2. *^amêl ušparu*, 165:2.
3. s. *Nabû-dannu*, 166:32.
4. s. *Šulâ*, gs. *^amêl kudimmu*, 174:39.
5. 21:5; 32:4; 57:4; 85:5.
ᵈIn-nin-zêr-ušallim, in *Bît ^md In-nin-zêr-ušallim*, 118:4.
Ina-E-sag-ila-zêr, f. *Nabû-uballiṭ*, 174:75.
Ina-eši-êṭir, (*êṭir(-ir)*),
1. s. *Ḫûnsû*, f. *Nergal-nâdin-šum*, 104:11.
2. s. *Nabû-aḫ-êreš*, 159:10.
3. s. *Nabû-zêr-iddin*, 114:13.
4. s. *Zabidâ*, 157:2.
5. f. *ᵈLugal-Banda(-da)-šum-ibni*, 109:5.
6. f. *Šamaš-dannu*, 109:9.
Ina-pa-an-da-nu, f. *Nabû-uballiṭ*, 129:5.
Ina-pa-ni(?)..., 158:28.
Ina-ṣilli-ᵈBêl-ab-ni, s. *Kuddîa*, 151:18.
Ina-ṣilli-E-an-na,
1. s. *Innina-nâdin-aḫu*, 99:18.
2. s. *Iqîsâ*, 163:4.
3. 163:1.
Ina-ṣilli-ᵈNa-na-a,
1. *ša Bît ^m Amêl-ᵈNabû*, 25:48.
2. s. *Nabû-šûzib-anni*, 136:6.
3. s. *Nanâ-êreš*, 151:13.
4. 90:6; 136:8; 163:15.
Ina-ṣilli..., f. ..., 131:18.
ᵈInnina-a-lik-pâni, 143:22.
ᵈInnina-aḫ-iddin, *^amêl âtû*, s. *Eanna-šum-lîšir*, 174:41.
ᵈInnina(-na)-aḫê^meš-iddin, 16:1.
ᵈInnina-dûr-e-du, 131:9.
ᵈInnina(-na)-nâdin-aḫu,
1. f. *Ina-ṣilli-Eanna*, 99:18.
2. 92:1.
ᵈInnina-ri-ṣu-u-a,
1. *^amêl ašaridu*, 131:11.
2. *^amêl mu-ša-gur iṣṣur^meš*, 174:26.
3. s. *Marduk-bêlšunu*, 174:27.
4. 163:16.
ᵈInnina-šum-êreš,
1. s. *Ea-ilûtu-ibni*, f. *Nabû-bêlšunu*, 105:17; 110:16; 111:14; 115:15; 125:20.
2. f. *Ardîa*, 168:10.
ᵈInnina-šum-lîšir, s. *Nergal-šum-ibni*, 127:40.
ᵈInnina(-na)-tab-ni-uṣur, s. *Gimil-Nanâ*, f. *Anûm-mukîn-aplu*, 97:14.
ᵈInnina-zêr-ibni, (*ᵈInnina(-na)*, *ᵈIštar*),
1. *^amêl râb-bânî* s. *Bêl-iqbi*, gs. *Ḫanap*, 169:8.
2. s. *Bulluṭa*, 154:16.
3. s. *Taqîš-Gula*, 174:54.
4. f. *Mušêzib-Šamaš*, 109:17; 113:23.
5. f. *Nâdina-aḫu*, 151:16.
6. f. *Nanâ-aḫ-iddin*, 129:14.
7. 158:2.
ᵈInnina(-na)-zêr-iddin, s. *Nâdin-aḫu*, 163:12.
ᵈInnina(-na)-zêr-iqîša(-ša), s. *Nergal-uballiṭ*, 36:27.
ᵈInnina(-na)-zêr-ušabši(-ši),
1. *ša eli gi-qûppi ša ^amêl šatammu*, s. *Ṭâb-šar-Ištar*, 150:1.
2. s. *Ibni-Ištar*, 168:18.

3. f. *Balṭîa*, 102:7.
4. 38:7; 75:1, 2; 139:8; 168:14.
^{d}*Innina(-na)-zêr-uṣur*, s. *Nergal-êṭir*, 157:9.
Iqîša, *Iqîša(-ša)*, *Iqîša(-ša)-a*,
1. s. *Bêl-zêr*, 142:8.
2. s. *Dinâ*, 156:5.
3. s. *E[-gi?-bi?]*, 177:9.
4. s. *Murranu*, 177:4.
5. s. *Ṣillâ*, 130:6.
6. f. *Ina-ṣilli-Eanna*, 163:4.
7. f. *Kalbâ*, 161:4.
8. 25:17; 79:12; 85:3; 156:8.
Iqîša(-ša)-^{d}*Marduk*,
1. s. *Nâdin-šum*, 141:3.
2. 141:12, 22, 26.
I-sin-na-a-a,
1. ^{amêl}*ašlaku*, s. *Bêl-aḫê-êriba*, 142:19.
2. 91:3.
Iškun-^{d}*Nabû*, 46:11.
^{d}*Ištar-âlik-pâni*, 151:12.
^{d}*Ištar-šar-uṣur*, 165:8.
^{d}*Iš-tar-šum-êreš*, (^{d}*Ištar*),
1. ^{amêl}*nangaru*, 173:9.
2. s. *Gimillu*, 142:16.
3. s. *Šâkin-šum*, 93:7.
Iṣ-ṣur, 166:12.
It-ti-^{d}*Bêl-li-im-mir*, 9:1.
Itti-E-an-na-GID-DI-iá, s. *Bêl-zêr*, 164:5.
Itti-ili-ia, s. *Ilu-nadannu*, 100:1, 7.
Itti-^{d}*Nabû-gu-u-su*, s. ^{d}*Tur-Esagila-riṣûa*, 120:6.
It-ti-^{d}*Nabû-i-ni-iá*, *Itti(KI)-*^{d}*Nabû-inî(ŠI)-iá*, 77:6, 15, 28.
Itti-^{d}*Šamaš-balâṭu*,
1. s. *Bêl-apal-uṣur*, f. *Bêl-supê-muḫur*, 113:18.
2. 110:2.
Itti-šarri-balâṭu, ^{amêl}*râb pît-qa*, 69:1.
I. . ., in *Bît* ^{m}*I*. ., 129:16.
Ka-lu-mu, *Ka-lum-u(?)*,
1. s. *Nabâ*, 114:13.
2. f. *Bêl-šum-iškun*, 159:14, 41.
3. f. *Nabû-aḫê-ušallim*, 14:8; 127:37.
Kal-ba-a,
1. s. *Gimillu*, gs. . . .*di*, 100:11.
2. s. *Iqîšâ*, 161:4.
3. s. *Nergal-šum-ibni*, 97:5.
4. f. *Bânîa*, 113:4, 9.
5. f. *Bêlšunu*, 174:64.
6. 136:4; 158:9; 161:5.
Kam-bu-zi-ia, *šar Bâbili*^{ki}, *šar mâtâti*, 98:18; 102:22; *passim*.
Kan-da-la-nu, *šar Bâbili*^{ki}, 159:3.
Ki-bi-^{d}*Bêl*, f. *Bêl-rîmanni*, 126:19.
Ki-din-^{d}*Marduk*,
1. gf. *Bêl-kâṣir*.
2. gf. *Imbîa*.
3. gf, *Innin-nâdin-aḫu*.
4. gf. *Lâbâši*.
5. gf. *Šamaš-napištim-uṣur*.
6. gf. . . ., 130:33.
7. 41:18.
^{amêl}*KIM-A*,
1. gf. *Nergal-nâṣir*.
2. gf. *Rîmût*.
Ki-na-a,
1. ^{amêl}*šatammu Eanna*, 47:3.
2. s. *Ibâ*, 168:26.
3. f. *Amurru-bêl-uṣur*, 126:18.
4. f. *Balâṭsu*, 175:23.
5. f. *Bêl-ibni*, 171:5.
6. f. *Sin-ibni*, 151:4.
7. in *Bît* ^{m}*Ki-na-a*, 166:18.
8. 16:2; 20:1.
Ki-ne-na-a-a,
1. f. *Ardi-Innin*, 164:1.
2. 94:1.
Ki-nu-na-a-a, f. *Ša-Nabû-šû*, 163:6.
Ki-rib-ti, f. *Balâṭu*, 174:45.
Ki-sik-^{d}*Nabû*, 10:2, 7; 21:1.
Kud-a-a, 153:12.
Kud-da-a, f. *Nâdina-aplu*, 177:7.
Kud-di-ia, *Kud-di-iá*, *Kud-di-a*,
1. ^{amêl}*râb-bânî*, 151:22.
2. s. *Aplâ*, 126:4.
3. s. *Nergal-ibni*, 157:14.
4. s. *Šamaš-êriba*, 157:20.
5. f. *Balâṭsu*, 94:36; 108:16; 148:6.
6. f. *Bêl-aḫê*^{meš}*-iddin*, 151:9.
7. f. *Ina-ṣilli-Bêl-abni*, 151:18.
8. f. *Nabû-êriba*, 177:35.
9. 156:11; 175:47.

^{amêl}*kudimmu*, gf. *Innin-zêr-ušabši*.
Kudurru,
1. s. *Balâṭsu*, 159:40.
2. s. *Nabû-nâṣir*, 25:43; 46:8.
3. s. *Nadnâ*, 157:7.
4. f. *Innina-zêr-ušabši*, 126:21.
5. f. *Nabû-ušallim*, 148:4.
6. 46:20; 175:29.
Ku-na-a, *Kun-a*,
1. f. *Šumâ*, 177:28.
2. gf. *Bêl-iddin*.
3. 175:20.
Ku-raš, *Ku-ra-aš*, *Kur-aš*, *Kur-ra-aš*, *šar Bâbili*^{ki}, *šar mâtâti*, 106:1, 20; 109:3, 18; 111:17; 118:22; 167:4.
Ku-ri-gal-su, s. *Nergal-ibni*, 159:34.
Ku-ri-i, *Kur-i*,
1. gf. *Nabû-êṭir-napšâti*^{meš}.
2. gf. *Rîmût*.
3. gf. *Šamaš-rê'ušunu*.
Kur-ban-ni-^{d}*Marduk*, 24:2.
La-a-ba-ši, *La-ba-ši*,
1. s. *Nabû-bâni(?)-aplu(?)*, gs. *Kidin-Marduk*, 125:19.
2. f. *Bêl-riba*, 159:5.
3. 153:16; 158:1, 5; 168:6.
La-ba-ši-^{d}*Marduk*, (*La-a-ba-ši*),
1. s. *Ardi-Bêl*, gs. *Egibi*, 118:18.
2. 19:3.
La-bi-ri-ia, in *Bît* ^{m}*La-bi-ri-ia*, 166:14.
La-kip, f. *Nanâ-êreš*, 99:17.
Lib-luṭ,
1. ^{amêl}*nuḫatimmu bît-ḫi-ri*, 174:15.
2. ^{amêl}*šaqû šarri amêl ša eli qûppi ša šarri*, 120:20.
3. 4:13; 8:6; 69:11(?); 170:22(?).
Li-pa-', in *Bît* ^{m}*Li-pa-'*, 130:3.
Li-ši-ru, *Li-ši-ri*,
1. s. *Bêl-ibni(?)*, gs. ^{amêl}*šangû-*^{âl}*Šallat*, 122:12.
2. 33:2.
^{d}*Lugal-Banda(-da)-šum-ibni*, s. *Ina-eši-êṭir*, 109:5.
Lu-li-ia, 176:9.
Lu-li.., s. *Ṣu-u..*, 176:5.
Lu-ṣu-a-na-nûr, *Lûṣi-ana-nûr*,
1. ^{amêl}*ardi-ekalli*, 174:29.
2. 4:1; 170:13.
Lu-ut-tu-u-a, *ša bît-qâti*, 174:28.
Man-na-a-ki-i-ar-ba-il, ^{amêl}*bêl-piqitti ša* ^{amêl}*qîpi*, 108:14.
Man-na-ki-i-ummu, f. *Bânia*, 177:32.
Man ..., f, *Nanâ-iddin*, 177:29.
Mar-duk,
1. s. *Kidin-Marduk*, f. *Bêl-kâṣir*, 101:17.
2. s. *Mušêzib-Marduk*, 127:36.
3. f. *Šamaš-bêl-ilâni*, 168:23.
4. f. *Zêr-ukîn*, 177:20.
5. 21:4; 70:1.
^{d}*Marduk-abu-šu*, gf. *Nabû-aḫê-iddin*.
^{d}*Marduk-apal-uṣur*,
1. s. *Mukîn-zêr*, 174:5.
2. s. *Mušêzib-Marduk*, gs. *Amêl-Ea*, 129:12.
^{d}*Marduk-bêl-ilâni*^{meš}, s. *Nabû-mušallim*, 159:24.
^{d}*Marduk-bêl-šu-nu*,
1. f. *Innina-riṣûa*, 174:27.
2. 2:1; 25:1(?); 33:1.
^{d}*Marduk-êreš(-eš)*, (*êreš* (*KAM*)),
1. s. *Nabû-ušallim*, 159:4.
2. 175:28.
^{d}*Marduk-êriba*,
1. s. *Eanna-ibni*, 157:42.
2. s. *Inî-ilu*, 177:31.
3. 23:1; 37:5; 81:33.
^{d}*Marduk-êṭir*,
1. ^{amêl}*dupsar Bît* ^{m}*Balâṭsu*, s. *Bêl-šum-iškun*, 108:4.
2. s. *Bêl-šum-iškun*, 96:7; 144:4.
3. f. *Nabû-bâni-aḫi*, 112:13.
4. f. *Niqudu*, 168:17.
5. 40:3; 96:11.
^{d}*Marduk-nâdin-aḫu*,
1. ^{amêl}*râb-bânî*, s. *Bêl-uballiṭ*, gs. *Bûṣu*, 169:4.
2. ^{amêl}*ša-ku Uruk*^{ki} s. *Nabû-šum-iškun*, gs. *Ḫûnsû*, 130:26.
3. s. *Bûṣu*, 153:3.
4. s. *Mušêzibi*, gs. ^{amêl}*râb-bânî*, 101:19.

5. s. *Nabû-iddin*, gs. ^{amêl}*šangû-*^{d}*Enurta*, 49:8.
6. s. *Nabû-šum-ibni*, 101:9.
7. 48:1.
^{d}*Marduk-nâdin-šum*,
1. s. *Bêl-apal-uṣur*, f. *Suqâi*, 174:10.
2. s. *Nâdin*, gs. *Sutî(a)*, 98:12; 105:15, 115:13.
3. s. *Nâdin*, gs. *Šutîa*, 102:15; 103:15.
4. s. *Nergal-ibni*, 159:6, 8.
5. 153:9; 170:5, 24.
^{d}*Marduk-nâṣir*, (*nâṣir(-ir)*),
1. ^{amêl}*šatam-Eanna*, 114:10.
2. s. *Bêl-šum-iškun*, 159:22.
3. f. *Gimillu*, 174:58.
4. 11:23; 56:2; 61:1.
^{d}*Marduk-šâkin-šum*,
1. s. *Sin-lîq-unnînni*, f. *Nergal-ina-ešî-êṭir*, 159:48.
2. 9:2; 11:2; 42:1; 70:3.
^{d}*Marduk-šâpik-zêr*,
1. ^{amêl}*šatam Eanna*, 126:10; 133:13.
2. s. *Balâṭu*, gs. *Miṣirai*, 103:14.
3. 88:2.
^{d}*Marduk-šar-a-ni*,
1. s. *Rîmût*, gs. *Sin-lîq-tešliti*, 130:35.
2. f. *Zêrîa*, 142:5.
3. 18:1; 151:25.
^{d}*Marduk-šum-ibni*,
1. s. *Nabû-iddin*, 36:26.
2. s. *Nabû-nâṣir*, 132:12.
3. s. *Nabû*..., 142:13.
^{d}*Marduk-šum-lîšir*, s. *Rîmût*, gs. *Bêl-usatti*, 127:32.
^{d}*Marduk-šum-u-ṣur*, s. *Bêlšunu*, 142:1.
^{d}*Marduk-uballiṭ(-iṭ)*,
1. s. *Nâdin*, gs. *Sutîa*, 111:12.
2. 82:10.
^{d}*Marduk-zêr-ibni*,
1. s. *Bêl-apal-uṣur*, f. *Bêl-iddin*, 124:15.
2. 175:5.
Meš-ša-na-du-u, f. *Nabû-nâdin-šum*, 23:7.
Mi-ia-a-ši, s. *Ṣi-ia-ki-'(?)*, 177:17.
Mi-ṣir-a-a, gf. *Marduk-šâpik-zêr*.
Muk-ki-e-a, *Muk-e-a*,
1. f. *Nanâ[-êreš]*, 99:6.
2. in *Bît* ^{m}*Muk-e-a*, 166:25.
3. 168:6.
Mukîn-aplu, s. *Nabû-aḫê-bulluṭ*, 27:4, 18.
Mukîn-šum, s. *Nabû-udammiq*, 159:28.
Mukîn-zêr,
1. s. *Nanâ-uballiṭ*, 159:21.
2. s. *Zabidâ*, 159:19.
3. f. *Marduk-apal-uṣur*, 174:5.
4. 41:1; 151:25.
Mun-na-bit-ti, *Mun-na-bit-tu*,
1. s. ^{amêl}*addupu*, f. *Bêl-iddin*, 107:11.
2. f. *Bêl-iddin*, 121:7.
3. 134:15.
Mu-ra-nu,
1. ^{amêl}*irrišu ša Šum-ukîn*, 166:29.
2. s. *Šamaš-zêr-ibni*, 164:3.
3. 16:3.
Mur-ra-nu, f. *Iqîšâ*, 177:4.
Mu-šal-li-mu, *Mu-šal-lim*,
1. s. *Amât-ilu*, 127:9.
2. 51:24.
Mu-šal-lim-^{d}*Marduk*, (*Mušallim(GI)*),
1. s. *Ardi-Nabû*, 65:6; 174:11.
2. s. *Nabû-gâmil*, 142:20.
3. s. *Nanâ*..., 142:12.
4. f. *Ṭâb-šar-Innina*, 164:4.
5. 94:6; 125:2.
Mušêtiq-aḫu-u-a, f. *Nabû-uraššî*, 127:5.
Mu-še-zi-bi, s. ^{amêl}*râb-bânî*, f. *Marduk-nâdin-aḫu*, 101:20.
Mu-še-zib-^{d}*Bêl*, (*Mušêzib(KAR)*),
1. ^{amêl}*nappaḫu*, f. *Eribšu*, 174:25.
2. ^{amêl}*râb-bânî*, s. *Balâṭsu*, gs. *Amêl-Ea*, 169:7.
3. s. *Balâṭsu*, 174:13.
4. s. *Balâṭsu*, gs. *Amêl-Ea*, 98:13; 110:14.
5. s. *Nûr-Sin*, f. *Šadûnu*, 106:14.
6. s. *Šamaš-dannu*, gs. *Êpeš-ilu*, 120:21.
7. f. *Balâṭu*, 3:9; 71:10.
8. 21:4; 25:2; 32:2; 33:3; 53:1, 37; 57:2; 85:2; 95:9.
Mu-še-zib-^{d}*Marduk*, (*Mušêzib (KAR)*),
1. s. *Amêl-Ea*, f. *Marduk-apal-uṣur*, 129:12.
2. s. *Bêlîa*, gs. *Šigûa*, 100:12.
3. s. *Egibi*, f. *Bêl-aḫê-iqîša*, 133:16.

4. s. *Sin-ibni*, f. *Bêl-aḫê-iqîša*, 133:21.
5. f. *Marduk*, 127:36.
Mutîr-aplu, 15:1.
Na-ba-a, *Na-ba-a-a*,
1. f. *Kalumu*, 114:13.
2. gf. *Balâṭsu*.
^{d}*Nabû-aḫ-êreš*, (*êreš*(*-eš*)),
1. f. *Aḫ-lûmur*, 46:6; 108:17.
2. f. *Ina-ešî-êṭir*, 159:10.
3. f. *Nabû-šum-êreš*, 152:8.
^{d}*Nabû-aḫ-iddin*,
1. ^{amêl}*šaqû šarri* ^{amêl}*bêl-piqitti Eanna*, 106:7; 113:11; 118:16; 169:10.
2. s. *Nanâ-êreš*, 46:7; 122:10; 144:8.
3. s. *Nanâ-iddin*, 157:17.
4. s. *Nanâ-šar-uṣur*, 150:10; 151:8.
5. f. *Ana-Innina-taklak*, 163:2.
6. f. *Êṭir-Šamaš*, 174:67.
7. 4:3; 7:1; 10:4; 20:3, 7; *passim*.
^{d}*Nabû-aḫ-ušabši*(*-ši*), f. *Na*[*bû*(*?*)*-bê*]*lšunu*, 174:49.
^{d}*Nabû-aḫê*^{meš}*-bul-luṭ*, (*bulliṭ*, *aḫê*$^{pl.}$),
1. ^{amêl}*dupsar*, 131:10.
2. s. *Ša-Nabû-šû*, 120:9.
3. f. *Bunanu*, 123:15.
4. f. *Mukîn-aplu*, 27:5, 19.
5. 2:2; 14:1; 120:12, 14, 15, 16, 17; 174:22; 175:26.
^{d}*Nabû-aḫê* ^{meš}*-êreš*, f. *Šamaš-êriba*, 142:17.
^{d}*Nabû-aḫê*^{meš}*-iddin*,
1. s. *Egibi*, f. *Bêlšunu*, 124:14.
2. s. *Ezida-šum-ukîn*, gs. *Marduk-abu-šu*, 109:13.
3. s. *'I-bad*, 175:11.
4. s. *Nabû*..., 157:37.
5. s. *Nâdin-šum*, f. *Nabû-nâṣir*, 108:7.
6. s. *Nergal-nâṣir*, gs. ^{amêl}..., 120:24.
7. s. *Nergal-ušallim*, 133:1.
8. f. *Nabû-nâṣir*, 142:4.
9. f. *Nabû-šum-ibni*, 175:11.
10. 22:4, 37; 26:1; 33:15; 45:1; 60:1; 74:2; 77:2; 92:2; 95:1, 7, 22.
^{d}*Nabû-aḫê*^{meš}*-ušabši*(*-ši*), 175:24.
^{d}*Nabû-aḫê*^{meš}*-ušallim*,
1. ^{amêl}*ràb-irrišti ša* ^{d}*Bêlit ša Uruk*^{ki}, s. *Nabû-dannu*, 123:3.
2. s. *Balâṭu*, 97:11.
3. s. *Kalumu*, 14:7; 127:37.
4. s. *Nabû-šum-ukîn*, gs. ^{amêl}*šangû-*^{d}*En-urta*, 101:15.
5. f. *Innin-zêr-ibni*, 118:5.
6. 154:14, 18.
^{d}*Nabû-aḫê*^{meš}..., 82:1; 93:9.
^{d}*Nabû-apal-iddin*, s. *Bêl-uballiṭ*, gs. ^{amêl}*ša ṭâbti* ^{zun}*-šu*, 113:20.
^{d}*Nabû-apal-uṣur*, *šar Bâbili*^{ki}, 96:2, 13; 107:15; 121:15; *passim*.
^{d}*Nabû-balâṭ-su-iqbi*,
1. s. *Sin-lîq-unnînni*, f. *Bânîa*, 120:28.
2. s. *Ša-Nabû-šû*, 103:7.
3. f. ^{f}*Šarrâ*, 111:6.
4. f. ...*iqîša*, 174:63.
^{d}*Nabû-balâṭ-šarri-iqbi*, 8:1.
^{d}*Nabû-ba-ni*,
1. s. *Šullummu*, 114:3.
2. 114:7.
^{d}*Nabû-bâni-aḫi*,
1. s. *Ardi-Nabû*, gs. ^{amêl}..*gi-na*, 124:6.
2. s. *Ḫapirku*, 51:5.
3. s. *Ibnâ*, gs. *Ekur-zâkir*, 133:19.
4. s. *Ibni-Ištar*, gs. ^{amêl}*agâru*, 101:17.
5. s. *Marduk-êṭir*, 112:13.
6. s. *Nabû-iqîša*, 163:7.
7. s. *Rîmût-Ea*, f. *Ardîa*, 98:4; 102:4; 103:5; 105:4; *passim*.
8. f. *Bêl-êṭir*, 103:3.
9. f. *Nûr-Sin*, 137:6.
10. 6:19; 26:2; 50:2; *passim*.
^{d}*Nabû-bâni*(*?*)*-aplu*(*?*), s. *Kidin-Marduk*, f. *Lâbâši*, 125:19.
^{d}*Nabû-bêl-šu-nu*,
1. ^{amêl}*bêl-piqitti ša Marduk-šâpik-zêr* ^{amêl}*šatam Eanna*, s. *Nabû-šum-ukîn*, 126:9.
2. ^{amêl}*ràb-bânî*, s. *Bêl-aḫ-ušubši*, gs. *Amêl-Ea*, 169:6.
3. ^{amêl}*ràb-bânî*, s. *Nâdinu*, gs. *Aḫ'utu*, 169:5.
4. s. *Balâṭu*, 170:7.
5. s. *Innina-šum-êreš*, gs. *Ea-ilûtu-ibni*, 105:16; 111:13; 115:14.
6. s. *Nabû-aḫ-ušabši*, 174:49(?).

7. s. *Nabû-šum-ukîn*, 122:1; 126:2; 145:7.
8. f. *Balâṭu*, 174:73.
9. f. *Nanâ-aḫ-iddin*, 136:5.
10. 122:7.

^{d}*Nabû-bêl-uṣur*,
1. f. *Ea-zêr-iddin*, 119:5.
2. 80:2.

^{d}*Nabû-bît(?)-ia-a-ši*, f. *Ṣillâ*, 177:6.

^{d}*Nabû-dan*(or *dannu*),
1. s. *Balâṭsu*, 156:25.
2. s. *Nabû-zêr-lîšir*, 174:66.
3. f. *Innin-zêr-ušabši*, 166:32.
4. f. *Nabû-aḫê-ušallim*, 123:4.
5. f. *Šâkin-šum*, 157:43.

^{d}*Nabû-dûr-pâni-iá*, 150:7.

^{d}*Nabû-edu-uṣur*,
1. f. ^{f}*Abîddi*, 120:2.
2. f. ^{f}*Basurâ*, 120:2.
3. f. ^{f}*Bêlti-abušu*, 120:2.
4. f. ^{f}*Ina-qâti-Nanâ-šâkin*, 120:2.
5. f. *Nâdin-šum*, 174:43.
6. f. ^{f}*Nanâ-aili*, 120:2.

^{d}*Nabû-e-ḫi(iḫ)-im-me-e*,
1. f. *Nabû(?)-enatannu*, 177:16.
2. f. *Nâdina-aḫu*, 151:7.

^{d}*Nabû-e-na-ta-nu*, (*e-na-tan-nu*),
1. s. *Nabû-eḫîmme*, 177:15.
2. s. *Tâlla*, 108:2.

^{d}*Nabû-êpuš(-uš?)*, 156:39.

^{d}*Nabû-êriba*,
1. s. *Bulluṭa*, 108:19.
2. s. *Kuddia*, 177:35.

^{d}*Nabû-êṭir*, (*êṭir(-ir)*),
1. ^{amêl}*si-pi-ri Nabû-aḫ-iddin*, 95:3.
2. s. *Amêl-Ea*, f. *Nabû-nâdin-šum*, 102:18.
3. s. *Aplâ*, 174:7.
4. s. *Bêl-aḫ-iddin*, 157:13.
5. s. *Nanâ-iddin*, 2:17.
6. s. *Ukumu*, 159:33.
7. s. . . ., 128:13.
8. f. *Šamaš-iqîša*, 128:5.
9. f. *Šum-ukîn*, 153:5.
10. 89:7(?); 93:11; 170:14; 175:7, 15.

^{d}*Nabû-êṭir-napšâti*^{meš},
1. ^{amêl}*pu-ṣa-a-a*, 174:47.
2. s. *Ardi-Bêl*, gs. . . ., 120:26.
3. s. *Bânia*, 126:17.
4. s. *Bêl-li'u*, 108:9.
5. s. *Ea-kurbanni*, f. *Ea-kurbanni*, 169:13.
6. s. *Egibi*, f. *Gimil-Šamaš*, 113:21.
7. s. *Ibni-Ištar*, gs. *Kurî*, 106:16.
8. s. *Nergal-uballiṭ*, 133:8.
9. s. . . .*ia*, gs. *Rîmût-Bêl*, 103:6.
10. f. *Nabû-šum-lîšir*, 100:10.
11. 30:1; 34:1; 131:13; 156:33; 170:4, 25.

^{d}*Nabû-ga(?)-mil(?)*, f. *Mušallim-Marduk*, 142:20.

^{d}*Nabû-ibni*, 66:6; 175:66(?).

^{d}*Nabû-iddin*,
1. ^{amêl}*mu-ša-kil alpu*, s. *Nanâ-iddin*, 174:24.
2. s. *Ardi-Innin*, 164:2.
3. s. ^{amêl}*šangû-*^{d}*Enurta*, f. *Marduk-nâdin-aḫu*, 49:9.
4. f. *Bêl-šum-iškun*, 159:23.
5. f. *Marduk-šum-ibni*, 36:26.
6. f. *Nabû-kîn-uballiṭ*, 174:34.
7. f. *Riḫêti*, 157:19.
8. f. *Zêrîa*, 97:10; 166:10.
9. 156:18, 31.

^{d}*Nabû-ina-na-kut-ti-al-si*, 163:16.

^{d}*Nabû-iq-ṣur*, s. *Nergal-šum-ibni*, 137:3.

^{d}*Nabû-iqîša(-ša)*,
1. s.*Nanâ-iddin*, gs. *Nûr-Sin*, 127:33.
2. f. *Nabû-bâni-aḫi*, 163:7.
3. in ^{nâr}*sa-ḫi-ru ša* ^{md}*Nabû-iqîša*, 116:2.
4. 28:10, 14.

^{d}*Nabû-ka-ṣir*,
1. s. *Ârrabtum*, f. *Nabû-zêr-ukîn*, 113:19.
2. s. *Balâṭu*, 117:4.
3. f. *Zêr-ukîn*, 153:1.

^{d}*Nabû-kib-su-šar-uṣur*, 50:1.

^{d}*Nabû-kil-la-an-ni*, 158:13.

^{d}*Nabû-kîn-uballiṭ(-iṭ)*, s. *Nabû-iddin*, 174:34.

^{d}*Nabû-kudurri-uṣur*, *šar Bâbili*^{ki}, 99:21; 101:23; 108:21; *passim*.

^{d}*Nabû-li'u*, f. *Nabû-zêr-ušabši*, 159:17.

^{d}*Nabû-lu-u-da-a-ri*, 59:1.

^{d}*Nabû-ma-lik*, 83:26.

^{d}*Nabû-muk-e-lip*, s. *Nabû-šum-ukîn*, 157:21.

^{d}*Nabû-mukîn-aplu,*
1. ^{amêl}*šatam Eanna,* s. *Nâdinu,* gs. *Dabibi,* 106:6; 113:10; 118:14; 169:9.
2. s. *Nâdin,* gs. *Dabibi,* 109:12.
3. f. *Šullum,* 174:12.
4. 4:2; 19:1; 69:3; 158:22.

^{d}*Nabû-mu-še-ti-iq(NI)-urra,*
1. s. *Balâṭsu,* gs. *Da'iqu,* 101:1.
2. s. *Nûr-Sin,* f. *Ardi-Marduk,* 120:22.
3. f. *Nidinti,* 165:15.
4. 45:4; 62:25; 75:3; 90:2; 91:1; 101:11, 13; 163:15.

^{d}*Nabû-na-din-aḫu, (nâdin),*
1. ^{amêl}*apal-šipri ša Šum-ukîn,* 166:2.
2. s. *Ḫûnsu',* f. *Šâpik,* 107:8.
3. s. *Ia-ḫu,* 97:12.

^{d}*Nabû-nâdin-šum, (na-din),*
1. ^{amêl}*mu. . .,* 175:46.
2. ^{amêl}*šatammu,* 73:22.
3. [^{amêl}*šatam Eanna*] s. *Bêl-šum-iškun,* gs. *Dabibi,* 130:28.
4. s. *Bânitu-šu-lîšir,* 140:3.
5. s. *Iddin-Papsukal,* f. *Nâdin-aplu,* 130:7, 10, 40.
6. s. *Meššanadû,* 23:6.
7. s. *Nabû-êṭir,* gs. *Amêl-Ea,* 102:18.
8. s. *Nanâ-êreš,* 168:24; 172:3.
9. f. *Nâdin-aplu,* 130:18.
10. 23:25; 61:2; 175:40.

^{d}*Nabû-nâ'id,*
1. s. *Aplâ,* 177:39.
2. *šar Bâbili*^{ki}, 3:15; 71:13; *passim.*

^{d}*Nabû-nâṣir,*
1. ^{amêl}*kudimmu,* s. *Nergal-iddin,* 132:10.
2. s. *Ardîá,* 163:11.
3. s. *Nabû-aḫê*^{meš}*-iddin,* 142:4.
4. s. *Nabû-aḫê*^{meš}*-iddin,* gs. *Nâdin-šum,* 108:7.
5. s. *Nûr-Sin,* f. *Bêl-ušallim,* 107:10.
6. s. *Zabidâ,* 112:12.
7. f. *Balâṭsu,* 154:8.
8. f. *Kudurru,* 25:43; 46:8.
9. f. *Marduk-šum-ibni,* 132:10.
10. f. *Rîmût,* 139:6.
11. 95:17; 132:15; 156:6.

^{d}*Nabû-na. . .,* 68:1.

^{d}*Nabû-nûr,* f. *Nabû-zêr-ibni,* 157:23.

^{d}*Nabû-qat-šu-ṣa-bat,* 158:14.

^{d}*Nabû-qâtâ-ṣa-bat,* in *Bît* ^{md}*Nabû-qâtâ-ṣa-bat,* 166:8.

^{d}*Nabû-ri-man-ni,*
1. ^{amêl}*TIL-LA-GID-DA* (= *qîpu*), 114:11.
2. s. ^{amêl}*ša ṭâbti*^{zun}*-šu,* f. . . .*ŠEŠ,* 98:14.

^{d}*Nabû-šar-aḫê*$^{pl.}$*-šu,* 156:21, 23.

^{d}*Nabû-šar-ḫi-ilâni*$^{pl.}$, f. . . .*a,* 130:31.

^{d}*Nabû-šar-ilâni*$^{pl.}$,
1. f. *Ardîa,* 108:18.
2. 175:14.

^{d}*Nabû-šar-uṣur,*
1. ^{amêl}*apal-šipri Nergal-uballiṭ,* 133:4.
2. ^{amêl}*šaqû šarri* ^{amêl}*bêl-piqitti Eanna,* 104:7; 120:19.
3. 32:1; 54:2; 55:2; 65:1; 85:1.

^{d}*Nabû-šar-ut-su,* ^{amêl}*qîpu ša E-apzu,* 47:1.

^{d}*Nabû-šum-êreš,*
1. s. *Âlu-lûmur,* 139:4.
2. s. *Nabû-aḫ-êreš,* 152:8.
3. s. *Zîbi,* 157:40.
4. f. *Bêl-ušallim,* 142:7.
5. f. *Zêrûtu,* 142:6.
6. 41:18; 60:13; 79:1(?); 139:2; 152:23; 156:16, 26.

^{d}*Nabû-šum-ibni,*
1. ^{amêl}*aškapu,* s. *Amêl-Nanâ,* 151:23.
2. s. *Amêl-Nanâ,* 151:17.
3. s. *Nabû-aḫê-iddin,* 175:12.
4. s. *Ša-Nabû-šû,* 157:4.
5. s. . . ., 112:1.
6. f. *Amêl-Nanâ,* 157:16.
7. f. *Ardi-Innina,* 157:10.
8. f. *Ibni-Innina,* 154:21.
9. f. *Marduk-nâdin-aḫu,* 101:10.
10. 44:3; 60:13; 154:3; 156:10, 12, 23.

^{d}*Nabû-šum-iškun(-un), (iš-kun),*
1. s. *Ḫûnsû,* f. *Marduk-nâdin-aḫu,* 130:26.
2. s. *Šullummu,* 114:14.
3. f. *Innin-ina-ešî-êṭir,* 127:38.
4. 9:8, 14.

^{d}*Nabû-šum-lîšir,*
1. s. *Kurî,* f. *Rîmûtu,* 118:4.
2. s. *Nabû-êṭir-napšâti*^{meš}, 100:9.
3. in ^{nâr}*ḫar-ri ša* ^{md}*Nabû-šum-lîšir,* 166:24.

^{d}*Nabû-šum-ukîn*,
1. $^{am\hat{e}l}$*bêl-piqitti ša Marduk-šâpik-zêr* $^{am\hat{e}l}$*šatammu ša Eanna*, f. *Nabû-bêl-šunu*, 126:9.
2. $^{am\hat{e}l}$*kudimmu*, 138:6.
3. s. *A*..., 157:36.
4. s. *Êṭeru*, f. *Ili'-Marduk*, 98:5.
5. s. $^{am\hat{e}l}$*šangû-*^{d}*Enurta*, f. *Nabû-aḫê-ušallim*, 101:15.
6. f. *Nabû-bêlšunu*, 122:2; 126:2; 145:8.
7. f. *Nabû-muk-elip*, 157:21.
8. f. ...*bêl-šu*, 174:53.
9. 28:2, 13; 45:2.

^{d}*Nabû-šum-uṣur*,
1. s. *Ea-êpuš*, 157:5.
2. s. *Uruk*^{ki}*-a-a*, 157:12.
3. s. ..., 157:28.

^{d}*Nabû-šu-zib-an-ni*, f. *Ina-ṣilli-Nanâ*, 136:7.
^{d}*Nabû-ṣu-li-e-ši-ma*, 12:2, 14.
^{d}*Nabû-tak-lak*, $^{am\hat{e}l}$*gal-la Nabû-aḫê-bulliṭ*, 120:15.
^{d}*Nabû-târiṣ(-iṣ)* (*LAL-IṢ*), 135:3.
^{d}*Nabû[-tu]-kul-ti*, 61:19.
^{d}*Nabû-ub-ni-ia*, $^{am\hat{e}l}$*nuḫatimmu bît-ḫi-ri*, 174:17.

^{d}*Nabû-uballiṭ(-iṭ)*,
1. s. *Ina-Esagila-zêr*, 174:75.
2. s. *Ina-pân-danu*, 129:4.
3. 64:18.

^{d}*Nabû-udammiq(-iq)*,
1. s. *Zibâ*, 159:39.
2. f. *Mukîn-šum*, 159:28.
3. 93:10.

^{d}*Nabû-unammir(-ir)*, f. *Nabû-zêr-ibni*, 156:7, 20.
^{d}*Nabû-urašši(-ši)*, s. *Mušêtiq-aḫûa*, 127:5.

^{d}*Nabû-ušabši(-ši)*,
1. s. *Iddina*, 156:15.
2. 22:1; 156:41.

^{d}*Nabû-ušallim*,
1. $^{am\hat{e}l}$*dupsar ši-pir-ti*, 46:9.
2. $^{am\hat{e}l}$*rê'u-sattukkû*, s. *Kudurru*, 148:4.
3. s. *Bêl-êriba*, 157:15.
4. f. *Aḫ-iddin-Marduk*, 127:13, 19.
5. f. *Ardia*, 156:14.
6. f. *Marduk-bêl-ilâni*, 159:24.
7. f. *Marduk-êreš*, 159:4.
8. 68:2; 78:9; 148:3; 174:22.

^{d}*Nabû-u-še-zib*,
1. s. *Tabbanêa*, 114:4.
2. f. *Aplâ*, 159:35.
3. f. *Balâṭsu-ilu*, 156:9.
4. 62:2; 114:7; 156:36.

^{d}*Nabû-u-ṣal-la*, (*u-ṣal-li*),
1. f. *Aḫḫûtu*, 114:17.
2. f. *Amêl-Nabû*, 157:18.
3. f. *Iddîa*, 177:5.

^{d}*Nabû-u-ṭir-ra*, 163:5.
^{d}*Nabû-uznâ (PI)-iddin*, 175:53.

^{d}*Nabû-zêr-ibni*,
1. s. *Iddin-Nergal*, 177:19.
2. s. *Nabû-nûr*, 157:23.
3. s. *Nabû-unammir*, 156:7, 20.
4. s. .., 157:30.
5. f. *Amêl-Nanâ*, 142:18.
6. f. *Bêl-aḫê-iddin*, 127:14, 18, 24, 44.
7. 31:15; 156:17, 29.

^{d}*Nabû-zêr-iddin*,
1. $^{am\hat{e}l}$*nappaḫu-parzilli*, 173:7.
2. s. *Nanâ-êreš*, 155:18.
3. s. *Ubar*, 155:13.
4. f. *Balâṭsu*, 108:5.
5. f. *Ina-eši-êṭir*, 114:14.
6. f. *Silim-Bêl*, 151:5.
7. 18:2; 156:5, 8; 175:62; 177:36.

^{d}*Nabû-zêr-iqîša(-ša)*,
1. s. *Nanâ*..., 135:8.
2. f. *Balâṭu*, 41:16.
3. 31:1.

^{d}*Nabû-zêr-lîšir*,
1. f. *Nabû-dannu*, 174:66.
2. 57:18.

^{d}*Nabû-zêr-ukîn*,
1. $^{am\hat{e}l}$*kudimmu*, 138:6.
2. s. *Abiri-ilu*, 177:33.
3. s. $^{am\hat{e}l}$*ašlaku*, f. *Ibni-Innina*, 133:22.
4. s. *Bêl-uballiṭ*, 93:18.
5. s. *Bêl-usatu*, 159:31.
6. s. *Nabû-kâṣir*, gs. *Ârrabtum*, 113:19.
7. s. *Šumâ*, 171:6.
8. s. ..*šâkin-šum*, 142:10.
9. f. *Ardi-Innina*, 142:21.

10. f. *Bêlšunu*, 157:6.
11. f. *Nâdin*, 28:29.
12. f. *Nanâ-aḫ-iddin*, 177:34.
13. f. . ., 93:15.

^{d}*Nabû-zêr-ušabši(-ši)*,
1. s. *Bêl-ušallim*, 161:3.
2. s. *Nabû-li'u*, 159:17.
3. s. *Ša-Nabû-šû*, 157:11.

^{d}*Nabû-zêr* . . ., 156:38.

^{d}*Nabû* . . .,
1. f. *Marduk-šum-ibni*, 142:13.
2. f. *Nabû-aḫê-iddin*, 157:37.
3. 76:1.

Na-din, Na-di-nu,
1. ^{amêl}*irrišu*, 158:29.
2. *ša bît-*^{amêl}*bêl-paḫâti*, 33:25.
3. s. *Aḫ'ûtu*, f. *Nabû-bêlšunu*, 169:5.
4. s. *Aplâ*, 170:11.
5. s. *Bêl-aḫê-iqîša*, gs. *Egibi*, 120:27.
6. s. *Bêl-li'u*, gs. *Sin-lîq-unnînni*, 104:3.
7. s. *Bunâ*, gs. ^{amêl}*ušparu*, 146:2.
8. s. *Dabibi*, f. *Nabû-mukîn-aplu*, 106:7; 109:12; 113:11; 118:15; 169:10.
9. s. *Nabû-zêr-ukîn*, 28:29.
10. s. *Nergal-nâṣir*, gs. ^{amêl}*šangû*, 124:5.
11. s. *Nergal-nâṣir*, gs. ^{amêl}*ušparu*, 133:20.
12. s. *Sutî(a)*, f. *Marduk-nâdin-šum*, 98:12; 105:16; 115:14.
13. s. *Sutîa*, f. *Marduk-uballiṭ*, 111:13.
14. s. *Šulâ*, 177:14.
15. s. *Šutîá*, f. *Marduk-nâdin-šum*, 102:16; 103:16.
16. f. *Zuzuzu*, 174:61.
17. h. ^{f}*Emuqtum*, 106:3.
18. 2:4; 5:2; 6:13, 17; *passim*.

Nad-na-a,
1. ^{amêl}*man-di-di*, 108:13.
2. ^{amêl}*šu-ša-nu*, 157:7.
3. f. *Bêl-ibni*, 177:26.
4. f. *Kudurru*, 157:7.
5. 175:63.

Nâdina(-na)-aḫu, Nâdin-aḫu,
1. s. *Gašura*, f. *Nabû-šum-ukîn*, 98:15; 105:18; 111:15; 115:16.
2. s. *Innina-zêr-ibni*, 151:16.
3. s. *Nabû-êḫîmme*, 151:7.
4. f. *Ḫar* (or *Mur*). ., 142:23.
5. f. *Innina-zêr-iddin*, 163:10.
6. f. *Šullum*, 177:21.
7. 20:9, 17; 67:1; 154:19.

Nâdina(-na)-aplu, Nâdin-aplu,
1. s. *Iddin-Nergal*, 177:22.
2. s. *Kuddâ*, 177:7.
3. s. *Nabû-nâdin-šum*, 130:18.
4. s. *Nabû-nâdin-šum*, gs. *Iddin-Papsukal*, 130:7, 10, 40.

Nâdin-šum,
1. ^{amêl}*pu-ṣa-a-a*, s. *Nabû-edu-uṣur*, 174:43.
2. s. *Nergal-ušallim*, gs. *Sin-lîq-unnînni*, 104:12.
3. s. . . ., 157:35.
4. f. *Iqîša-Marduk*, 141:3.
5. gf. *Nabû-nâṣir*.
6. 3:1; 71:1.

^{d}*Na-na-a-aḫ-iddin*,
1. ^{amêl}*âtû ša bît-alpê*$^{pl.}$, 174:33.
2. ^{amêl}*ušparu* . . . *mu*, 174:46.
3. s. *Ár-rab*, 162:18.
4. s. *Innina-zêr-ibni*, 129:14.
5. s. *Nabû-bêlšunu*, 136:5.
6. s. *Nabû-zêr-ukîn*, 177:34.
7. f. *Nidinti*, 125:6.
8. 152:10; 175:43.

^{d}*Na-na-a-e-pu-uš*, (*êpuš*(*-uš*)),
1. ^{amêl}*gal-la*, 141:9.
2. s. *Bêl-aḫê-ušallim*, 141:5.
3. b. *Ištar-šum-êreš*, 93:8.
4. 141:8, 14, 22.

^{d}*Na-na-a-êreš*, (*êreš*(*-eš*)),
1. s. *Bânia*, 177:13,
2. s. *Ina-ṣilli-Nanâ*, 151:13.
3. s. *Lakip*, 99:17.
4. s. *Mukkêa*, 99:6.
5. s. *Nabû-zêr-iddin*, 155:18.
6. s. *Nanâ-ibni*, 157:3.
7. f. *Balâṭsu*, 142:9.
8. f. *Nabû-aḫ-iddin*, 46:7; 122:11; 144:8.
9. f. *Nabû-nâdin-šum*, 168:24; 172:3.
10. f. *Sin-ibni*, 168:27.
11. 175:27, 45.

^{d}*Na-na-a-ibni*,
1. f. *Bulluṭa*, 112:4; 157:1.
2. f. *Nanâ-êreš*, 157:3.
3. f. *Nergal-nâṣir*, 174:51.

^{d}*Na-na-a-iddin*,
1. ^{amêl}*mu-ša-kil alpu*, s. *Nabû-iddin*, 174:24.
2. ^{amêl}*râb-šanû*, s. *Ardi-Innin*, 174:44.
3. ^{amêl}*širqu ša* ^{d}*Belit ša Uruk*^{ki}, s. ^{f}*Emuqtum*, 106:4.
4. s. *Ammanu*, 125:5.
5. s. *Gimillu*, 157:26.
6. s. *Ḫârmaṣu*, 24:9.
7. s. *Man*.., 177:29.
8. s. *Nûr-Sin*, f. *Nabû-iqîša*, 127:33.
9. f. *Êribšu*, 165:3.
10. f. *Innin-nâdin-aḫu*, 109:8.
11. f. *Nabû-aḫ-iddin*, 157:17.
12. f. *Nabû-êṭir*, 2:12.
13. f. *Šamaš-zêr-ibni*, 118:2.
14. f. *Zêrîa*, 155:14.
15. 27:26; 41:7, 11; 122:6.

^{d}*Na-na-a-itti-ia*, ^{amêl}*šu-ša-nu*, 155:16.

^{d}*Na-na-a-karâbi*, f. *Aḫê*^{meš}*-ša-a*, 159:44.

^{d}*Na-na-a-šar-uṣur*, f. *Nabû-aḫ-iddin*, 150:10; 151:8.

^{d}*Na-na-a-uballiṭ(-iṭ)*, f. *Mukîn-zêr*, 159:21.

^{d}*Na-na-a*...,
1. s. *Mušallim-Marduk*, 142:12.
2. f. *Nabû-zêr-iqîša*, 135:8.

Nâ'id-^{d}*Ištar*,
1. b. *Silim-Bêl*, 151:6.
2. 62:3.

Nâ'id-^{d}*Marduk*,
1. s. *Ûmu-19*^{kan}*-nâṣir*, 159:18.
2. 175:9.

^{d}*Nergal-abu-uṣur*, ^{amêl}*gal-la ša Raḫîm*, 166:16.

^{d}*Nergal-êpuš(-uš)*,
1. ^{amêl}*malaḫu*, 155:6.
2. s. *Bêl-zêr*, 158:13.
3. 5:1; 24:1; 64:1; 158:8.

^{d}*Nergal-êṭir*,
1. s. ^{amêl}..., 37:16.
2. s. *Bêl-êpuš*, 157:22.
3. f. *Innina-zêr-uṣur*, 157:9.
4. 175:19, 34.

^{d}*Nergal-ibni, (ib-ni)*,
1. s. ^{amêl}*šangû-*^{d}*Adad*, f. *Innin-šum-iškun*, 106:16.
2. f. *Kuddîa*, 157:14.
3. f. *Kurigalsu*, 159:34.
4. f. *Marduk-nâdin-šum*, 159:6, 8.
5. f. *Silim-ilu*, 159:25.
6. 175:4, 33.

^{d}*Nergal-iddin*,
1. s. *Kunâ*, f. *Bêl-iddin*, 110:13.
2. s. *Ša-Nabû-šû*, 157:8.
3. s. ..., 119:14; 157:31.
4. f. *Nabû-nâṣir*, 132:10.
5. 35:11; 155:5.

^{d}*Nergal-ina-ešî-êṭir*,
1. s. *Marduk-šâkin-šum*, gs. *Sin-lîqunnînni*, 159:48.
2. s. *Zadunâ*, 112:2.
3. 44:2; 60:12; 154:5, 20.

^{d}*Nergal-nâdin-šum*, s. *Ina-ešî-êṭir*, gs. *Ḫûnsû*, 104:11.

^{d}*Nergal-nâṣir, (nâṣir(-ir), na-ṣir)*,
1. s. *A-qar*.., 108:10.
2. s. *Bêl-usatu*, gs. ^{amêl}*KIM-A*, 141:1.
3. s. *Nanâ-ibni*, 174:51.
4. s. *Šamaš*..., 114:15.
5. s. ^{amêl}*šangû*, f. *Nâdin*, 124:5.
6. s. ^{amêl}*ušparu*, f. *Nâdin*, 133:20.
7. s. ^{amêl}.., f. *Nabû-aḫê-iddin*, 120:24.
8. f. *Innina-nâdin-aḫu*, 99:19.
9. 131:1, 21; 141:6, 7, 13.

^{d}*Nergal-šar-uṣur*,
1. *šar Bâbili*^{ki}, 123:19; 131:4; 166:1, 5; 170:2, 3.
2. 44:32; 60:6, 8, 26, 32.

^{d}*Nergal-šum-ibni*,
1. s. *Innina-šum-lîšir*, 127:40.
2. f. *Kalbâ*, 97:6.
3. f. *Nabû-iqṣur*, 137:3.

^{d}*Nergal-ṭâbu*, f. *Innina-zêr-iqîša*, 36:27.

^{d}*Nergal-uballiṭ(-iṭ)*,
1. s. *Balâṭu*, 108:12.
2. s. *Bêl-li'u*, 133:2, 10.
3. s. ^{amêl}*šangû-parakki*, f. *Šamaš-šum-lîšir*, *Sin-kîšir* and *Gimil-Nanâ*, 101:5.

4. f. *Innin-zêr-iqîša*, 49:8.
5. f. *Innina-zêr-iqîša*, 36:27.
6. f. *Nabû-êṭir-napšâti*^{meš}, 133:8.
7. f. *Šamaš-iqbi*, 115:11.
8. 44:9, 20; 95:2; 101:9; 133:5; 156:43.

^{d}*Nergal-u-sip-pi*, s. *Ḫûnsû*, f. *Nûrea*, 125:17.

^{d}*Nergal-ušallim*,
1. s. *Sin-lîq-unnînni*, f. *Innin-nâdin-aḫu*, 124:16.
2. s. *Sin-lîq-unnînni*, f. *Nâdin-šum*, 104:13.
3. f. *Bânia*, 166:21.
4. f. *Nabû-aḫê-iddin*, 133:2.
5. 131:15; 170:10.

^{d}*Nergal-u-še-zib*, 37:15; 168:10.

^{d}*Nergal*.., 72:1; 154:27.

Ni-din-ti, *Ni-din-tum*,
1. ^{amêl}*ušparu*, 165:4.
2. s. *Ardîa*, gs. *Šâkin-zêr*, 174:9.
3. s. *Ḫâḫḫuru*, 174:56.
4. s. *Nabû-mušêtiq-urra*, 165:15.
5. s. *Nanâ-aḫ-iddin*, 125:6.
6. 174:55.

Ni-din-tu-^{d}*Bêl*, 80:3.

Ni-qu-du, s. *Marduk-êṭir*, 168:16.

Nu-ḫa-a, 158:15.

Nu-uḫ-ḫu-ki, f. *Bulluṭa*, 156:13.

Nûr-e-a,
1. s. *Nergal-usippi*, gs. *Ḫûnsû*, 125:17.
2. s. *Šamaš-uballiṭ*, 174:50.
3. 158:23; 168:16.

Nûr-^{d}*Nabû*, 84:16.

Nûr-^{d}*Sin*,
1. s. *Nabû-bâni-aḫi*, 137:6.
2. gf. *Ardi-Marduk*.
3. gf. *Bêl-ušallim*.
4. gf. *Nabû-iqîša*.
5. gf. *Šadûnu*.
6. 153:13.

^{d}*Nusku-iddin*, f. *Rîmût-Bêl*, 113:1.

Pir-', s. *Šamaš-zêr-iqîša*, 168:12.

Qurdi (AM)-^{d}*Ea*, gf. *Šamaš-aḫ-iddin*.

^{amêl}*râb-bânî*, gf. *Nabû-nâdin-aḫu*.

Ra-ḫi-im, 166:16.

^{amêl}*rê'u-sattukkû*, gf. ..., 130:32.

Ri-ḫi-e-ti, *Ri-ḫi-e-tu*,
1. s. *Nabû-iddin*, 157:19.
2. 95:4, 10, 13, 16, 28.

Ri-ḫi-im, 108:3; 166:16.

Ri-mut, *Ri-mu-tu*,
1. ^{amêl}*apal-šipri Nabû-šum-iškun*, 9:6.
2. ^{amêl}*nuḫatimmu bît-ḫi-ri*, 165:1; 174:14.
3. ^{amêl}*paḫḫaru*, 174:23.
4. ^{amêl}*širqu ša* ^{d}*Belit ša Uruk*^{ki}, s. ^{f}*Emuqtum*, 106:4.
5. ^{amêl}*te-ba-a-a*, 151:14.
6. s. *Balâṭu*, gs. *Ḫânbi*, 107:6.
7. s. *Bêl-uballiṭ*, 157:39.
8. s. *Bêl-usatu*, gs. ^{amêl}*KIM-A*, 141:1.
9. s. *Bêl-usatti*, f. *Marduk-šum-lîšir*, 127:32.
10. s. *Kurî*, f. *Šulâ*, 118:19.
11. s. *Nabû-nâṣir*, 139:5.
12. s. *Nabû-šum-lîšir*, gs. *Kurî*, 118:3.
13. s. *Sin-lîq-tešliti*, f. *Marduk-šarani*, 130:35.
14. s. *Šâkin-šum*, 114:12.
15. s. ^{f}*zakitu*, 161:7.
16. s. .., 157:33.
17. f. *Ubar*, 174:36.
18. gf. *Ardia*.
19. 18:7, 31; 139:2; 141:20, 21, 26; 170:18.

Ri-mut-^{d}*Bêl*,
1. s. *Nusku-iddin*, 113:1.
2. gf. *Nabû-êṭir-napšâti*^{meš}.
3. 113:6, 7, 13, 15, 16, 17.

Ri-mut-^{d}*Ea*, gf. *Ardîa*.

Si-lim-^{d}*Bêl*,
1. ^{amêl}*irrišu*, 158:22.
2. s. *Aplâ*, 112:3.
3. s. *Nabû-zêr-iddin(?)*, 151:5.
4. s. .., 157:32.
5. f. *Guzanu*, 174:52.
6. 35:1; 44:1; 51:1; 154:22.

Si-lim-ilu,
1. *amêl ša eli qu-pu*, 7:20.
2. ^{amêl}*šaqû šarri amêl ša eli qu-ub-bu*, 169:2.
3. s. *Nergal-ibni*, 159:25.

Si(?)-lim(?)-^{d}*Na-na-a*, ^{amêl}*rê'u*, 91:6.

Si(?)-na(?)-me-lum, 175:56.
^{d}*Sin-aḫ-iddin*, s. *Ṣillâ*, 129:13.
^{d}*Sin-êreš*,
1. s. *Ibni-ilu*, f. . ., 117:22.
2. 153:11.
^{d}*Sin-ibni*,
1. s. *Kinâ*, 151:4.
2. s. *Nanâ-êreš*, 168:27.
3. gf. *Bêl-aḫê-iqîša*.
^{d}*Sin-iddin*, ^{amêl}*qîpu ša Eanna*, 124:7.
^{d}*Sin-ki-šir*, s. *Nergal-uballiṭ*, gs. ^{amêl}*šangû-parakki*, 101:4.
^{d}*Sin-lîq-tešliti* (*A-RA-ZU*), gf. *Marduk-šarani*.
^{d}*Sin-lîq-unnînni*,
1. gf. *Bânîa*.
2. gf. *Nâdinu*.
3. gf. *Nâdin-šum*.
4. gf. *Nergal-ina-ešî-êṭir*.
5. gf. *Nergal-ušallim*.
^{d}*Sin-muk-ki-e-lip*, 30:2.
^{d}*Sin-šar-uṣur*, 12:1.
^{d}*Sin-šum(?)-êreš(?)*, 80:1.
^{d}*Sin-udammiq(-iq)*, 85:16.
^{d}*Sin*. ., 124:12.
Su-qa-a-a,
1. s. *Balâṭi*, 174:65.
2. s. *Marduk-nâdin-šum*, gs. *Bêl-apal-uṣur*, 174:10.
Su-ti-ia, *Su-ti-i*,
1. gf. *Marduk-nâdin-šum*.
2. gf. *Marduk-uballiṭ*.
Ša-al-mu(?), f. *Šamaš-tabni-uṣur*, 174:76.
Ša-ba-ḫi-ilu, in ^{âl}*Bît* ^{m}*Ša-ba-ḫi-ilu*, 97:15.
Ša-^{d}*Bêl-liš-ši*, in *Bît* ^{m}*Ša-*^{d}*Bêl-liš-ši*, 174:55.
Ša-du-nu,
1. s. *Mušêzib-Bêl*, gs. *Nûr-Sin*, 106:14.
2. s. ^{amêl}[ ], f. *Anu-zêr-ušabši*, 118:8.
3. 153:14.
Ša(or *A*)*-gur(?)-ru*, 79:12.
Ša-^{d}*Innina-tak-lak*, s. *Bânia*, 151:24.
Šâkin-šum,
1. s. *Nabû-dannu*, 157:43.
2. s. *Šamaš[-šum(?)]-lîšir*, 135:4.
3. s. *Ṣillâ*, 157:27.
4. f. *Ardîa*, 170:16.
5. f. *Ištar-šum-êreš*, 93:7.
6. f. *Rîmûtu*, 114:12.
7. 154:15.
Šâkin-zêr, gf. *Nidinti*.
Ša-la-da-a-ta, 155:10.
Ša-lam-El, 16:19.
Šal-ti-ilu, 87:1.
Ša-ma-'-gu-nu,
1. s. *Êṭir*, 177:25.
2. 175:54.
^{d}*Šamaš-aḫ-iddin*,
1. ^{amêl}*paqudu ša Uruk*^{ki}, s. *Šamaš-nâdin-šum*, gs. *Qurdi-Ea*, 169:11, 18.
2. ^{amêl}*ušparu*, 165:4.
3. s. *Ardia*, 157:41.
4. s. *Šamaš-balâṭsu*, 117:5.
5. 21:2; 39:23.
^{d}*Šamaš-aḫê*^{meš}*-ušallim*, 175:10.
^{d}*Šamaš-balâṭ-su*, f. *Šamaš-aḫ-iddin*, 117:5.
^{d}*Šamaš-bêl-ilâni*^{meš}, s. *Marduk*, 168:22.
^{d}*Šamaš-dan* (or *dannu*),
1. s. *Êpeš-ilu*, f. *Mušêzib-Bêl*, 120:21.
2. s. *Ina-ešî-êṭir*, 109:9.
3. 32:3; 65:2.
Šamaš-êreš, 13:2.
Šamaš-êriba,
1. ^{amêl}*ša-qu-u*, 155:3.
2. s. *Bêl-iddin*, 107:2.
3. s. *Nabû-aḫê-êreš*, 142:17.
4. s. *Šarid*, 159:29.
5. f. *Kuddîa*, 157:20.
6. f. *Zêrûtu*, 172:4.
^{d}*Šamaš-êṭir*, 28:23.
^{d}*Šamaš-GAL-LU-lu-mur*, s. *Kidin-Marduk*, f. *Šamaš-napištim-uṣur*, 106:11.
^{d}*Šamaš-ibni*,
1. in *Bît* ^{md}*Šamaš-ibni*, 111:2.
2. 87:11.
^{d}*Šamaš-iddin*,
1. s. *Šu'atu*, f. *Bêl-ušallim*, 101:19.
2. 30:17.
^{d}*Šamaš-'-id-ri*, (*id-ri-'*),
1. ^{amêl}*qîpu ša Larsum*^{ki}, 169:1.
2. 10:1.

^{d}*Šamaš-iqbi*,
1. s. *Nergal-uballiṭ*, 115:10.
2. 115:12.

^{d}*Šamaš-iqîša(-ša)*, s. *Nabû-êṭir*, 128:5.

^{d}*Šamaš-li'u*,
1. s. *Šamaš-šum-lîšir*, 105:11.
2. 105:14.

^{d}*Šamaš-mukîn-aplu*,
1. s. *Bânîa*, 109:15.
2. 19:2.

^{d}*Šamaš-nâdin-aplu*, f. *Nabû-ušallim*, 101:19.

^{d}*Šamaš-nâdin-šum*,
1. s. *Qurdi-Ea*, f. *Šamaš-aḫ-iddin*, 169:12.
2. 158:11, 12; 166:3.

^{d}*Šamaš-napištim(-tim)-uṣur*, s. *Šamaš-GAL-LU-lûmur*, gs. *Kidin-Marduk*, 106:11.

^{d}*Šamaš-rê'u-šu-nu*, s. *Imbîa*, gs. *Kuri*, 125:18.

^{d}*Šamaš-šum-ibni*, s. *Ta*..., 142:14.

^{d}*Šamaš-šum-lîšir*,
1. s. *Nergal-uballiṭ*, gs. ^{amêl}*šangû-parakki*, 101:4.
2. f. *Šâkin-šum*, 135:4(?).
3. f. *Šamaš-li'u*, 105:12.

^{d}*Šamaš-šum-ukîn*,
1. ^{amêl}*pu-ṣa-a-a*, 165:9.
2. b. *Bêl-aḫê-iddin*, 151:10.

^{d}*Šamaš-tab(?)-ni-uṣur*, s. *Ša-al-mu(?)*, 174:76.

^{d}*Šamaš-uballiṭ(-iṭ)*,
1. f. *Ibni-Innina*, 174:70.
2. f. *Nûr(?)-ea*, 174:50.
3. 66:1.

^{d}*Šamaš-zêr-ibni*,
1. s. *Nanâ-iddin*, 118:1.
2. f. *Muranu*, 164:3.
3. f. *Šulâ*, 174:2.
4. f. ..*dannu*, 174:35.
5. in *Bît* ^{md}*Šamaš-zêr-ibni*, 166:26.
6. 25:39.

^{d}*Šamaš-zêr-iqîša(-ša)*,
1. s. *Ibâ*, 149:7.
2. f. *Pir'*, 168:12.
3. f. *Šulâ*, 105:5.
4. 63:1.

^{d}*Šamaš*...,
1. f. *Nergal-nâṣir*, 114:16.
2. 85:4; 158:29(?).

Ša-^{d}*Nabû-êriba*, ^{amêl}*bêl-pi-qit-ni-ti*^{meš} *ša*—, 151:26.

Ša-^{d}*Nabû-i-šal-lim*, 165:12.

Ša-^{d}*Nabû-ša-lim*, (*šal-lim*), 24:25; 157:45.

Ša-^{d}*Nabû-šu-u*,
1. ^{amêl}*irrišu ša* ^{amêl}*ša-ku*, 142:2.
2. s. *Kinunâi*, 163:6.
3. f. *Nabû-aḫê-bulluṭ*, 120:9.
4. f. *Nabû-balâṭsu-iqbi*, 103:8.
5. f. *Nabû-šum-ibni*, 157:4.
6. f. *Nabû-zêr-ušabši*, 157:11.
7. f. *Nergal-iddin*, 157:8.
8. 46:11; 175:16, 37, 49.

^{amêl}*šangû*, gf. *Nâdin*.

^{amêl}*šangû-*^{d}*Adad*, gf. *Innin-šum-iškun*.

^{amêl}*šangû-*^{d}*Enurta*,
1. gf. *Marduk-nâdin-aḫu*.
2. gf. *Nabû-aḫê-ušallim*.

^{amêl}*šangû-parakki*,
1. gf. *Anûm-mukîn-aplu*.
2. gf. *Gimil-Nanâ*.
3. gf. *Sin-kîšir*.
4. gf. *Šamaš-šum-lîšir*.

^{amêl}*šangû-*^{al}*Šal-lat*, gf. *Lîširi*.

Ša-pik,
1. s. *Nabû-nâdin-aḫu*, gs. *Ḫûnsû*, 107:8.
2. f. *Bêl-ibni*, 159:26.

Ša-rid, f. *Šamaš-êriba*, 159:29.

Šarru-êṭir(-ir), f. *Ardîa*, 123:6.

Šarru(?)..*iá(?)*, 28:28.

^{amêl}*ša ṭâbti*^{zun}*-šu*,
1. gf. *Nabû-apal-iddin*.
2. gf. ...*ŠEŠ*.

Šêlibu(LUL-A), s. *Bânîa*, 174:8.

Ši-gu-u-a,
1. gf. *Gimillu*.
2. gf. *Mušêzib-Marduk*.

Šu-la-a,
1. s. *Ardia*, 151:2.
2. s. *Bêl-êpuš*, 122:2.
3. s. *Bêl-iqîša*, 121:10.
4. s. *Gimillu*, 168:8.
5. s. ^{amêl}*kudimmu*, f. *Innin-zêr-ušabši*. 174:40.
6. s. *Nabâi*, f. *Balâṭsu*, 133:17.
7. s. *Nabû-zêr-iqîša*, 41:15.

8. s. *Rîmût*, gs. *Kurî*, 118:19.
9. s. *Šamaš-zêr-ibni*, 174:1.
10. s. *Šamaš-zêr-iqîša*, 105:5.
11. s. *Zabdi-ilu*, 177:30.
12. f. *Árrab*, 119:3; 168:14.
13. f. *Bêl-šum-iškun*, 159:11.
14. f. *Iddin-nu-nu*, 174:21.
15. f. *Nâdin*, 177:14.
16. 17:1; 31:21; 52:4; *passim*.

Šul-lu-mu, Šul-lum, Šul-lum-mu,
1. s. *Balâṭsu*, 159:12.
2. s. *Nabû-mukîn-aplu*, 174:12.
3. s. *Nâdina-aḫu*, 177:21.
4. f. *Bêl-êṭir*, 157:38.
5. f. *Nabû-bâni*, 114:4.
6. f. *Nabû-šum-iškun*, 114:15.
7. 58:1.

Šu-ma-a,
1. s. *Kunâ*, 177:28.
2. s. *Zabunu*, 159:27.
3. s. *Zîbu*, 159:15, 45.
4. f. *Nabû-zêr-ukîn*, 171:6.
5. 175:1.

Šum-ukîn, (*ukîna*(*-na*)),
1. *amêl ša eli giš-bar ša* ^{d}*Bêlit*, s. *Bêl-zêr*, gs. *Basîa*, 97:3.
2. s. *Aḫêa*, 152:16.
3. s. *Bêl-aḫ-iddin*, 127:34.
4. s. *Nabû-êṭir*, 153:5.
5. f. *Gilûa*, 159:16.
6. in *Bît* ^{m}*Šum-ukîn*, 166:16.
7. 33:27, 55:1; *passim*.

Šu-ra-nu,
1. ^{amêl}*šu-ša-nu ša nak-kan-du*, 48:25.
2. 48:29, 36.

Šu-ru-mu, 155:11.

Šu-ti-iá, gf. *Marduk-nâdin-šum*.

Šu-zu-bu,
1. s. *Bêl-iqîša*, 127:7.
2. f. *Gimillu*, 127:35.
3. 11:1; 37:1.

Šu'atu, gf. *Bêl-ušallim*.

Ṣi-ia-ki-'(*?*), f. *Mi-ia-a-ši*, 177:18.

Ṣil-la-a, Ṣilla-a,
1. ^{amêl}*nuḫatimmu bît-ḫi-ri*, 165:5.
2. ^{amêl}*nappaḫu-parzilli*, 142:15.
3. ^{amêl}*ràb-qa-na*, 61:15.
4. s. *Abi-iá*, 43:19.
5. s. *Nabû-bit*(*?*)*-iâši*, 177:6.
6. f. *Balâṭu*, 117:1.
7. f. *Balâṭsu*, 157:24.
8. f. *Iqîšâ*, 130:6.
9. f. *Sin-aḫ-iddin*, 129:13.
10. f. *Šâkin-šum*, 157:27.
11. f. . ., 163:10.
12. in *Bît* ^{m}*Ṣil-la-a*, 166:23.
13. 6:1; 43:22; 61:25.

Ṣu-u. . ., f. *Lu-li*. ., 176:6.

Ta-al-la, f. *Nabû-enatanu*, 108:2.

Tab-ba-ni-e-a, f. *Nabû-ušêzib*, 114:5.

Tab-ni-e-a,
1. s. ^{amêl}*bâ'iru*, f. *Ea-bâni-zêr*, 133:18.
2. f. *Balâṭu*, 153:2.
3. 21:9, 21; 175:3.

Ta-qiš-^{d}*Gu-la*, f. *Innina-zêr-ibni*, 174:54.

Tar-ba-ru-šu, f. *Aḫ-iddin*, 116:5.

Tar-bi, gf. *Balâṭsu*.

Ta. . .,
1. f. *Šamaš-šum-ibni*, 142:14.
2. 57:22, 29.

Te-rik-šarru-us-su, s. *Zâkir*, 151:11.

Tukulti(*-ti*)-^{d}*Marduk*,
1. ^{amêl}*rê'u-sattukkû*, 147:6.
2. s. *Dûmmuqu*, gs. *E-sag*[*-gil*]*-a*, 120:23.

^{d}*TUR*(or *Banda*)*-E-sag-ila-ri-ṣu-u-a*,
1. f. *Itti-Nabû-gûsu*, 120:5.
2. f. ^{f}*Itti-Nanâ-gûsu*, 120:5.
3. f. ^{f}*Nanâ-silim*, 120:5.
4. f. ^{f}*Šidati*, 120:5.
5. h. ^{f}*Ninlil-tabni*, 120:5.
6. 120:1; 165:11.

Ṭâb-šar-^{d}*Ištar*, (^{d}*Innina*),
1. ^{amêl}*addupu*, 151:20.
2. s. *Mušallim-Marduk*, 164:4.
3. f. *Innina-zêr-ušabši*, 150:2.

Ṭâb-šar-^{d}*Šamaš*, ^{amêl}*nuḫatimmu* ^{d}*TUR-Esagila-riṣûa*, 120:1.

Ṭâb-Uruk^{ki},
1. f. *Êribšu*, 174:18.
2. 158:7.

U-bar,
1. ^{amêl}*mu-ša-kil alpê*$^{pl.}$, 174:31.
2. ^{amêl}*nappaḫu-parzilli*, 174:74.

3. s. *Rîmût*, 174:36.
4. f. *Nabû-zêr-iddin*, 155:13.
U-ku-mu, f. *Nabû-êṭir*, 159:33.
Ûmu-19^{kan}-nâṣir, f. *Nâ'id-Marduk*, 159:18.
Uruk^{ki}-a-a, f. *Nabû-šum-uṣur*, 157:12.
^{amêl}*ušparu*, gf. *Nâdin*.
^{d}*Za-bâ-bâ-êriba*, f. *Bêl-ušallim*, 126:16.
^{d}*Za-bâ-bâ-nâdin-šum*, s. *Bêl-êpuš*, 122:3.
Za-bi-da-a,
1. s. *Bêl-êreš*, 157:25.
2. f. *Ina-ešî-êṭir*, 157:2.
3. f. *Mukîn-zêr*, 159:19.
4. f. *Nabû-nâṣir*, 112:12.
5. f. . . .*ibni*, 121:8.
6. 175:36, 38, 60.
Zab-di-ilu, f. *Šulâ*, 177:30.
Za-bu-nu,
1. f. *Šumâ*, 159:27.
2. in *Bît* ^{m}*Za-bu-nu*, 159:1.
Za-du-na-a, f. *Nergal-ešî-êṭir*, 112:2.
Za-kir,
1. f. *Balâṭu*, 174:37.
2. f. *Têrik-šarrûssu*, 151:11.
Zêri-ia, *Zêri-iá*,
1. ^{amêl}*bâni*, s. *Bulluṭ*, gs. *Balâṭu*, 133: 14.
2. s. *Bânia*, 73:11.
3. s. *Bêl-šum-iškun*, 148:1.
4. s. *Egibi*, f. *Ardi-Marduk*, 118:17; 169:3.
5. s. *Marduk-šarani*, 142:5.
6. s. *Nabû-iddin*, 97:10; 166:10.
7. s. *Nanâ-iddin*, 155:14.
8. s. *Šigûa*, f. *Gimillu*, 133:15.
9. s. . . .*na-a*, 123:14; 124:13.
10. f. *Bêl-iddin*, 33:12.
11. 8:6; 16:6, 21; 33:14; 90:1; 153:7.
Zêr-iddina(-na),
1. f. *Bêl-aḫê-iddin*, 159:42.
2. f. *Aḫê-ša-'*, 159:9.
Zêr-u-tu, *Zêru-tu*,
1. ^{amêl}*ṣa-ri-pi-*[ ], s. *Šamaš-êriba*, 172:4.
2. s. *Nabû-šum-êreš*, 142:6.
3. 175:59.
Zêr-ukîn,
1. s. *Marduk*, 177:20.
2. s. *Nabû-kâṣir*, 153:1.
3. 175:48.
Zi-ba-a,
1. f. *Nabû-udammiq*, 159:39.
2. 175:51.
Zib(?)-ka(?)-šu-^{d}*Na-na-a*, 175:35.
Zi-i-bi, f. *Nabû-šum-êreš*, 157:40.
Zi-i-bu, f. *Šumâ*, 159:15, 45.
Zîr-bi-bi, ^{amêl}*nuḫatimmu bît-ḫi-ri ša* ^{amêl}*šatam-mu*, 131:12.
Zu-zu-zu,
1. s. *Ibni-Ištar*, 174:6.
2. s. *Nâdinu*, 174:61.
^{amêl}. .*gi-na*, gf. *Nabû-bâni-aḫi*.
^{amêl}[ ], gf. *Anu-zêr-ušabši*.
^{amêl}. . ., gf. *Nabû-aḫê-iddin*.
. . .*a*, s. *Nabû-šarḫi-ilâni*$^{pl.}$, f. . . ., 130:31.
. . .*aḫ-iddin*, 125:2.
. . .*aḫê*^{meš}*-iddin*, 81:2.
. . .*bêl-šu*, s. *Nabû-šum-ukîn*, 174:53.
. . .*bît*, s. ^{amêl}*rê'u-sattukkû*, f. . ., 130:32.
. . .*dannu*, s. *Šamaš-zêr-ibni*, 174:35.
. . .*di*, gf. *Kalbâ*.
. . .*êriba*, 25:3.
. . .*êṭir-napšâti*^{meš}, 34:16.
. . .*ia*, s. *Rîmût-Bêl*, f. *Nabû-êṭir-napšâti*^{meš}, 103:7.
. . .*ibni*, s. *Zabidâ*, 121:8.
. . .^{d}*Innina*, 158:33.
. . .*iq-bi*, s. *Bêl-êriba*, 123:13.
. . .*iqîša(-ša)*, s. *Nabû-balâṭsu-iqbi*, 174:63.
. . .*iš* (or *mil*), s. *Bânitu-šu*, 121:9.
. . .*mukîn-zêr*, s. *Bêl-iqîša*, 142:11.
. . .*na-a*, f. *Zêria*, 123:14.
. . .*šâkin-šum*, f. *Nabû-zêr-ukîn*, 142:10.
. . .*ŠEŠ*, s. *Nabû-rîmanni*, gs. ^{amêl}*ša ṭâbti*^{zun}*-šu*, 98:14.
. . .*šir*, 39:1.
. . .*šum-ukîn*, 131:1.
. . .*ukîn*, 88:1.
. . .*ušabši(-ši)*, s. . . ., 79:23.
. . .*uṣur*, *šar Bâbili*^{ki}, 151:30.

Feminine Names.

^{f}*A-bi-id-di*, d. *Nabû-edu-uṣur*, 120:2.
^{f}*Ba-su-ra-a*,
1. d. *Nabû-edu-uṣur*, 120:2.
2. 120:4.
^{f}*Bêlti-abu-šu*, d. *Nabû-edu-uṣur*, 120:2.
^{f}*E-muq-tum*,
1. ^{amêl}*širqu* ^{d}*Innina Uruk*^{ki}, w. *Nâdinu*, 106:2.
2. m. *Nanâ-iddin*, 106:2.
3. m. *Rîmût*, 106:2.
4. 106:12.
^{f}*Ina-qâti-*^{d}*Na-na-a-ša-kin*, d. *Nabû-edu-uṣur*, 120:3.
^{fd}*Innina(-na)-e-ṭe-rat*, 28:1.
^{f}*Itti-*^{d}*Na-na-a-gu-u-su*, d. ^{d}*TUR-Esagila-riṣûa*, 120:6.
^{f}*Kal-ba-a*, ^{f}*Kalba-a*, 6:2, 21.
^{fd}*Na-na-a-ai-li*, d. *Nabû-edu-uṣur*, 120:3.
^{fd}*Na-na-a-si-lim*, d. ^{d}*TUR-Esagila-riṣûa*, 120:7.
^{fd}*Nin-lil-tab-ni*, w. ^{d}*TUR-Esagila-riṣûa*, 120:5.
^{f}*Šar-ra-a*, d. *Nabû-balâṭsu-iqbi*, 111:5.
^{f}*Ši-da-ti*, d. ^{d}*TUR-Esagila-riṣûa*, 120:7.

Names of Scribes.

^{d}*A-num-mukîn-aplu*, s. *Innina-tabni-uṣur*, gs. *Gimil-Nanâ*, 97:13.
Ba-ba-a, s. *Ibni-Ištar*, gs. ^{amêl}*ašlaku*, 120:29.
Ba-lat-su, s. *Bêl-aḫê-iddin*, gs. *Tarbi*, 101:21.
^{d}*Bêl-iqîša(-ša)*,
1. s. *Bânîa*, *gs.* ^{amêl}*bâ'iru*, 102:19; 129:15.
2. s. . . ., 117:24.
Bu-na-nu, s. *Nabû-aḫê-bulliṭ*, 123:15.
E-an-na-šum-ibni, s. *Aḫê-ša-a*, 100:13.
Gimillu, s. *Innin-zêr-iddin*, 106:18.
^{d}*In-nin-šum-uṣur*, s. *Bêl-aḫê-iddin*, 127:41.
^{d}*Innina(-na)-nâdin-aḫu*, s. *Nergal-nâṣir*, 99:19.
^{d}*Innina(-na)-zêr-ušabši(-ši)*, s. *Kudurru*, 126:20.
^{d}*Marduk-êṭir*,
1. ^{amêl}*dupsar Eanna*, s. *Bêl-šum-iškun*, gs. *Dabibi*, 130:36.
2. s. *Dabibi*, 107:12.
Mu-še-zib-^{d}*Šamaš*, s. *Ištar-zêr-ibni*, 109:16; 113:23.
Na-di-nu,
1. s. *Bêl-aḫê-iqîša*, gs. *Egibi*, 118:20.
2. s. *Bêl-limur*, gs. *Egibi*, 104:14.
^{d}*Nabû-bâni-aḫi*, s. *Ibni*. . ., 112:15.
^{d}*Nabû-bêl-šu-nu*, s. *Innina-šum-êreš*, gs. *Ea-ilûtu-ibni*, 110:15; 125:20.
^{d}*Nabû-nâdin-šum*, s. *Bêl-šum-iškun*, gs. *Dabibi*, 121:11.
^{d}*Nabû-šum-ukîn*, (*ukîna(-na)*), s. *Nâdina-aḫu*, gs. *Gašura*, 98:15; 105:18; 111:15; 115:16.
^{d}*Šamaš-mukîn-aplu*, s. *Eanna-nâdin-šum*, gs. *Babûtu*, 103:18; 116:15; 119:17; 128:14.
Ši-riq-tum-^{d}*AZAG-SUD*, s. *Balâṭu*, 169:24.

Names of Deities.

^{d}*Adad*, see names with ^{amêl}*šangû*—, and *abullu*—.
^{d}*Aja*, 21:6; 50:3.
^{d}*Amar*, see name with ^{d}*Amar*—.
^{d}*Amurru*, see names with ^{d}*Amurru*—.
An-ni-tum, 158:26.
^{d}*Anu*, ^{d}*A-nu*, ^{d}*A-nu-um*, ^{d}*A-num*, see names with ^{d}*Anu*—, and *E*—, also 63:3; 64:5.
^{d}*Aš-ka-i-ti*, 152:4, 20.

^{d}*AZAG-SUD*, see name *Širiqtum*—.
^{d}*Bau*, see name with ^{d}*Bau*—.
^{d}*Bêl*, see names with ^{d}*Bêl*—, *Ardi*—, *At-kal-ana*—, *Iddin*—, *Ina-ṣilli—ab-ni*, *Itti—limmir*, *Ki-bi*—, *Mušêzib*—, *Nidin-tu*—, *Rîmût*—, *Silim*—, *Ša—lišši*, and 5:3; 6:3; *passim*.
^{d}*Bêlit*, 152:4, 21; 153:15.
^{d}*Bêlit Larsum*^{ki} 10:9.
^{d}*Bêlit ša Uruk*^{ki}, 3:3; 13:3; *passim*.
^{d}*Bu-ne-ne*, 1:4; 10:5; 42:4.
^{d}*Dajân*, see names with ^{d}*Dajân*—.
^{d}*Ea*, see names with ^{d}*Ea*—, *Amêl*—, *Ardi*—, *Qurdi*—, *Rîmût*—, and 47:6, 16.
El, see name *Šalam*—, and *bît*—, *bâb*—, ^{nâr}*ša bît*—.
^{d}*Ellil*, see name *Iddin*—,
^{d}*Enurta*, see names with ^{amêl}*šangû*—, and *E*—, also 54:10(?); 60:16(?); 101:16.
^{d}*GID-DA-KI-AN-NA*, 47:6.
^{d}*Gu-la*, see names *Ardi*—, *Taqîš*—.
^{d}*Il-ta-meš*, see name with ^{d}*Il-ta-meš*—.
ilu ša amêlu-tu, 28:4.
^{d}*In-nin*, see names with ^{d}*Innin*—, and ^{nâr}—.
^{d}*Innina Uruk*^{ki}, 34:22; 98:2; *passim*.
^{d}*Ištar*, ^{d}*Innina*, see names with ^{d}*Ištar*—, ^{d}*Innina*—, *Aḫu-dân*—, *Ibni*—, *Nâ'id*—, *Ša—taklak*, *Ṭâb-šar*—, . .—, and ^{nâr}—, also 27:7; 43:3; *passim*.
^{d}*Lugal-Banda(-da)*, see name with ^{d}*Lugal-Banda*—.
^{d}*MA*(or *AŠ*)-*KUR*, 48:3.
^{d}*Marduk*, see names with ^{d}*Marduk*—, *Aḫ-iddin*—, *Amêl*—, *Ardi*—, *Dajân*—, *Iddin*—, *Ili'*—, *Iqîša*—, *Kidin*—, *Kurbanni*—, *Lâbâši*—, *Mušallim*—, *Mušêzib*—, *Nâ'id*—, *Tukulti*—, and 2:4; 4:4; *passim*.
Meš (or *Mešša*), see name with *Meš*—.
^{d}*Nabû*, see names with ^{d}*Nabû*—, *Amêl*—, *Ardi*—, *Iddin*—, *Iškun*—, *Itti—gûsu*, *Itti—inîa*, *Kisik*—, *Nûr*—, *Ša—êriba*, *Ša—išallim*, *Ša—šallim*, *Ša—šû*, and *E*—, also 2:4; 4:4; *passim*.
^{d}*Na-na-a*, see names with ^{d}*Nanâ*—, *Amêl*—, *Ardi*—, *Gimil*—, *Ina-qâti—šâkin*, *Ina-ṣilli*—, *Itti—gûsu*, *Silim(?)*—, *Zib(?)-ka(?)-šu*—, and ^{âl}*Kar*—, also 3:4; 13:4; *passim*.
^{d}*Nergal*, see names with ^{d}*Nergal*—, *Dannu*—, *Iddin*—, and 37:3.
^{d}*Nin-gal*, 12:3; 80:5.
^{d}*Nin-lil*, see name with ^{d}*Ninlil*—.
^{d}*Nusku*, see name with ^{d}*Nusku*—.
^{d}*Papsukal*, see name *Iddin*—.
^{d}*Sin*, see names with ^{d}*Sin*—, *Nûr*—, and 12:3; 30:4, 14, 21, 23, 28; 37:3; 80:5.
^{d}*Šamaš*, (^{d}*Šam-šu*), see names with ^{d}*Šamaš*—, *Êṭir*—, *Gimil*—, *Iddin*—, *Itti—balâṭu*, *Mušêzib*—, *Ṭâb-šar*—, and 1:4, 10, 14; 10:5, 17; *passim*.
^{d}*Šar-rat Kul-la-bu*, 28:3.
^{d}*TUR* (or *Banda*), see name with ^{d}*TUR*—.
^{d}*Za-bâ-bâ*,[1] see names with ^{d}*Za-bâ-bâ*—.

Names of Temples.

E-^{d}*A-num*, 127:3.
E-an-na, see names with *E-an-na*—, *Ina-ṣilla*—, *Itti—GID-DI-iá*, and *bît makkurru ša*—, also 2:7; *passim*.
E-apzu, 47:2.
E-bar-ra, 21:13.
E-^{d}*Enurta*, 152:5.
E-kur, see names with *Ekur*—, and 33:7; 80:23, 31; 82:6.
E-^{d}*Nabû*, 117:4.
E-sag-ila(-la), see names *Ina-Esagila-zêr*, ^{d}*TUR-Esagila-riṣua*, and 21:19; 138:3.
E-Uruk^{ki}, 127:42.
E-zi-da, see name with *Ezida*—, and 32:8.

[1] For this reading see Chicago Syllabary, l. 220, *American Journal of Semitic Languages and Literatures*, XXXIII, p. 169 ff.

Names of Places.

^{âl}*A-GA-DE*^{ki}, *mât Akkadu*^{ki}, 17:6, 11; 36:43.
Bâbili^{ki}, 1:15; 3:16; *passim.*
Bar-sip^{ki}, 59:8, 19.
Bît a-ki-tu, 170:19.
Bît ^{m}*Aḫê*^{meš}*-ša-a*, 159:44.
Bît ^{m}*Amêl- Nabû*, 25:49.
Bît ^{m}*Ár-rab*, 119:11.
Bît ^{m}*Bânîa*, 113:9; 166:21.
Bît ^{md}*Bêl-aḫ-šub-ši*, 166:27.
Bît ^{md}*Bêl-aḫê*^{meš}*-iddin*, 127:24.
Bît ^{amêl}*bêl-paḫâti*, 33:25.
Bît-El, Bît-ilu,
1. 114:8; 166:12.
2. in ^{nâr}*ša Bît El*, 44:24; 102:2; 105:2.
Bît-e-pi-nu, 117:16.
Bît-erinu^{meš}, 19:9, 20; 26:22.
Bît-^{iṣ}*gišimmaru ša ina E-*^{d}*Nabû*, 117:3.
Bît ^{amêl}*bâru(ḪAL)*, 166:26.
Bît-ḫi-ri, (*ḫi-ri-e*), *bît-ḫi-ri ša* ^{amêl}*šatammu*, 131:12; 150:9; 165:1, 6; 174:14, 15, 16, 17.
Bît ^{md}*In-nin-zêr-ušabši(-ši)*, 166:31.
Bît ^{md}*In-nin-zêr-ušallim*, 118:4.
Bît ^{m}*I...*, 129:16.
Bît-Ka-lak-ku in *bâb bît-Ka-lak-ku*, 121:4.
Bît-kal-lu-u, 23:25.
Bît-ka-ri-e, (*kar-ri*), 25:7; 54:20.
Bît ^{m}*Ki-na-a*, 166:17.
Bît ^{amêl}*ku-ra-am*, 166:30.
Bît ^{m}*La-bi-ri-ia*, 166:13.
Bît ^{m}*Li-pa-'*, 130:3.
Bît-makkuru ša Eanna, 126:7.
Bît-makkuru^{meš} *ša ṣabê*, 46:41.
Bît ^{m}*Muk-e-a*, 166:25.
Bît ^{m}*Mu-ra-nu*, 166:29.
Bît ^{m}*Mu-šal-lim*, 127:9.
Bît ^{md}*Nabû-qâtâ-ṣa-bat*, 166:8.
Bît ^{md}*Nabû-urašši(-ši)*, 127:5.
Bît ^{md}*Nabû-zêr-ukîn*, 93:18.
Bît ^{m}*Nâdin-aplu*, 130:18.
Bît ^{md}*Nergal-abu-uṣur*, 166:16.
Bît ^{amêl}*rê'i(-i)*, 94:4.
Bît ^{amêl}*rê'u-sattukkû*, 167:5.
Bît ^{m}*Rîmûtu*, 118:3.
^{âl}*Bît* ^{m}*Ša-ba-ḫi-ilu*, 97:15.
Bît ^{m}*Ša-*^{d}*Bêl-lišši*, 174:55.
Bît ^{md}*Šamaš-zêr-ibni*, 118:1; 166:26.
^{âl}*Bît-šap-ru-'*, 163:14.
Bît ^{m}*Šu-zu-bu*, 127:7.
Bît ^{m}*Šum-ukîn*, 166:6.
Bît ^{m}*Ṣil-la-a*, 166:23.
Bît ^{m}*Za-bu-nu*, 159:1.
^{âl}*Dûr-ša-i-ti-ri*, 168:2, 21, 29.
^{âl}*E-ku-šu*, 58:17.
^{âl}*Kap-ra*, 58:16.
^{âl}*Kar-Na-na-a*, 116:16; 123:16; 154:13 without the determinative *âlu*.
^{âl}*Kar(?)-ra-ma-nu-u-a*, 83:2.
^{âl}*Kul-la-bu*, 28:3, 31.
^{âl}*KUR-BAT*, 128:2, 15; 166:27.
^{âl}*La-giš-bar*, 119:2, 18.
^{âl}*La-su-u-tu*, 168:20.
Larsum^{ki}, 5:10, 18; 169:1.
^{âl}*pît-qa ša* ^{md}*Bêl-êṭir*, 102:20; 99:20; and 103:19; 117:25; 125:21 without the determinative *âlu*.
^{âl}*Nu-ḫa-nu*, 43:16.
Sippar^{ki}, 93:15.
^{âl}*Ša* ^{m}*A-mat-su-uṣur*, 166:7.
^{âl}*Šal-la-ta*,
1. 126:4, 6.
2. in ^{amêl}*šangû* ^{âl}*Šal-lat*, 122:13.
^{âl}*Ši-li-iḫ-ti(?)*, 168:26.
Uru^{ki}, 30:9.
Uruk^{ki}, see names with *Uruk*^{ki}—, *Ṭâb*—, and *abullu ša*—, *bâb ša*—, also 1:12; 5:7; *passim.*

Names of Canals.

^{nâr}*Eš-še-ti*, *Eš-šu*, 110:2; 111:16; 159:47; 166:13.

^{nâr}*ḫar-ri ša* ^{m}*Du*(or *Gub*)*-ba-a*, 101:8; 166:20.

^{nâr}*ḫar-ri ša* ^{md}*Nabû-šum-lîšir*, 166:24.

^{nârd}*In-nin*, 131:17; 166:6.

^{nârd}*Innina*(*-na*), 158:18.

^{nâr}*Ni-ḫi-šar*(*?*).., 29:10.

^{nâr}*Ni-ib-ta*, 35:19.

^{nâr}*pît-qa ša* ^{md}*Bêl-êṭir*, (*pît-qu*),
  1. 98:16; 105:19; 115:17.
  2. in *bâb* ^{nâr}*pît-qa ša* ^{md}*Bêl-êṭir*, 99:2.

^{nâr}*Sa-ḫi-ri*, 159:30.

^{nâr}*sa-ḫi-ru ša* ^{md}*Nabû-iqîša*(*-ša*), 116:2.

^{nâr}*Si*(*?*)*-ma-di-e*(*?*), 60:27.

^{nâr}*ša Bît-El*, 44:24; 102:2; 105:2.

^{nâr}*Ša-kil-la-at*, 97:9.

^{nâr}*Šarru*, 7:23; 44:27; 130:2.

^{nâr}*Tak-ki-ri*, *Ta-ki-ru*, 37:10; 98:2; 115:2.

^{nâr}*Tak-kil-bêl-lu-šar-ri-tu*, 55:12.

Names of Gates.

abullu ^{d}*Adad*, 32:18.

abullu ša Uruk^{ki}, 104:6.

bâb âlu, 117:6.

bâb Bît-Ka-lak-ku, 121:4.

bâb ekallu, 24:16.

bâb El, 42:8.

bâb nâri, 95:26.

bâb ^{nâr}*pît-qa ša* ^{md}*Bêl-êṭir*, 99:2.

bâb^{meš} *ša* ^{âl}*KUR-BAT*, 128:2.

bâb ša Uruk^{ki}, 23:26.

CATALOGUE.

A. List of Letters.

Text No.	Letter from	Addressed to	Catalog NBC
1	*[d]Il-ta-meš-id-ri-'* and *Iddin-[d]Šamšu.*	*šatammu.*	1138
2	*Marduk-bêlšunu* and *Nabû-aḫê-bulliṭ.*	*Balâṭsu, Dajân-Marduk* and *Nâdin.*	1071
3	*Nâdin-šum.*	*šatammu.*	1140
4	*Lûṣu-ana-nûr.*	*Nabû-mukîn-aplu* and *Nabû-aḫ-iddin.*	1116
5	*Nergal-êpuš.*	*Nâdin* and *Balâṭu.*	1129
6	*Ṣillâ.*	*[f]Kalbâ.*	1120
7	*Nabû-aḫ-iddin.*	*Nâdin.*	1153
8	*Nabû-balâṭ-šarri-iqbi.*	*Nâdinu.*	1147
9	*Itti-Bêl-limmir.*	*Marduk-šâkin-šum.*	1124
10	*Šamaš-'idri* and *Kisik-Nabû.*	*šatammu* and *Nabû-aḫ-iddin.*	1144
11	*Šûzubu.*	*Marduk-šâkin-šum* and *Nâdin.*	1149
12	*Sin-šar-uṣur.*	*Nabû-ṣu-li-e-ši-ma.*	1117
13	*Ab-di-iá.*	*Šamaš-êreš.*	1075
14	*Nabû-aḫê-bulliṭ.*	*Nâdin, Balâṭsu, Nâdin* and *belê pi-qit-e-tu.*	1154
15	*Mutîr-aplu.*	*šatammu.*	1081
16	*Innina-aḫê-iddin.*	*Nâdin, Kinâ, Balâṭu* and *Muranu.*	1112
17	*Šulâ.*	*dupsar-bîti.*	1085
18	*Marduk-šarani* and *Nabû-zêr-iddin.*	*Nâdin.*	1157
19	*Nabû-mukîn-aplu.*	*Šamaš-mukîn-aplu, Lâbâši-Marduk* and *Iddinâ.*	1146
20	*Kinâ.*	*šatammu* and *Nabû-aḫ-iddin.*	1152
21	*Kisik-Nabû* and *Šamaš-aḫ-iddin.*	*Amurru-zêr-ibni, Bêl-nâdin-aplu, Mušêzib-Bêl, Marduk* and *Innin-zêr-ušabši.*	1110
22	*Enurta-šar-uṣur.*	*Nabû-ušabši.*	1101
23	*Marduk-êriba.*	*qîpi, šatammu,* and *dupsar-bîti.*	1096
24	*Nergal-êpuš.*	*Kurbanni-Marduk.*	1141
25	*[Mard]uk-bêlšunu.*	*Mušêzib-Bêl,...-êriba, Nâdin* and *Nâdin.*	1099
26	*Nabû-aḫê-iddin.*	*Nabû-bâni-aḫu.*	1156
27	....	.... and *Mukîn-aplu* s. *Nabû-aḫê-bulluṭ.*	1159
28	*[f]Innina-êṭerat.*	*Nabû-šum-ukîn.*	1106
29	*Innin-aḫê-iddin.*	*Nâdinu.*	1103
30	*Nabû-êṭir-napšâti* and *Sin-mukki-elip.*	*šatammu.*	1078
31	*Nabû-zêr-iqîša.*	*qîpi, šatammu* and *dupsar-bîti.*	1115

Text No.	Letter from	Addres ed to	Catalog NBC
32	*Nabû-šar-uṣur.*	*Mušêzib-Bêl, Nâdin, Šamaš-dannu* and *Innin-zêr-ušabši.*	1136
33	*Marduk-bêlšunu.*	*Lîširu, Mušêzib-Bêl, Balâṭsu* and *Nâdin.*	1114
34	*Nabû-êṭir-napšâti.*	*Nâdin.*	1125
35	*Silim-Bêl.*	*šatammu.*	1132
36	*amêl Uruk*[ki]...	*amêl Uruk*[ki]...	1119
37	*Šûzubu.*	*šatammu.*	1105
38	*Enurta-šar-uṣur.*	*Balâṭsu.*	1111
39	....*šir.*	*qîpi, šatammu* and *dupsar-bîti.*	1108
40	*Enurta-šar-uṣur.*	*Nâdin* and *Marduk-êṭir.*	1123
41	*Mukîn-zêr.*	*qîpi, šatammu* and *dupsar-bîti.*	1127
42	*Marduk-šâkin-šum.*	*šatammu.*	1148
43	*Ibni-Ištar.*	*šangû-Eanna.*	1072
44	*Silim-Bêl, Nergal-ina-eši-êṭir* and *Nabû-šum-ibni.*	*šatammu.*	1131
45	*Nabû-aḫê-iddin.*	*Nabû-šum-ukîn* and *Nabû-mušêtiq-urra.*	1135
46	*Nabû-aḫ-iddin.*	*šatammu.*	1104
47	*Nabû-šar-ut-su qîpu ša E-apzu.*	*Kinâ šatam Eanna* and *Nabû-aḫ-iddin.*	1145
48	*Marduk-nâdin-aḫu.*	*Nabû-aḫ-iddin.*	1094
49	*amêl-Uruk*[ki]*-ai ṣab-tu-tu.*	*šatammu.*	1150
50	*Nabû-kibsu-šar-uṣur.*	*Nabû-bâni-aḫu.*	1134
51	*[Si]-lim-Bêl.*	*šatammu.*	1097
52	*Ardi-Nabû.*	*Bêl-iddin.*	1121
53	*Mušêzib-Bêl* and *Ibni-Ištar.*	*šatammu.*	1100
54	*Innin-šar-uṣur.*	*Nabû-šar-uṣur.*	1113
55	*Šum-ukîn.*	*Nabû-šar-uṣur.*	1093
56	.... and *Marduk-nâṣir.*	*Bêl-aḫê-êriba.*	1142
57	.....	*Mušêzib-Bêl, Bêlšunu, Bêl-nâdin-aplu, Innin-zêr-ušabši* and *Balâṭu.*	1130
58	*Šullumu.*	*šatammu.*	1118
59	*Nabû-lûdâri.*	*šatammu* and *qîpi.*	1109
60	*Nabû-aḫê-iddin.*	*Nabû-bâni-aḫi.*	1158
61	*Marduk-nâṣir.*	*Nabû-nâdin-šum.*	1155
62	......	*Nabû-ušêzib* and *Nâ'id-Ištar.*	1122
63	*Šamaš-zêr-iqîša.*	*Gimillu.*	1133
64	*Nergal-êpuš.*	*Nâdinu, Dinâ* and *Balâṭu.*	1091
65	*Nabû-šar-uṣur.*	*Šamaš-dannu.*	1070
66	*Šamaš-uballiṭ.*	*Nâdin* and *Balâṭsu.*	1074
67	*Nâdina-aḫu.*	*šatammu* and *Nabû-aḫ-iddin.*	1077
68	*Nabû-na*.....	*Nabû-ušallim.*	1126
69	*Itti-šarri-balâṭu* [amêl]*râb-pîtqa.*	*Nabû-mukîn-aplu.*	1143
70	*Marduk* and *Innin-nâdin-aḫu.*	*Marduk-šâkin-šum.*	1151
71	*Nâdin-šum.*	*Bêl-rîmanni.*	1139
72	*Nergal*.... and *Nabû-bâni-aḫu.*	*šatammu.*	1076

Text No.	Letter from	Addres ed to	Catalog NBC
73	*Balâṭu.*	*Innin-šum-ušabši.*	1080
74	*Balâṭsu.*	*Nabû-aḫê-iddin.*	1082
75	*Innina-zêr-ušabši.*	*Innina-zêr-ušabši* and *Nabû-mušêtiq-urra.*	1073
76	*Nabû.....*	*qîpi.*	1128
77	*Amurru-aḫê-iddin.*	*Nabû-aḫê-iddin.*	1107
78	......	......	1088
79	*Nabû-šum(?)-êreš.*	*šatammu.*	1084
80	*Sin-šum(?)-êreš(?)* and *Nabû-bêl-uṣur.*	*Nidintu-Bêl* and *Nabû-aḫ-iddin.*	1102
81	*Enurta-šar-uṣur.*	*...aḫê-iddin.*	1098
82	*Nabû-aḫê....*	*Balâṭsu.*	1053
83	*Isinâi.*	*šatammu.*	1086
84	.....	.....	1083
85	*Nabû-šar-uṣur.*	*Mušêzib-Bêl, Iqîšâ, Bêlšunu, Šamaš...* ..... and *Innin-zêr-ušabši.*	1079
86	......	......	1095
87	*Šalti-ilu.*	*dupsar-bîti.*	1052
88	*...ukîn.*	*Marduk(?)-šâpik-zêr.*	1090
89	......	......	1054
90	*Aplâ* and *Zêria.*	*Nabû-mušêtiq-urra.*	1087
91	*Nabû-bâni-aḫi.*	*Nabû-mušêtiq-urra.*	1092
92	*Nabû-aḫ-iddin, Ininna-šum-uṣur* and *amêlb[â'iru(?)].*	*Nabû-aḫê-iddin.*	1137
93	*Bêl-nâdin-aplu.*	*šar-mâtâti.*	1160
94	*Ki-ne-na-a-a.*	*qîpi, šatammu* and *šangû-Eanna.*	1089

B. List of Contracts, etc.

Text No.	Reign	Year	Month	Day	Catalog NBC	Contents
95	Undated.				1043	Payments made with the knowledge of the *šatammu.*
96	*Nabû-apal-uṣur.*	19	3	9	1039	Record concerning sesame.
97	*Nabû-nâ'id.*	1	1	12	1035	Record of a debt, specifying the place of payment.
98	*Kambuzia.*	2	6	23	1056	Record of tax to be paid.
99	*Nabû-kudurri-uṣur.*	1	7	13	1060	Record of a debt, specifying the time of payment.
100	*Nabû-nâ'id.*	11	1	12	1058	Rental of a boat.
101	*Nabû-kudurri-uṣur.*	40	5	25	1066	Mortgage. Certain fields are pledged as security for the payment of a debt.

Text No.	Reign	Year	Month	Day	Catalog NBC	Contents
102	*Kambuzia.*	4	6	4	1069	Promissory record. An individual promises to pay the tax of another.
103	*Kambuzia.*	5	6	1	1029	Record of tax to be paid.
104	*Nabû-nâ'id.*	8	9	13	1067	Record of a debt, specifying the time and place of payment.
105	*Kambuzia.*	2	6	24(?)	1064	Record of tax to be paid; the responsibility for paying is assumed by a second individual.
106	*Kuraš.*	7	5	5	1061	Two individuals go bond for a woman.
107	*Nabû-apal-uṣur.*	16	9	8	1068	Promissory note for grain, with interest at 20 per cent.
108	*Nabû-kudurri-uṣur.*	7	5	11	1020	Record of exchange.
109	*Kuraš.*	4	9	12	1055	Guarantee for the payment of delinquent taxes.
110	*Kambuzia.*	4	5	11	1065	Record of a debt, specifying the time of payment.
111	*Kuraš.*	2	5	16	1026	Record of tax to be paid by a woman.
112	*Nabû-kudurri-uṣur.*	19	6	25	1047	Document concerning oxen given to the *šatammu.*
113	*Kambuzia.*	1	1	30	1063	Obligation for the delivery of dates, with penalty attached in case of failure to bring them.
114	?	?	11	18	1051	Document concerning gold loaned to two individuals, with penalty attached if they do not pay it to the *bît-ilu* at a specified time.
115	*Kambuzia.*	?	6	27	1022	Record of a debt. Its payment at the specified time is guaranteed by another.
116	*Kambuzia.*	5	5	26	1059	Record of tax to be paid.
117	*Kambuzia.*	5	6	27	1044	Lease of certain fields.
118	*Kuraš.*	8	11	28	1057	Rental of a house, with the provision that the lessee pay the rent semi-annually and keep the house in repair.
119	*Kambuzia.*	5	5	18	1048	Record of tax to be paid.
120	*Nabû-nâ'id.*	3	2	21	1181	Document concerning slaves given by an individual to Eanna.
121	*Nabû-apal-uṣur.*	10	10	21	1025	Record of a debt, with interest at 20 per cent.
122	*Nabû-kudurri-uṣur.*	?	?	?	1028	Record of balancing an account.
123	*Nergal-šar-uṣur.*	Acc.	?	22	1032	Record of tax to be paid; also refers to a former debt.

Text No.	Reign	Year	Month	Day	Catalog NBC	Contents
124	*Nabû-kudurri-uṣur.*	6	10	8	1062	Record of precious stones brought to the temple.
125	?	?	?	?	1046	Lease of land.
126	*Nabû-kudurri-uṣur.*	23	12b	13	1040	Obligation for the safe delivery of bricks.
127	*Nabû-kudurri-uṣur.*	15	11	10	1196	Deed of sale of two houses belonging to the temple of Anu in Erech.
128	*Kambuzia.*	5	5	15	1023	Record of tax to be paid.
129	*Kambuzia.*	5	?	5	1034	Same. Also refers to an additional debt.
130	*Nabû-apal-uṣur.*	15	4	25	1193	Deed of sale of a field.
131	*Nergal-šar-uṣur.*	2	4	1	1179	Payments in grain.
132	*Nabû-apal-uṣur.*	15	11	27	1045	Receipt for objects in gold.
133	*Nabû-kudurri-uṣur.*	23	10	6	1036	Record of several transactions of an individual.
134	*Giššar-šum-ukîn.*	14	2	1	1185	Account of sheep.
135	*Nabû-nâ'id.*	1	12a	17	1031	Record of money received.
136	*Amêl-Marduk.*	Acc.	9	7	1166	Note stating that money given for an individual was received by him.
137	*Nabû-nâ'id.*	Acc.	12a	16	1169	Payments in sesame.
138	*Nabû-kudurri-uṣur.*	13	12a	1	1173	Note concerning gold brought for work on the temple Esagila.
139	*Nabû-kudurri-uṣur.*	8	6	7	1164	Record of a cargo of grain.
140	*Nabû-kudurri-uṣur.*	24	1	1	1167	Record of payments made by three men.
141	Undated.				1182	Legal document.
142	Undated.				1037	List of witnesses summoned for a specified time.
143	*Amêl-Marduk.*	2	1	21	1041	Account of an exchange of grain for money, and the various payments made with it.
144	*Nabû-kudurri-uṣur.*	4	8	5	1172	Record of money loaned to three men.
145	*Nabû-kudurri-uṣur.*	32	6	27	1170	Record of money delivered for building purposes.
146	*Nabû-kudurri-uṣur.*	?	8	17(?)	1175	Note concerning precious stones.
147	*Nabû-kudurri-uṣur.*	?	10	5	1165	Note concerning a sheep brought for sacrifice.
148	*Nabû-kudurri-uṣur.*	22	9	29	1161	Receipt for a kid.
149	*Nabû-apal-uṣur.*	12	3	15	1168	Account of money paid for wool.
150	*Nabû-kudurri-uṣur.*	17	2	13	1162	Record of payments in grain.
151	*?-uṣur.*	15	1	28	1042	Payments to soldiers.
152	*Nabû-apal[-uṣur].*	10(?)	5(?)	16(?)	1038	Record of various payments.
153	Undated.				1178	Temple record.
154	*Nabû-kudurri-uṣur.*	?	?	?	1050	Payments in dates.

Text No.	Reign	Year	Month	Day	Catalog NBC	Contents
155	Undated.				1018	Payments in silver.
156	?	8	1	13	1183	Record of payments in grain by the farmers of Eanna.
157	Undated.				1191	Temple list of farmers.
158	Undated.				1194	Record of payments in seed-grain.
159	*Kandalanu.*	8			1197	Document concerning the division of a seed field.
160	*Nabû-kudurri-uṣur.*	3	6	14	1033	Receipt for money.
161	*Nabû-nâ'id.*	2	2	15	1027	Record of various payments in silver.
162	*Nabû-kudurri-uṣur.*	31	8	3	1030	Receipt for silver as payment for different things.
163	*Nabû-kudurri-uṣur.*	14	9	5	1021	List of soldiers.
164	*Nabû-kudurri-uṣur.*	24	1	23	1024	Temple record concerning five soldiers.
165	*Nabû-nâ'id.*	8	10	10	1049	Receipt for wood.
166	*Nergal-šar-uṣur.*	2	7		1180	Account of cassia.
167	*Kuraš.*	?	?	?	1195	Record of the receipt of sheep for one month.
168	*Kambuzia.*	2	?	?	1177	Account of dates, including the tax, received from two cities.
169	*Kambuzia.*	Acc.	9	17	1184	Request made by temple officials to the mayors of Erech concerning the *širaqu.*
170	*Nergal-šar-uṣur.*	3	6	7	1019	Payments in dates to officials in the sixth month.
171	*Nabû-apal-uṣur.*	11	4	1	1171	Record of sheep given to an individual.
172	*Nabû-kudurri-uṣur.*	11	8	17	1163	Record of a loan, with penalty attached if not paid at a specified time.
173	*Nabû-apal-uṣur.*	16	9	16	1174	Receipt for iron.
174	*Nabû-nâ'id.*	14	4	27	1215	Account of ewes exchanged for grain and silver.
175	Undated.				1218	Temple record of payments to individuals.
176	*Nabû-kudurri-uṣur.*	31	5	21	1192	Temple record.
177	*Nabû-kudurri-uṣur.*	3	3	9	1204	Temple record of payments in wool.

AUTOGRAPHED PLATES

1

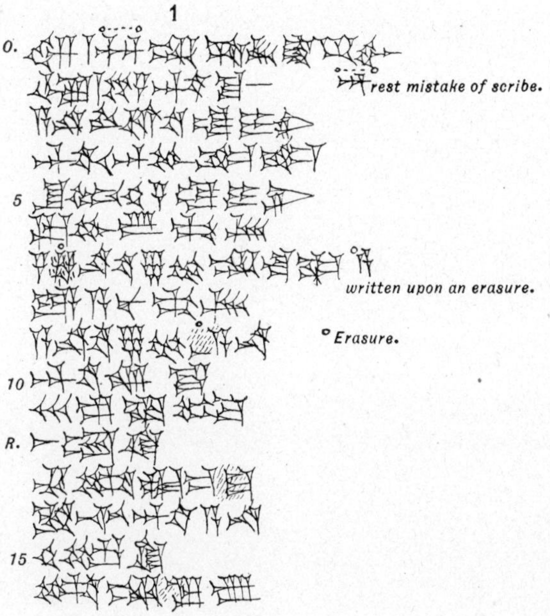
O.
rest mistake of scribe.
5
written upon an erasure.
Erasure.
10
R.
15

2

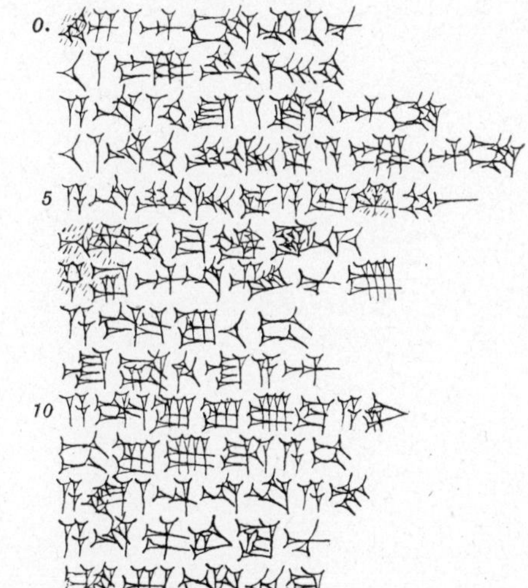
O.
5
10
Lo. E.
15
R.

3

O.

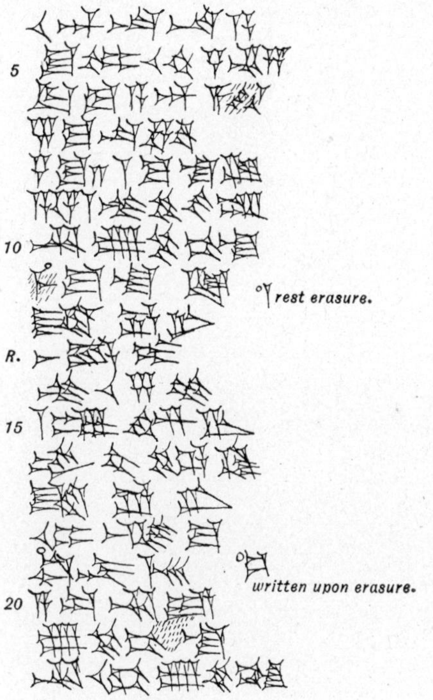
5
10
rest erasure.
R.
15
written upon erasure.
20

4

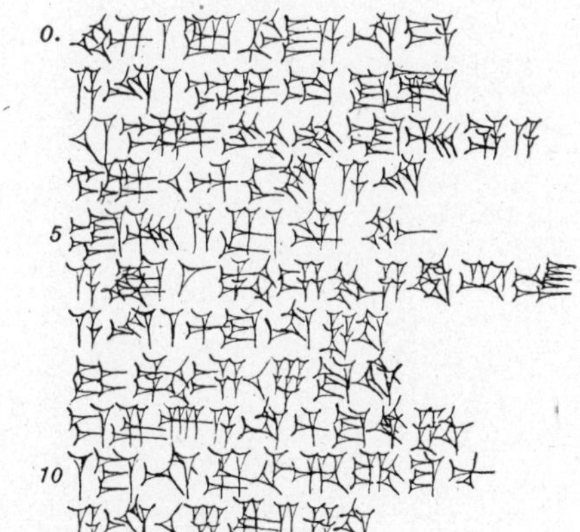
O.
5
10
Lo. E.
R.
15

5

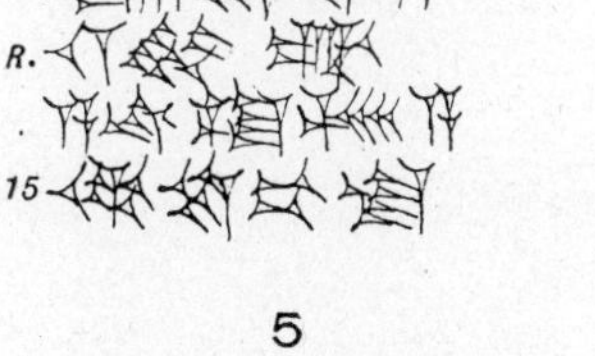
O.

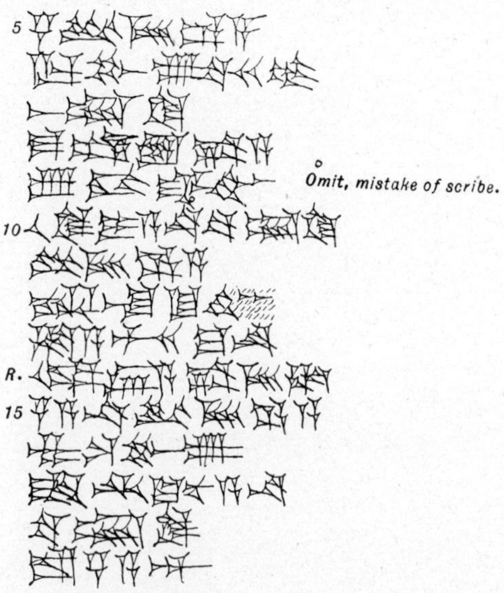

6

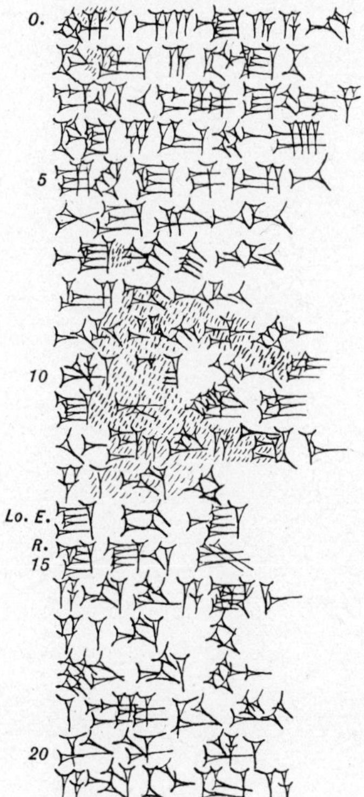

7

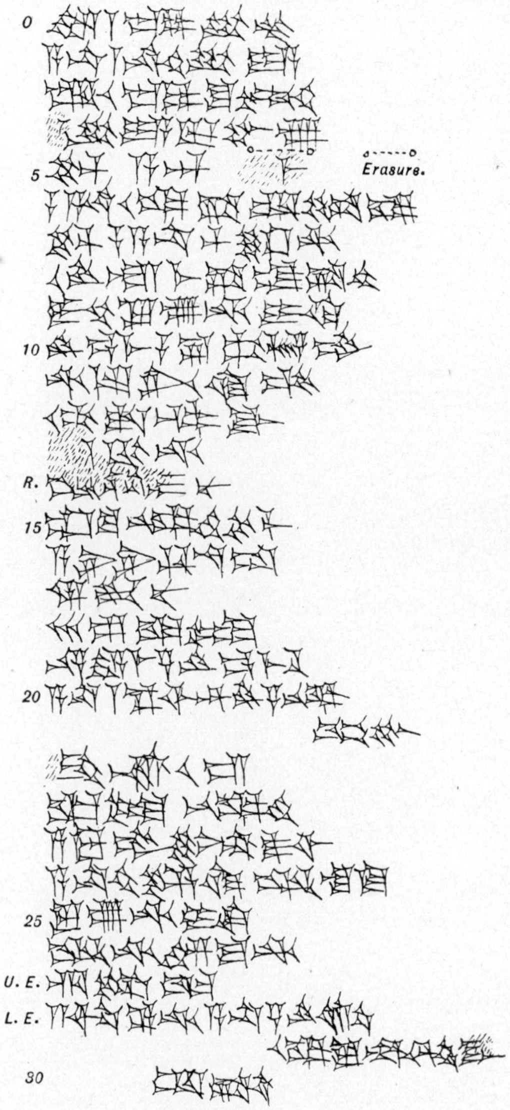

8

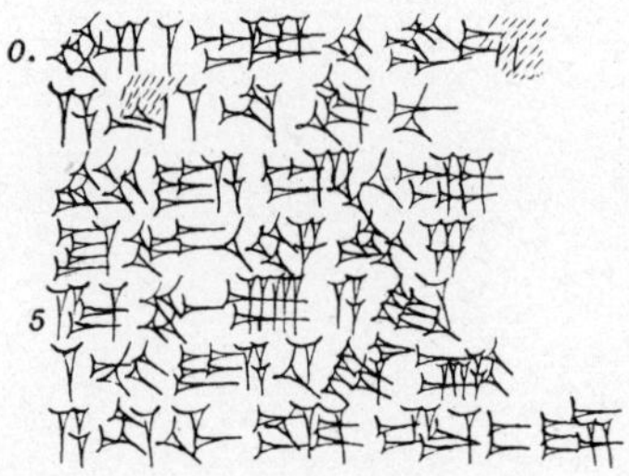

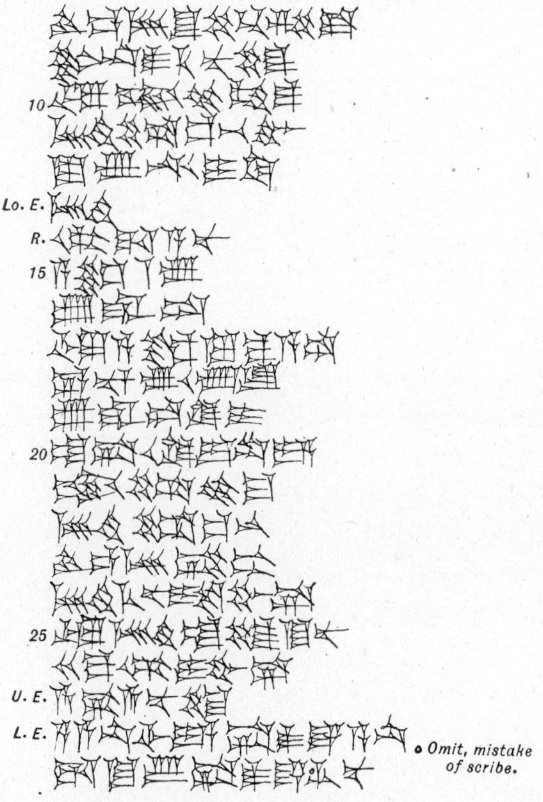
Omit, mistake of scribe.

9

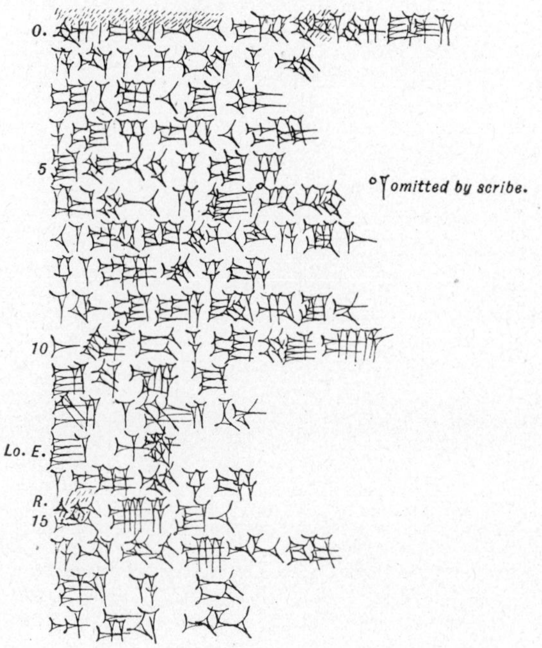
omitted by scribe.

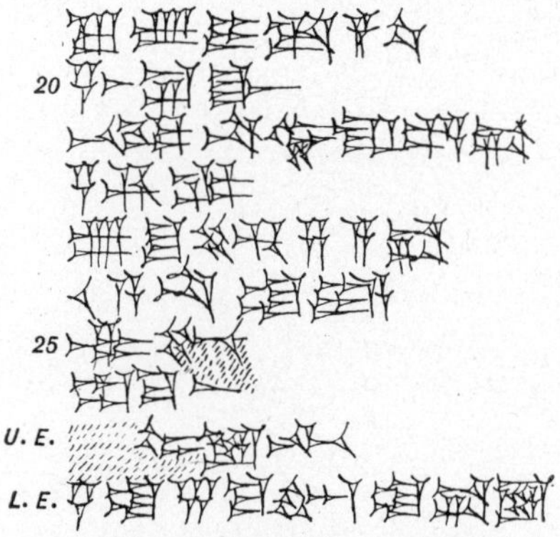

10

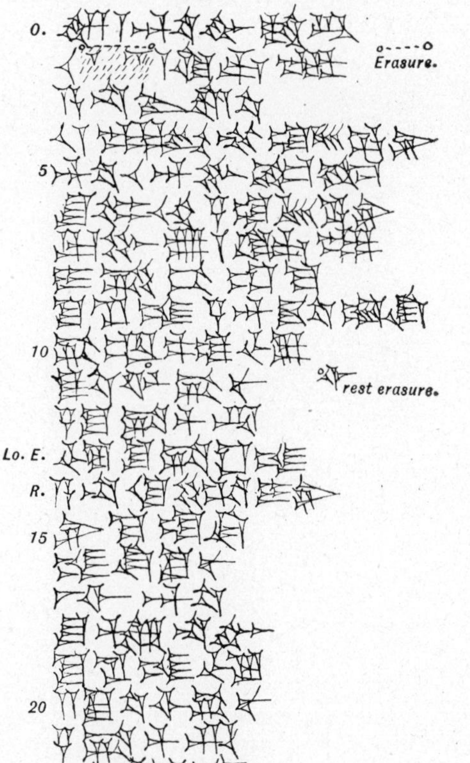
Erasure.
rest erasure.
rest erasure.

11

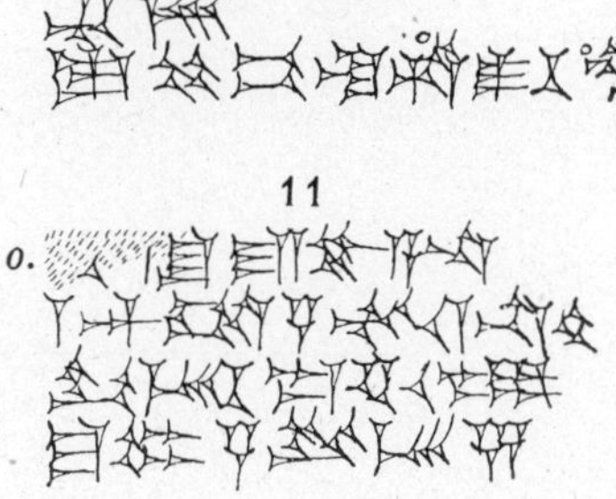

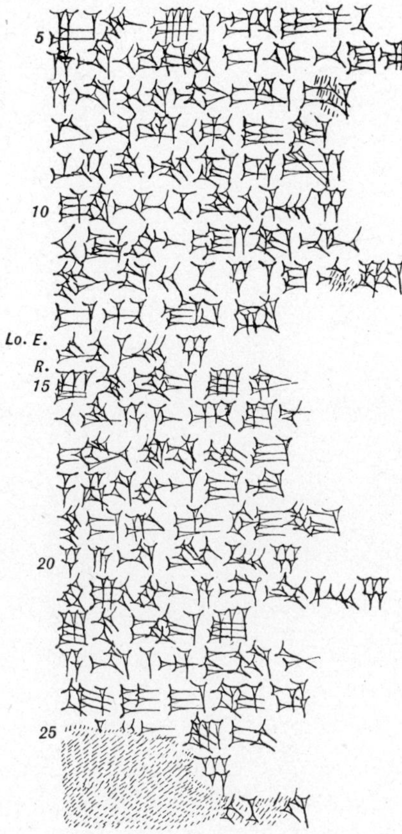

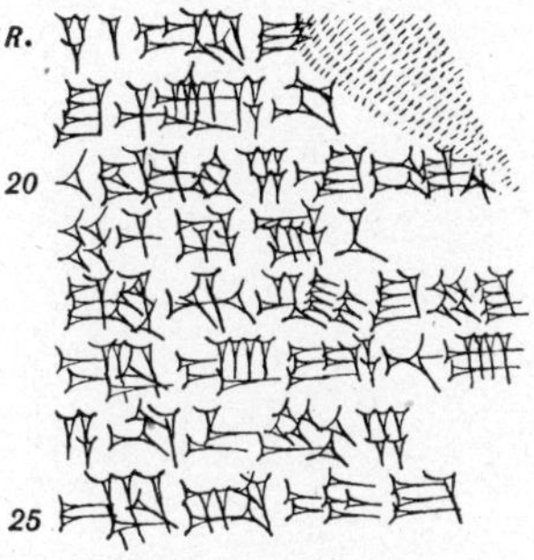

12

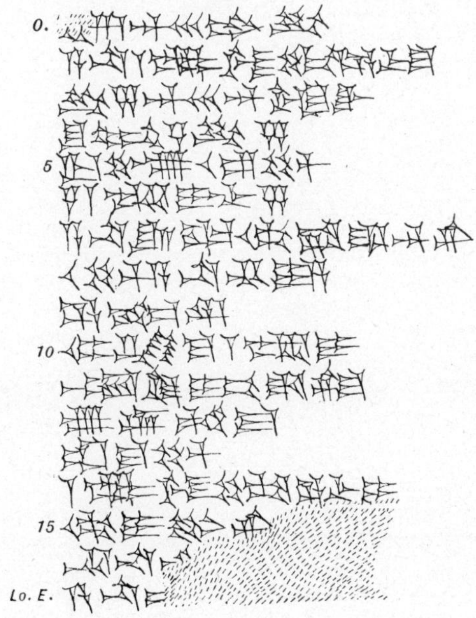

13

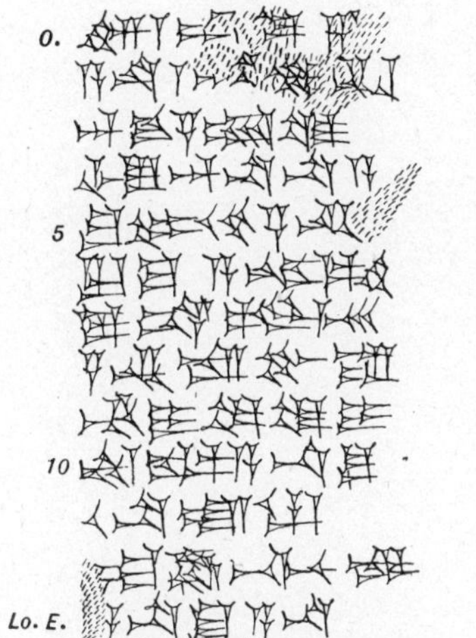

14

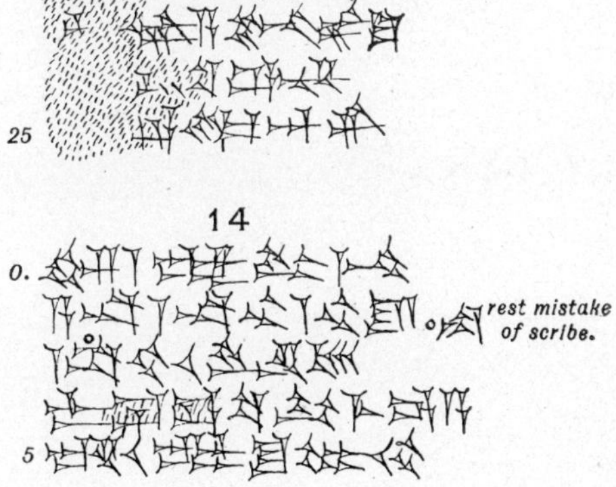

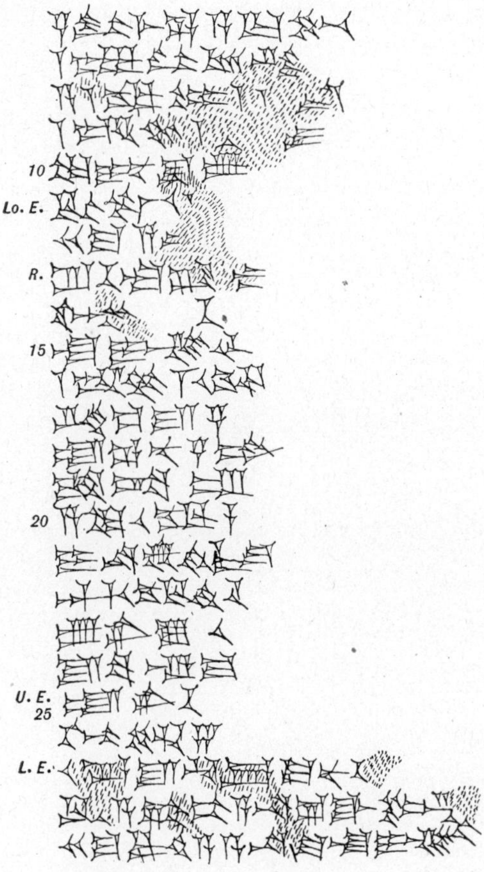

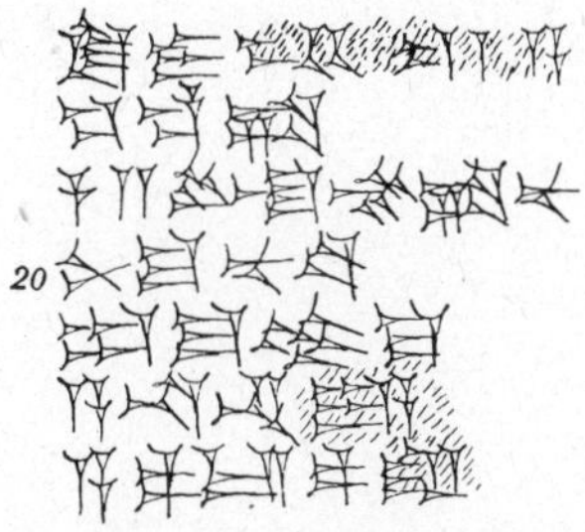

15

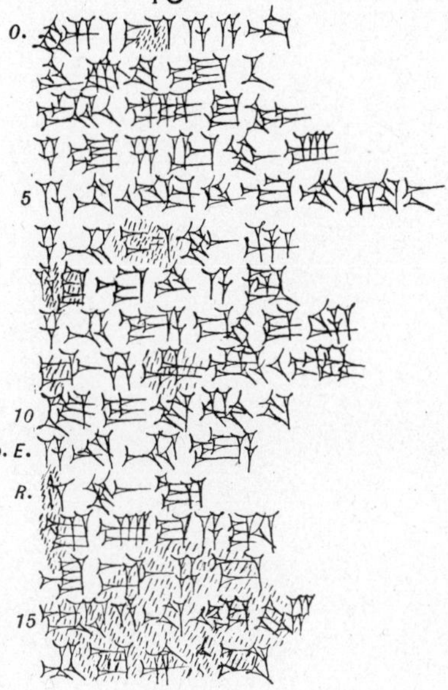

16

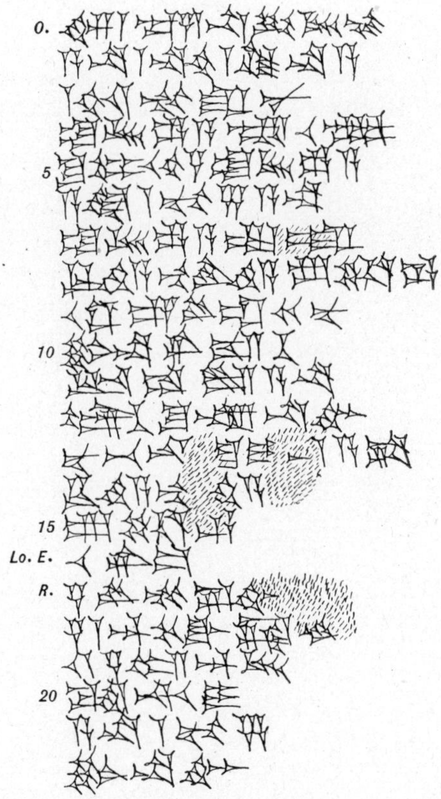

17

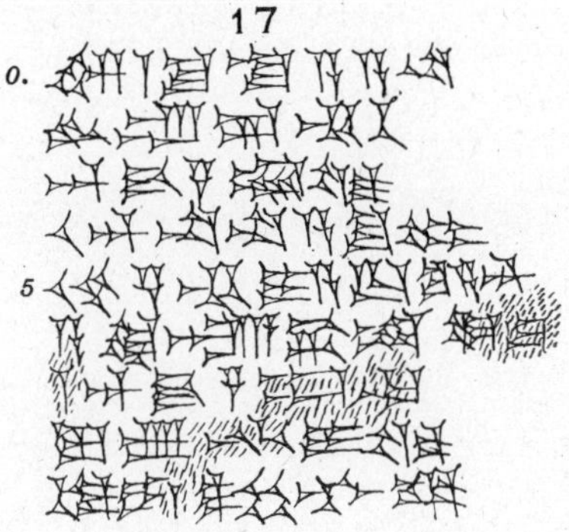

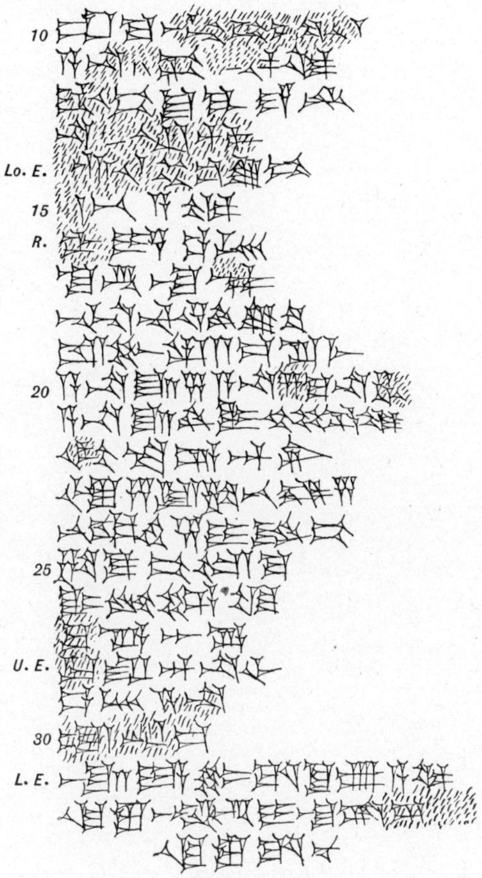
Lo. E.
R.
U. E.
L. E.

18

O.
Insert here.

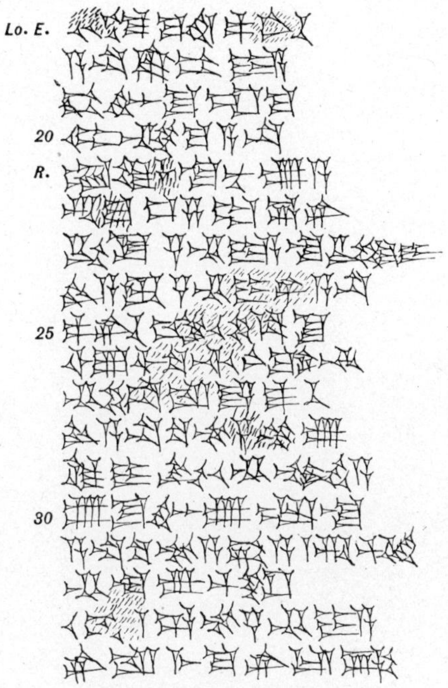
Lo. E.
R.

19

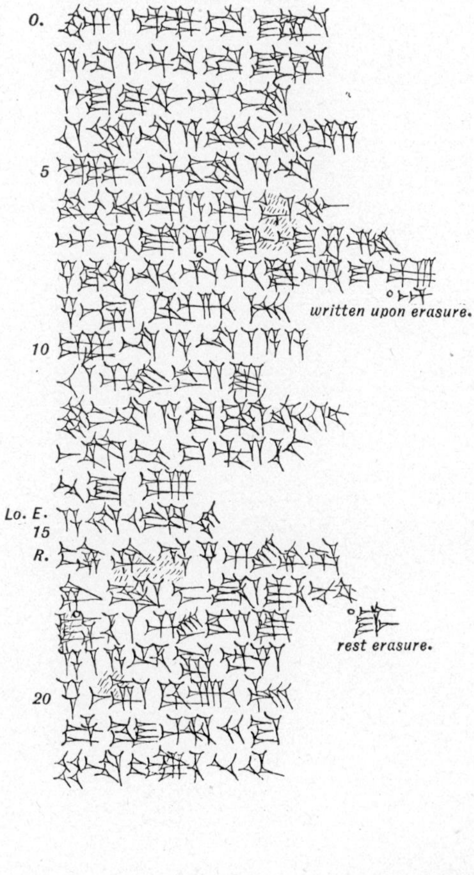
O.
written upon erasure.
Lo. E.
R.
rest erasure.

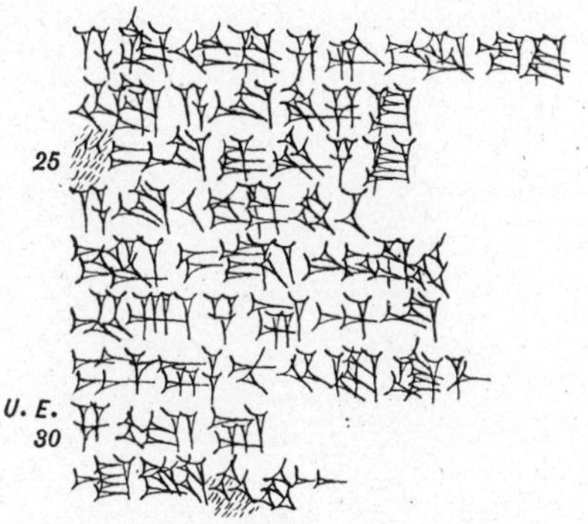

20

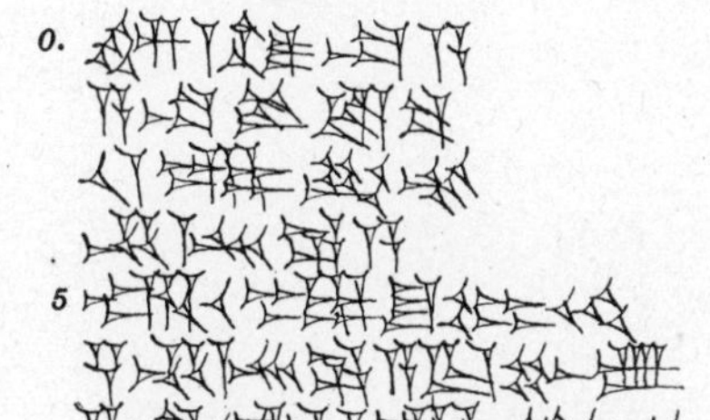

21

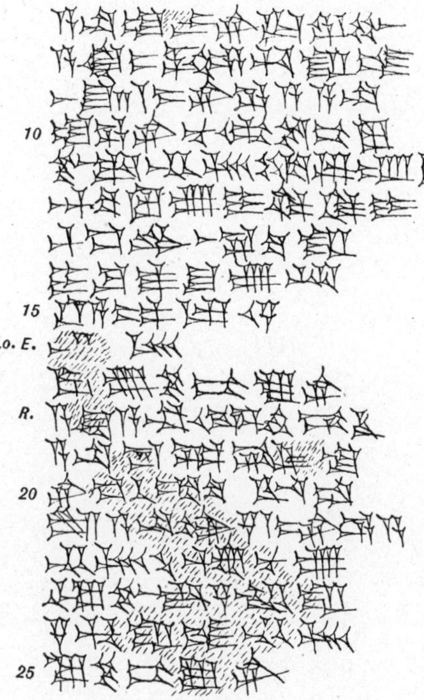

22

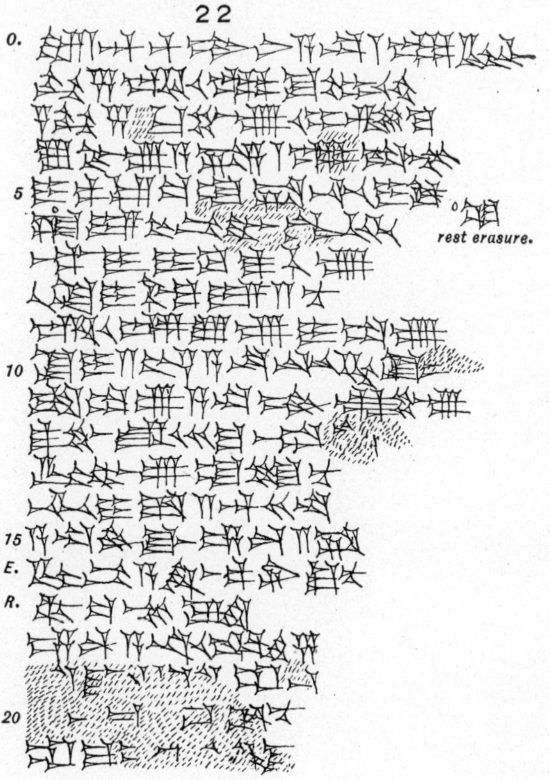

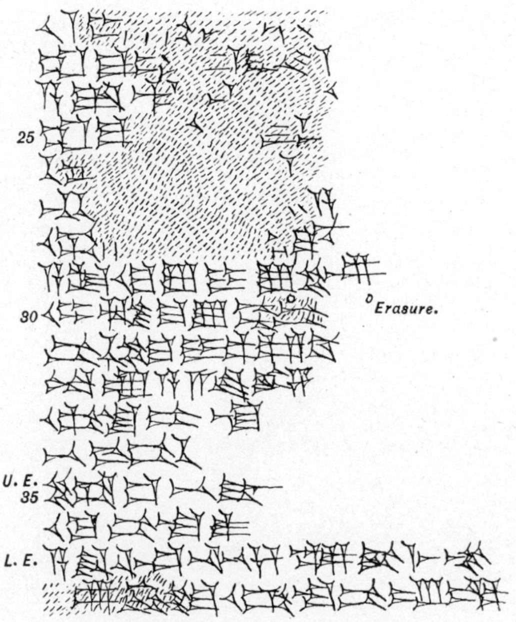

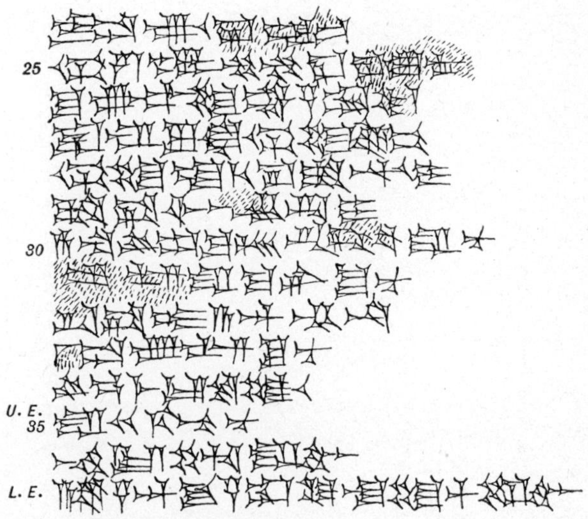

23

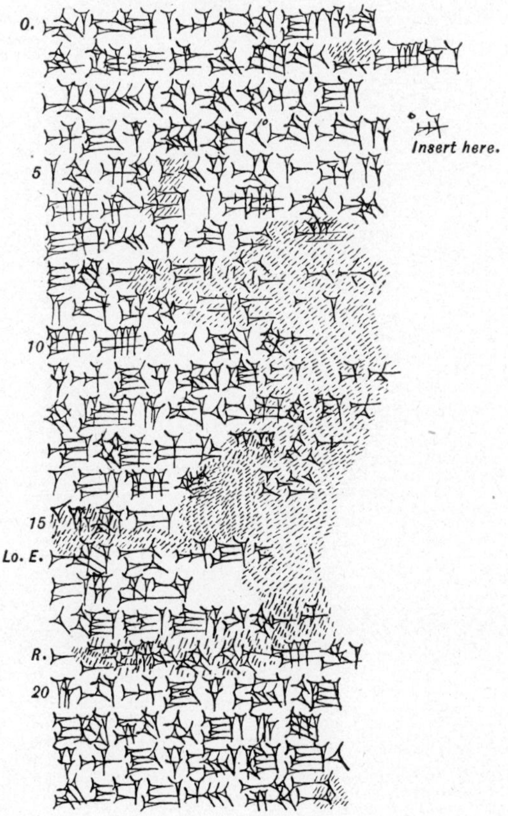

24

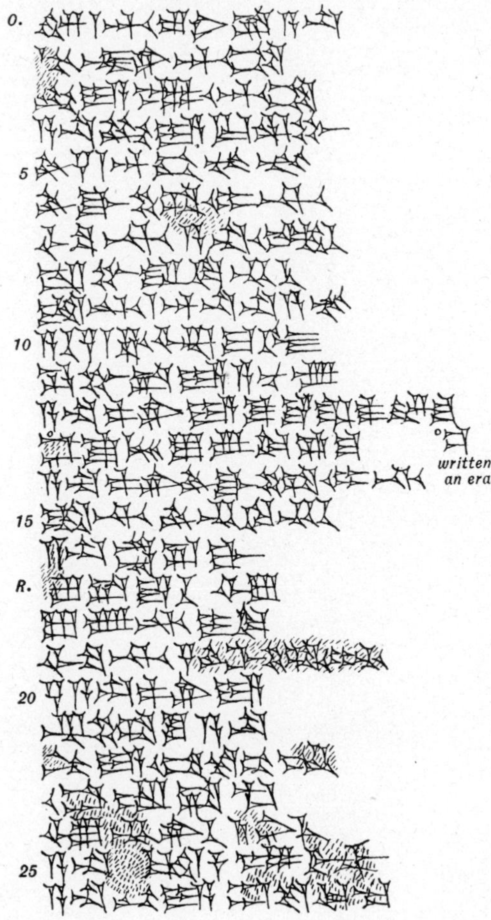

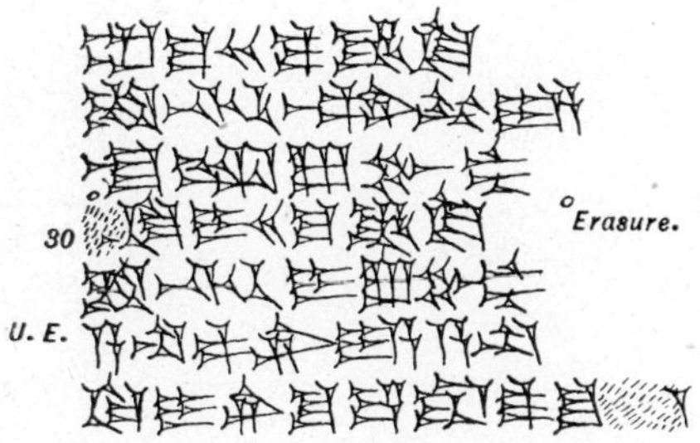

°Erasure.

25

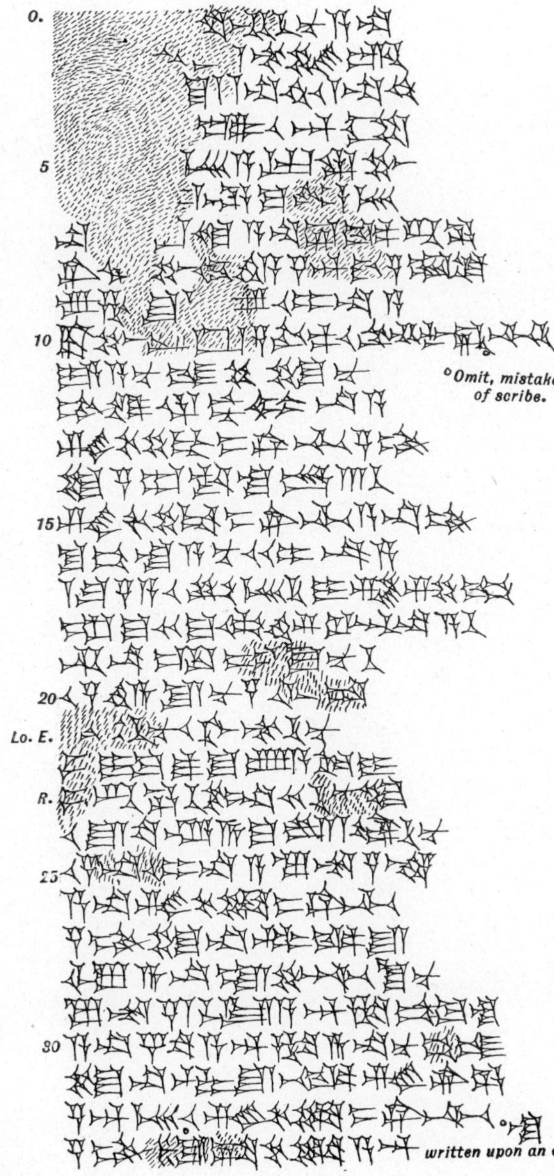

°Omit, mistake of scribe.

written upon an erasure.

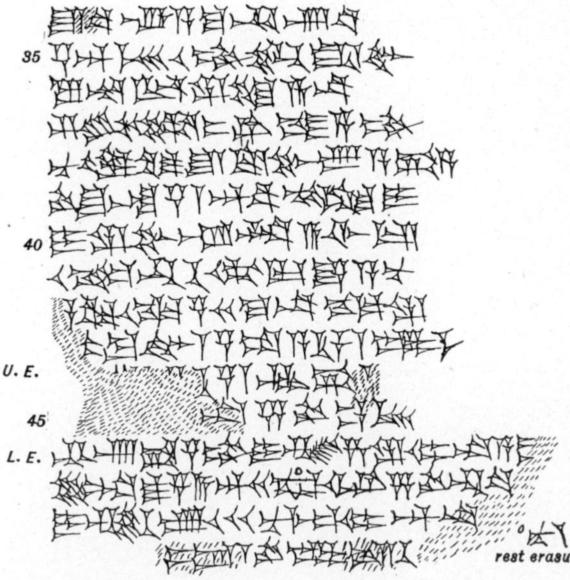

rest erasure.

26

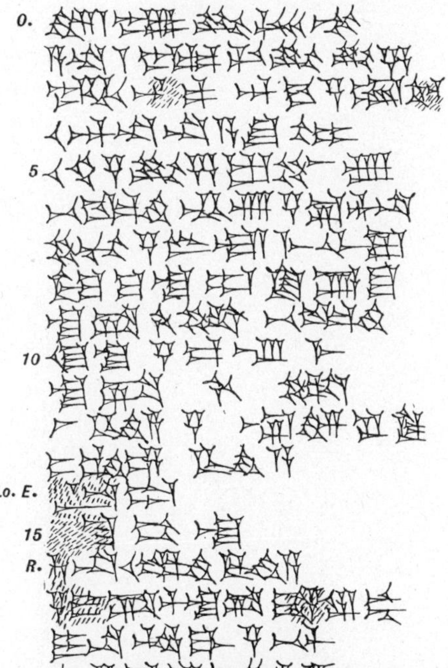

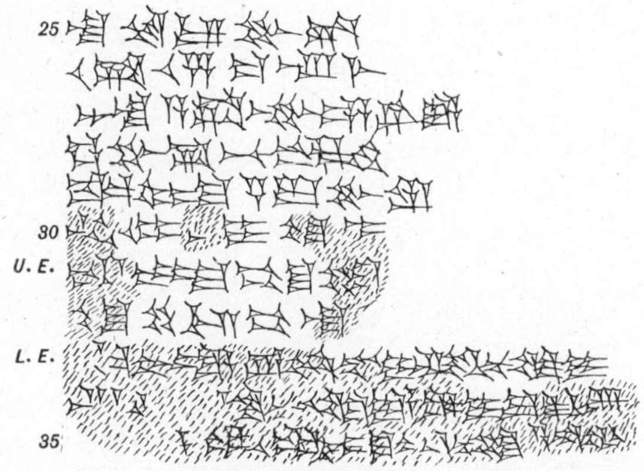

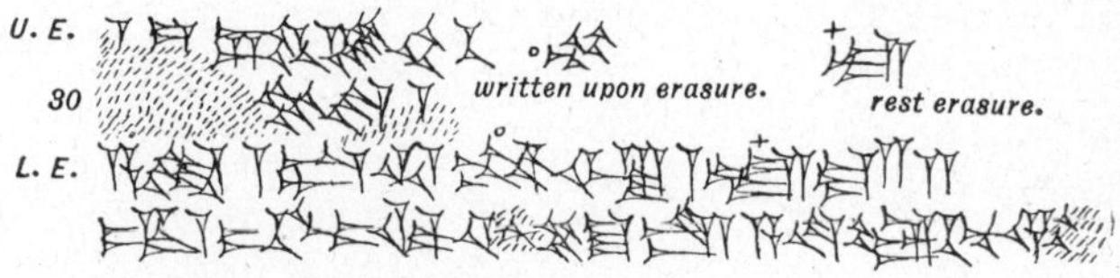
written upon erasure.
rest erasure.

27

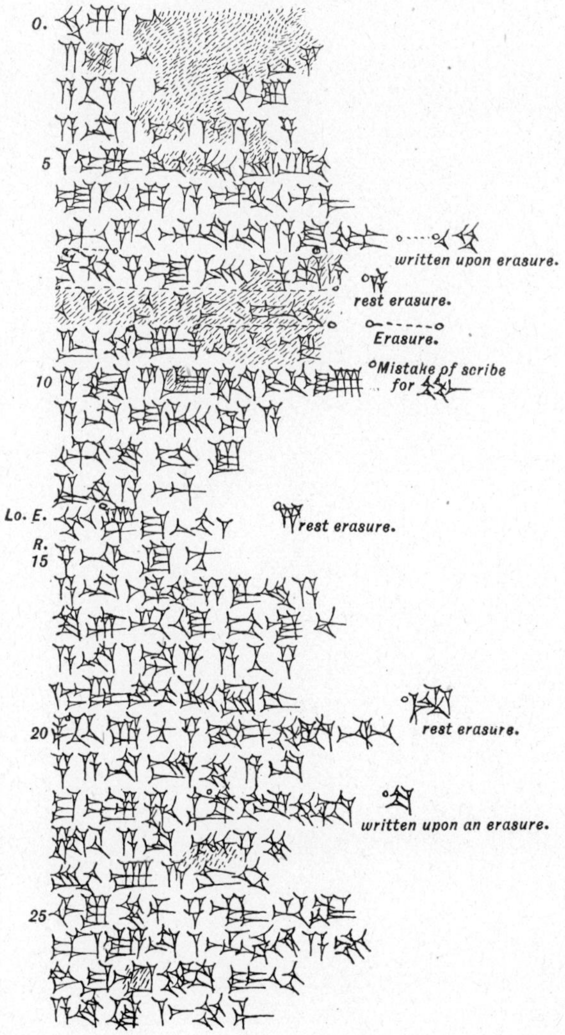
written upon erasure.
rest erasure.
Erasure.
Mistake of scribe for
rest erasure.
rest erasure.
written upon an erasure.

28

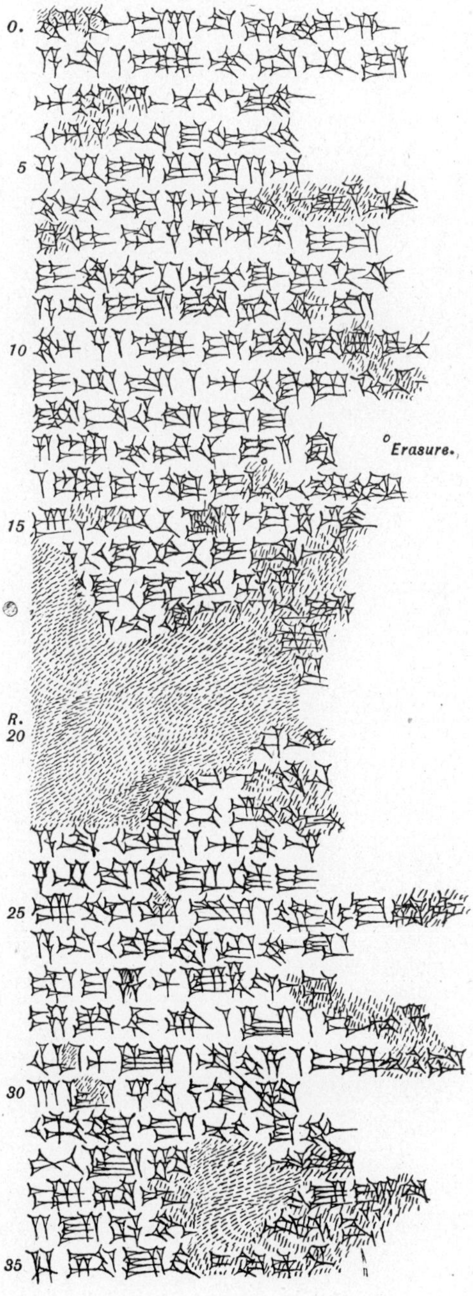
Erasure.

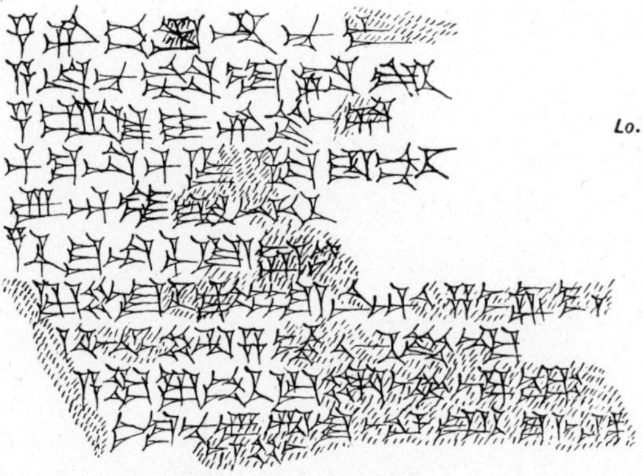

29

30

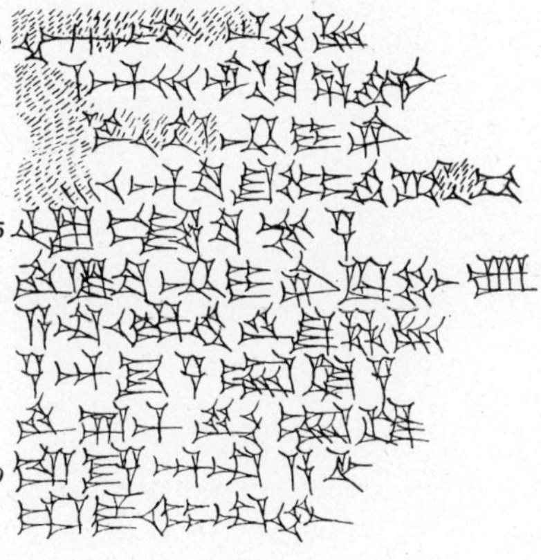

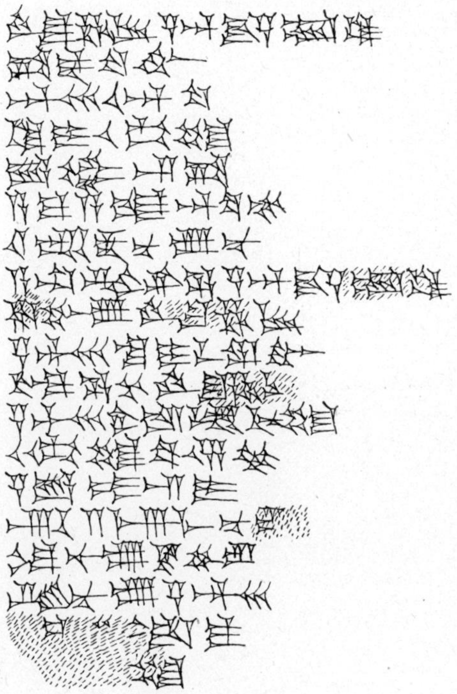

31

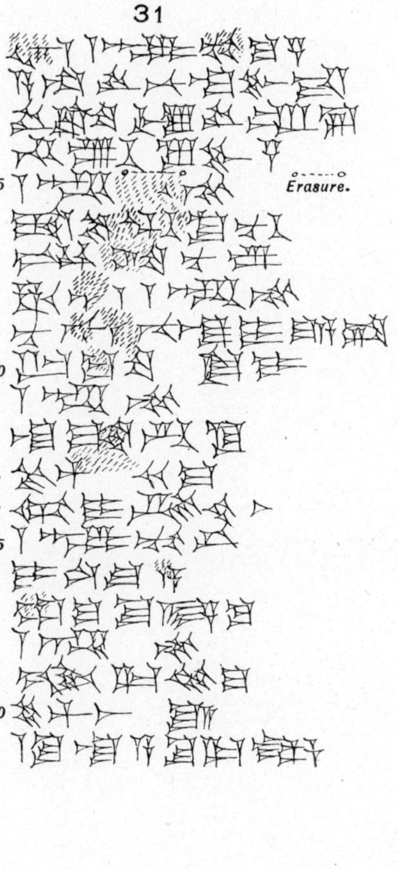

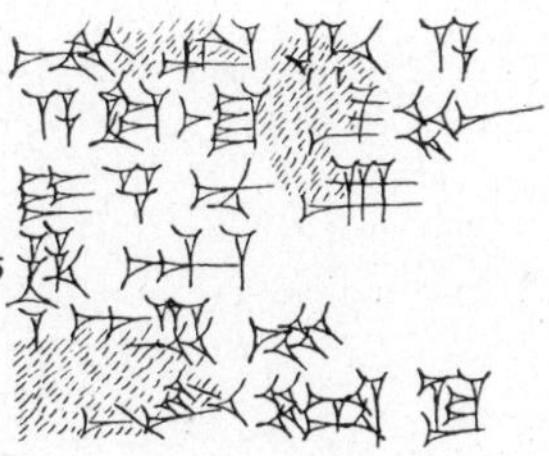

32

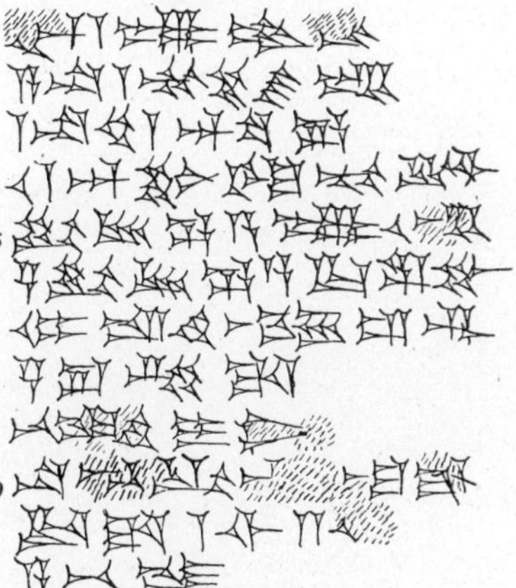

33

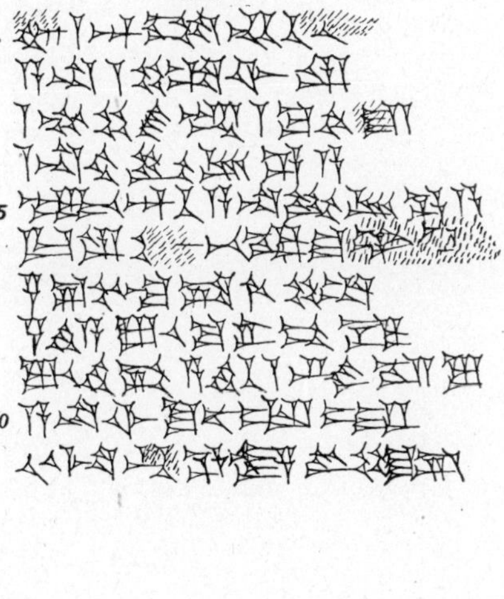

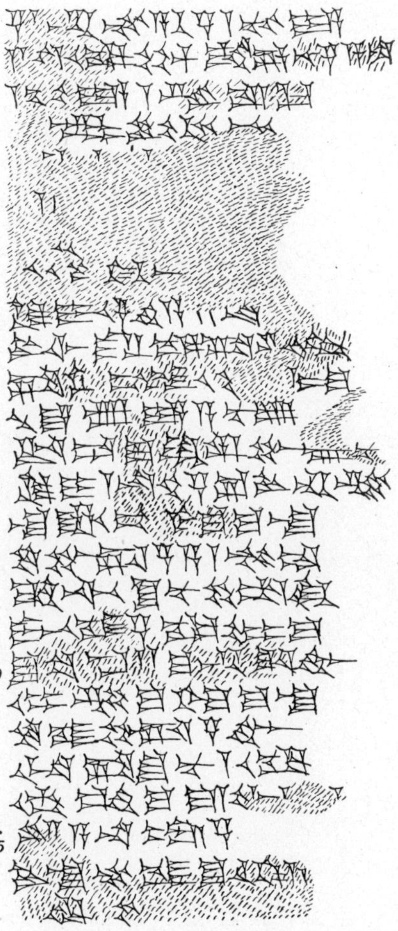

34

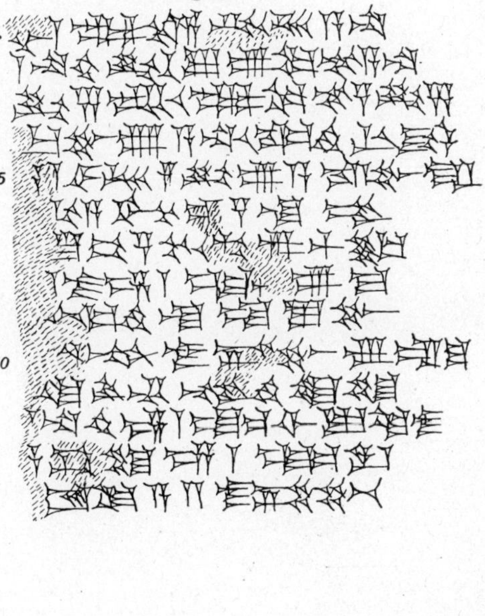

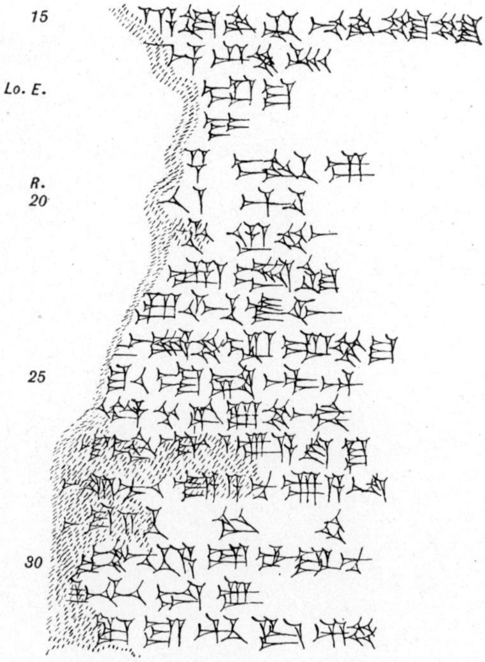

35

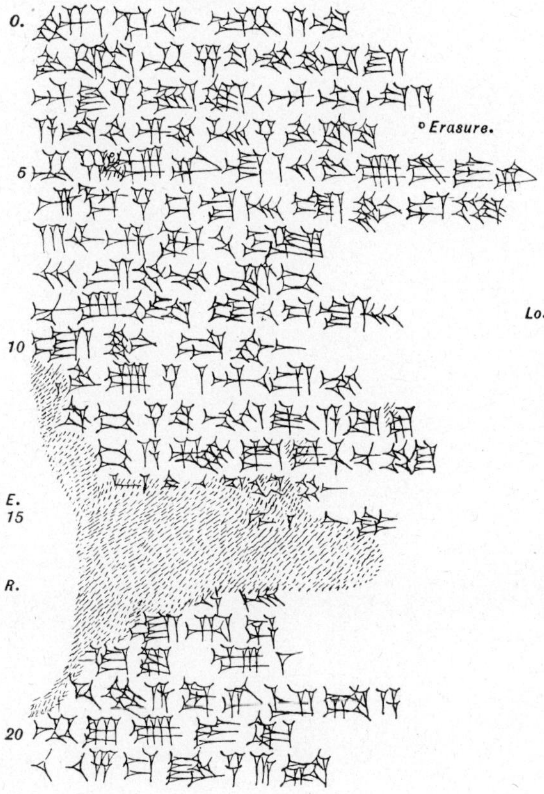

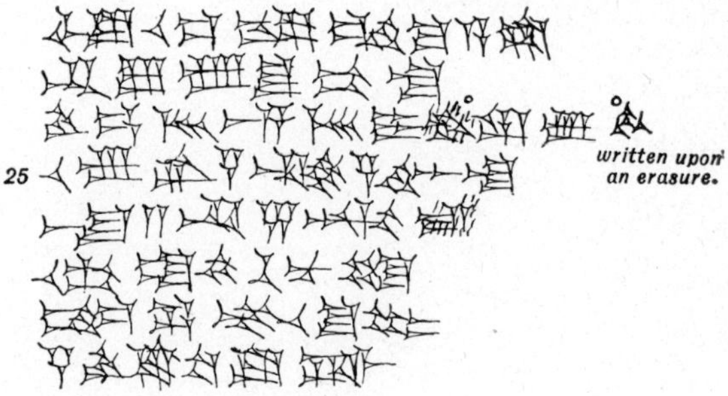

36

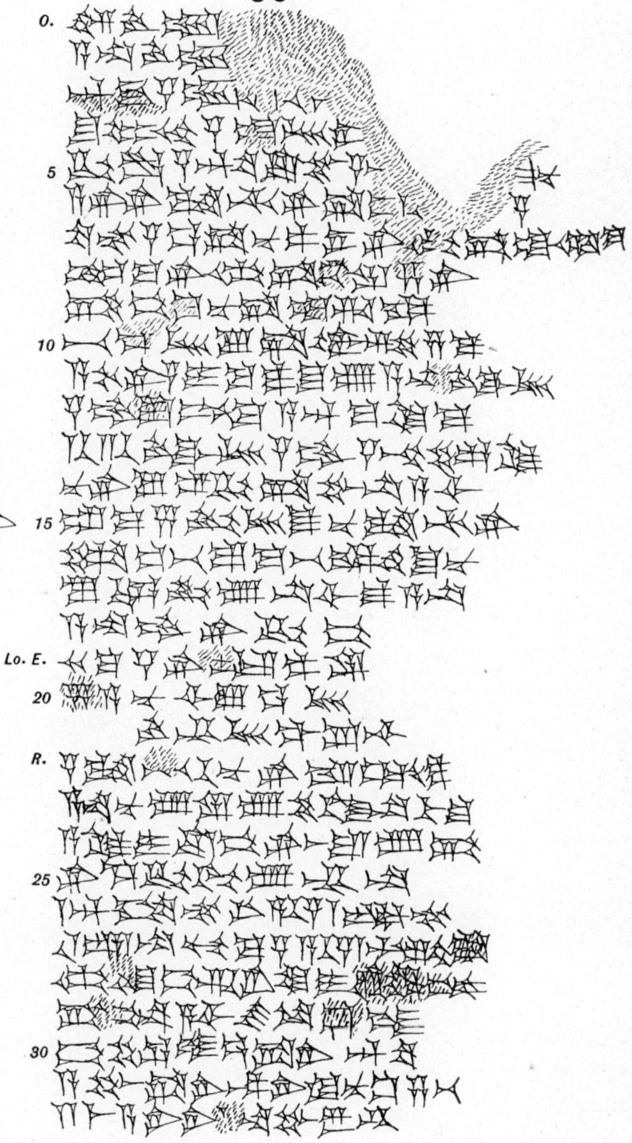

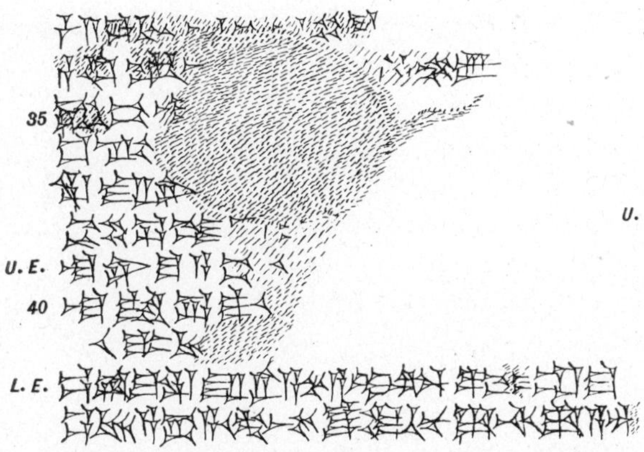

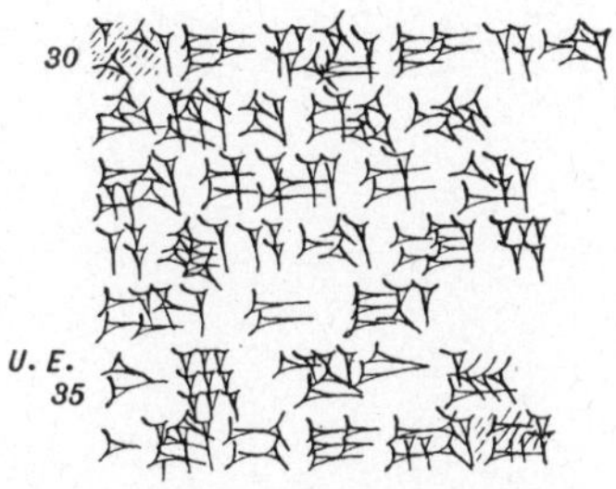

37

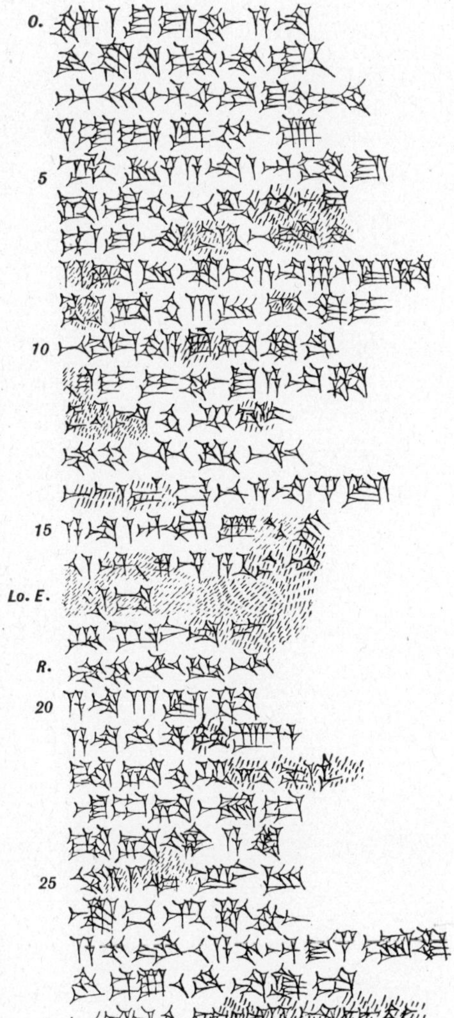

38

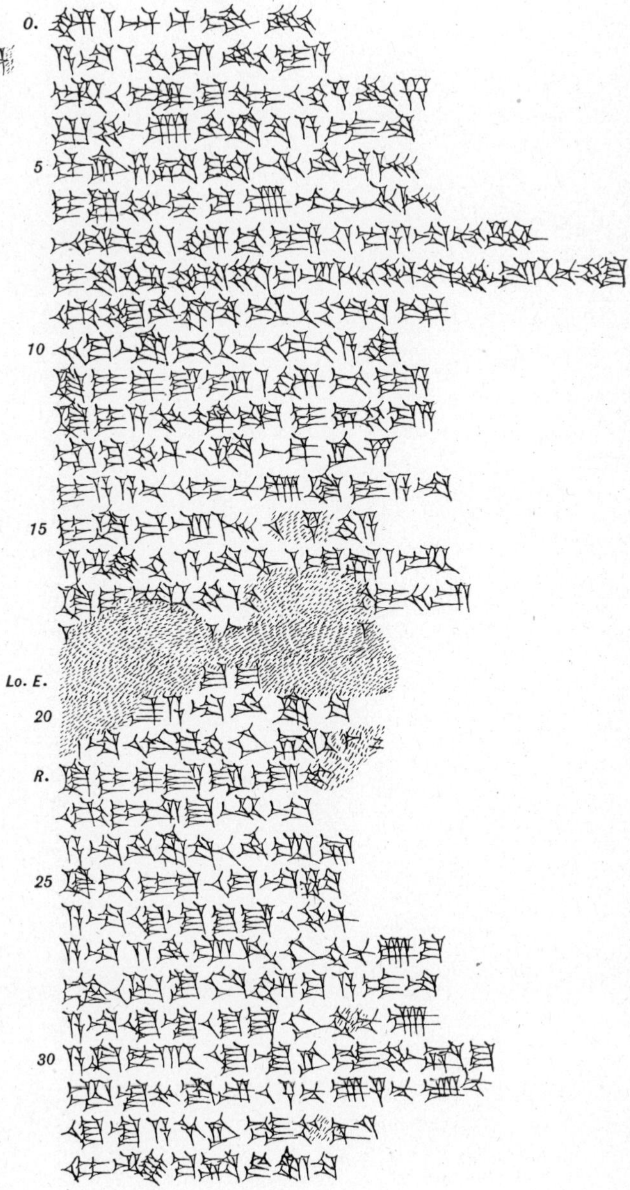

U. E.

L. E.

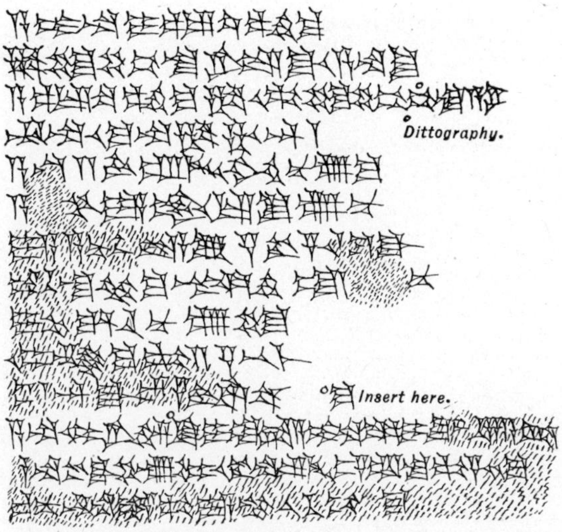

39

O.

R.

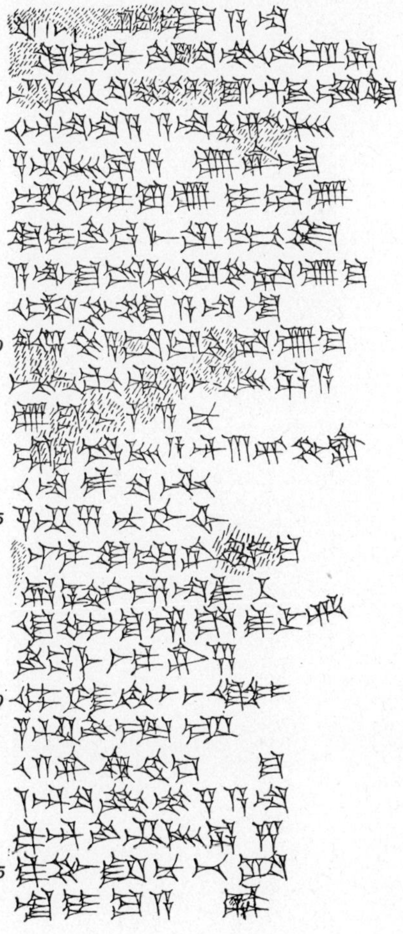

40

O.

Lo. E.

R.

U. E.

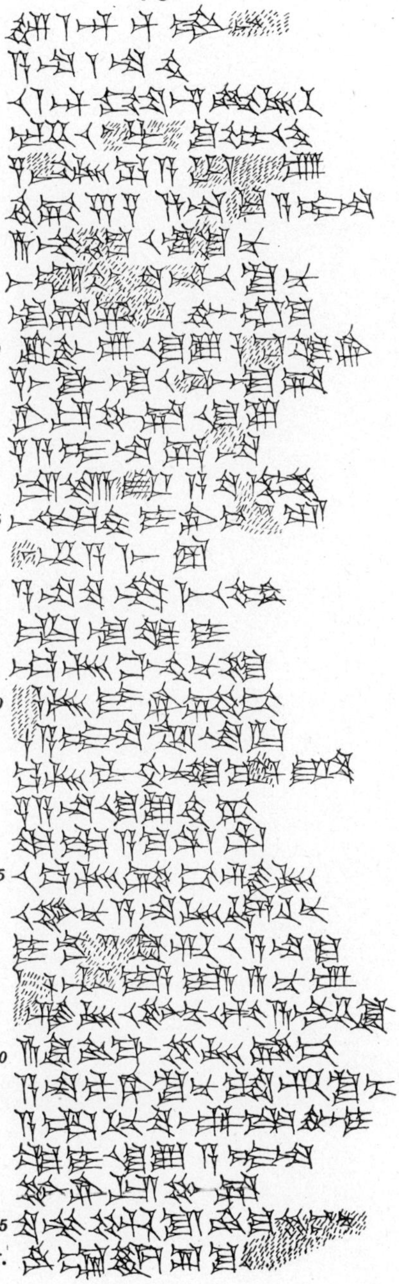

L.E.

40

41

0.

5

10

Lo. E.
R.
15

20

25

U.E.

42

0.

5

10

Lo. E.
R.
15

20

25

written upon an erasure.

43

0.

5

10

R.

15

Erasure.

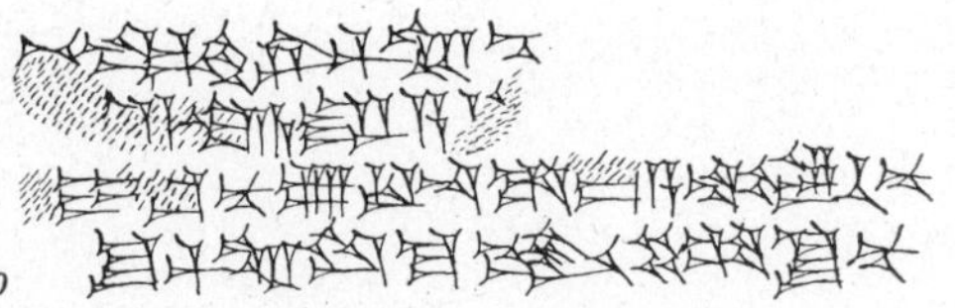

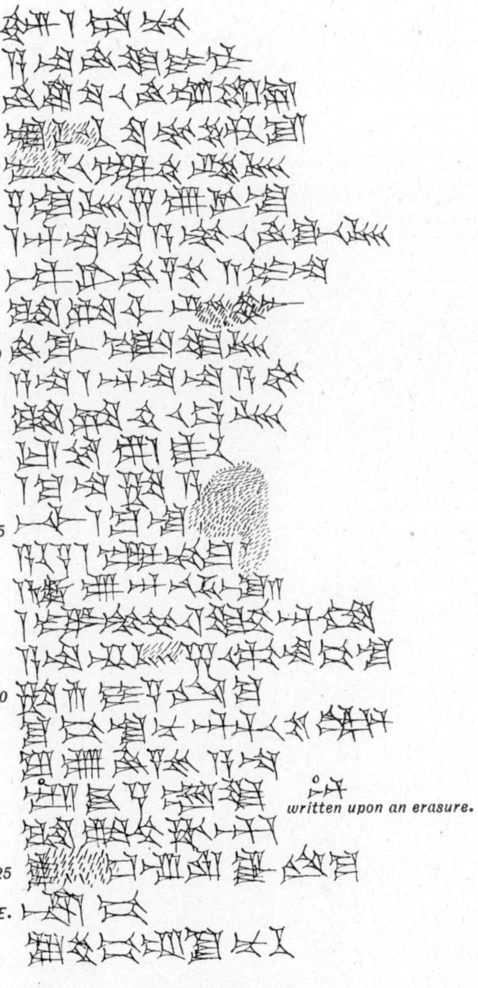

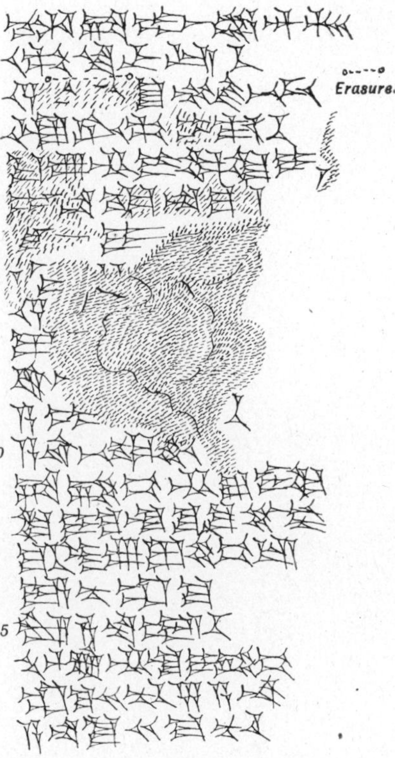

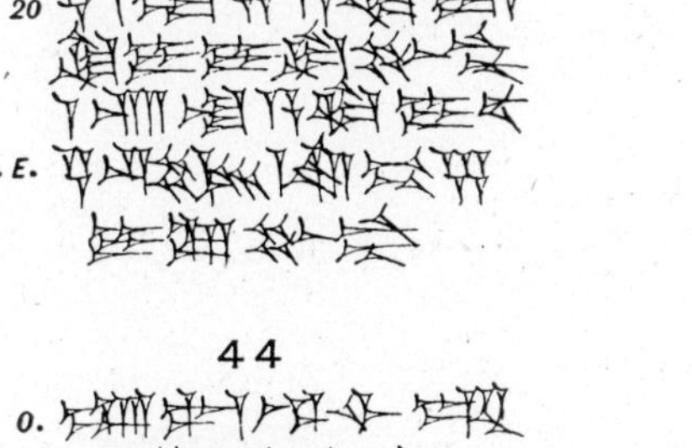
Erasure.
20
U. E.

44

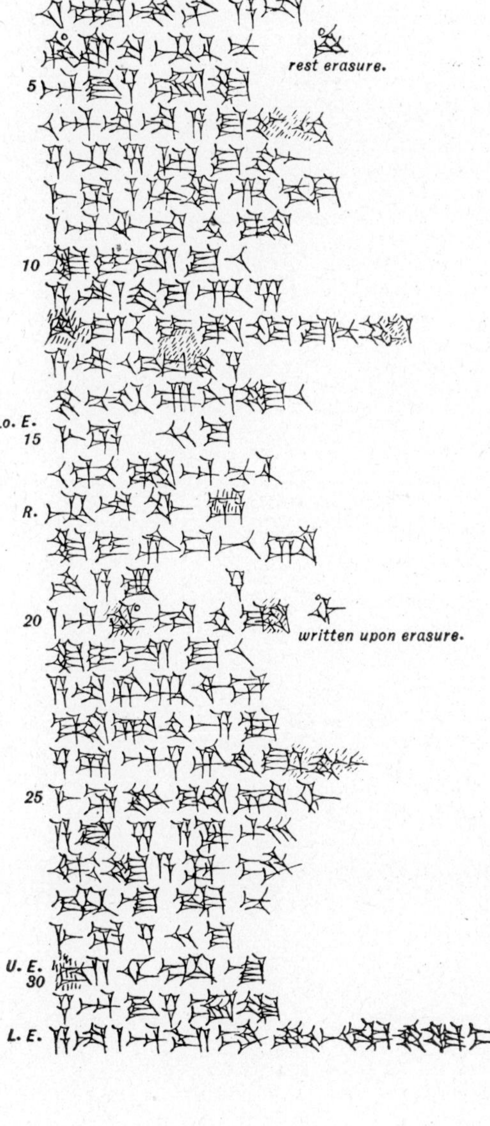
O.
rest erasure.
5
10
Lo. E.
15
R.
20
written upon erasure.
25
U. E.
30
L. E.

45

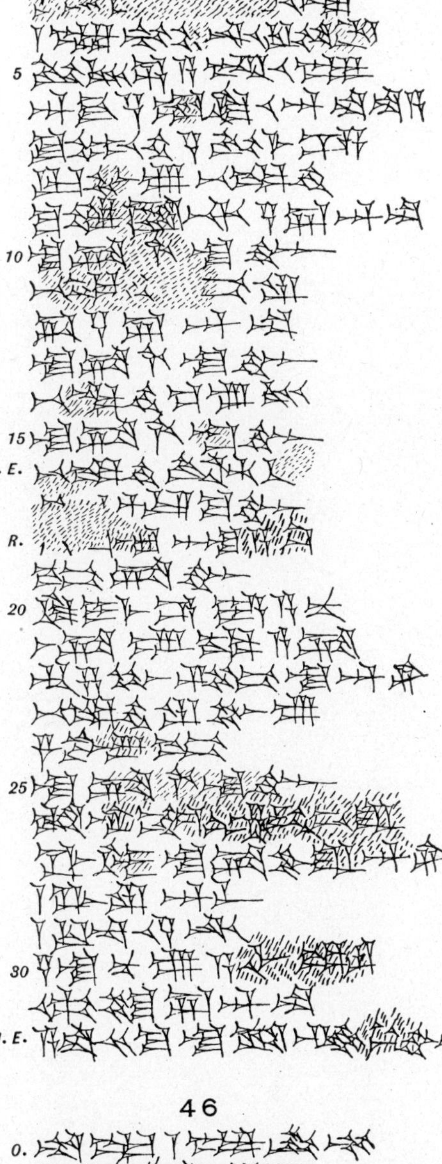
O.
Erasure.
5
10
15
Lo. E.
R.
20
25
30
U. E.

46

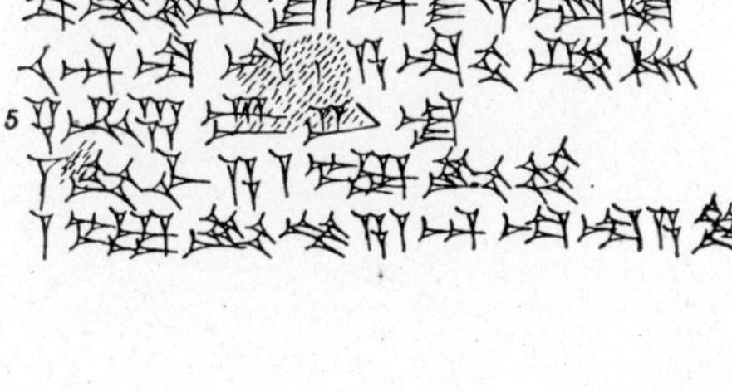
O.
5

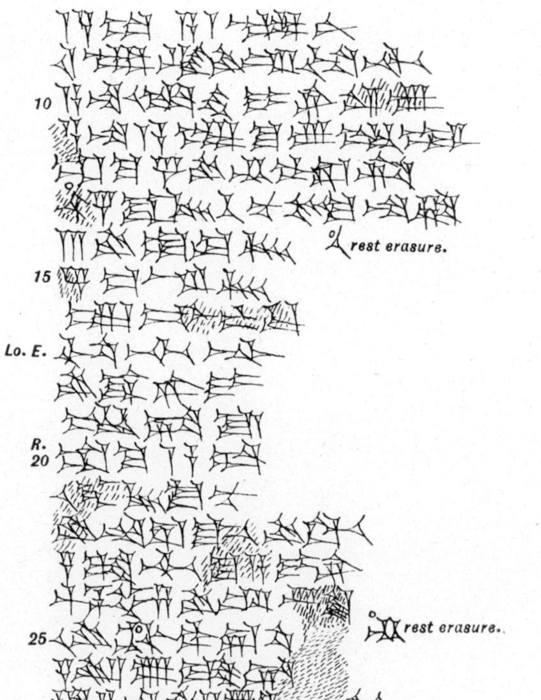
rest erasure.
Lo. E.
R.
rest erasure.
U. E.
L. E.

47

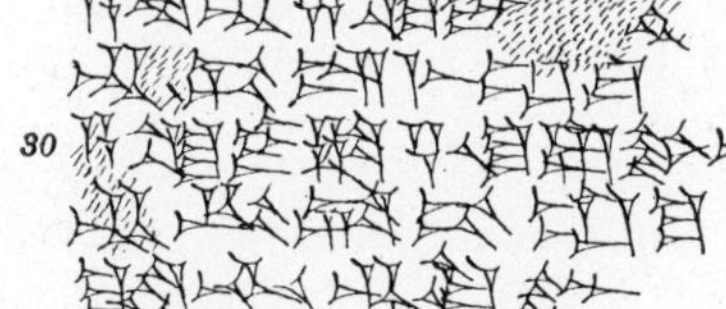
O.

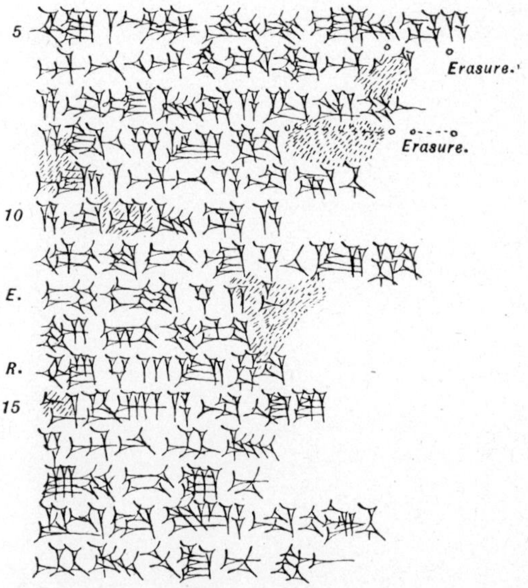
Erasure.
Erasure.
Lo. E.
R.

48

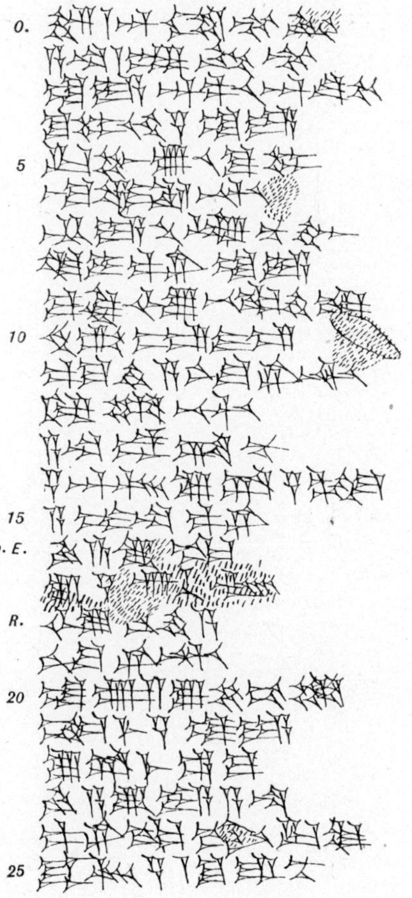
O.
Lo. E.
R.

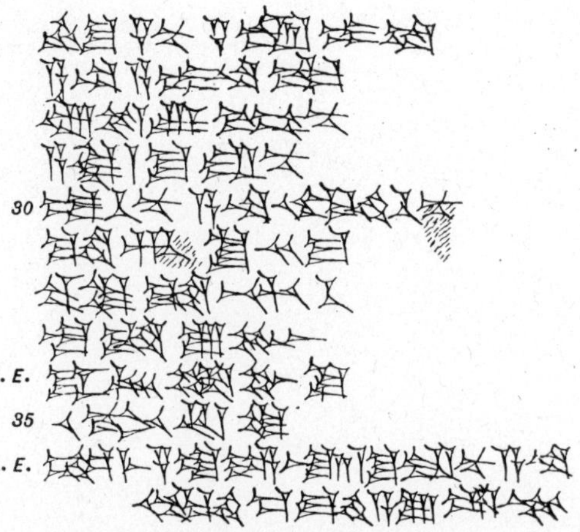

49

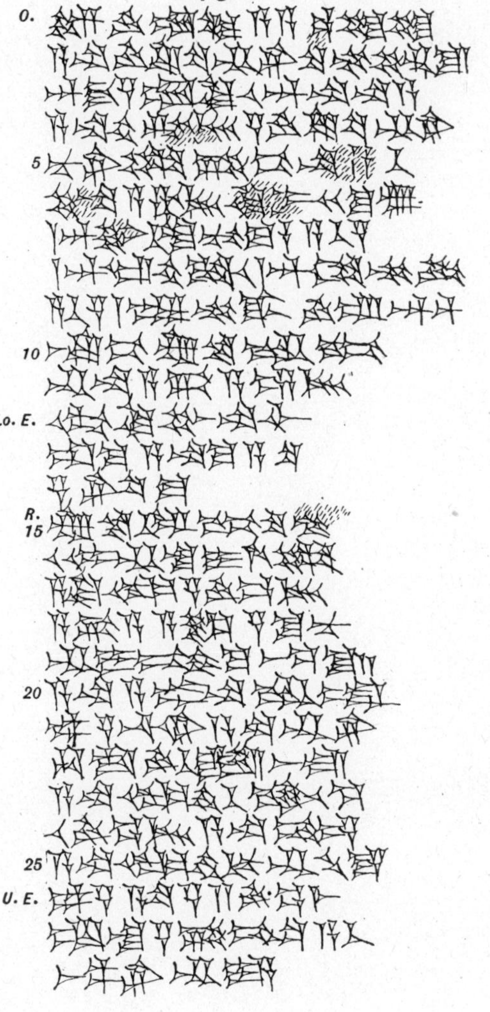

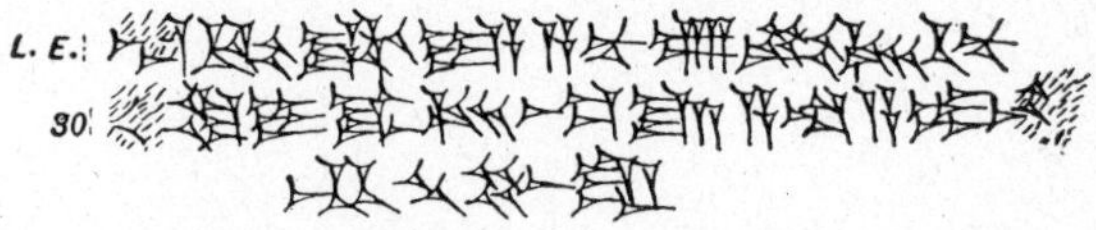

50

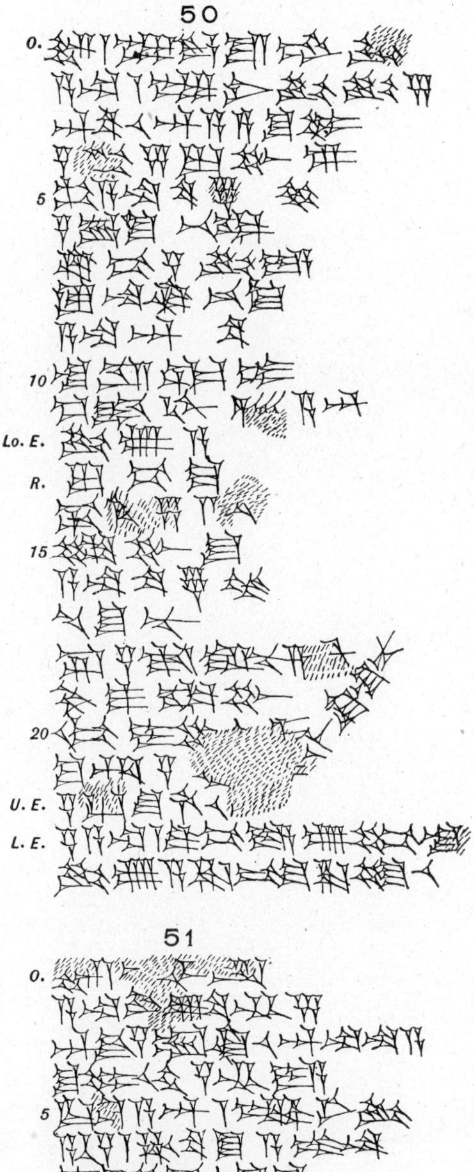

51

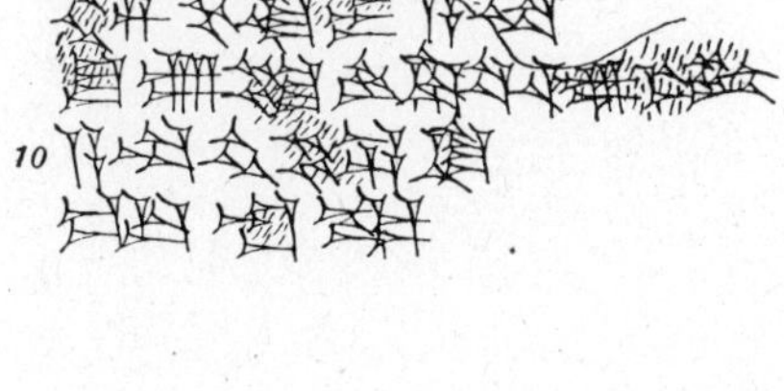

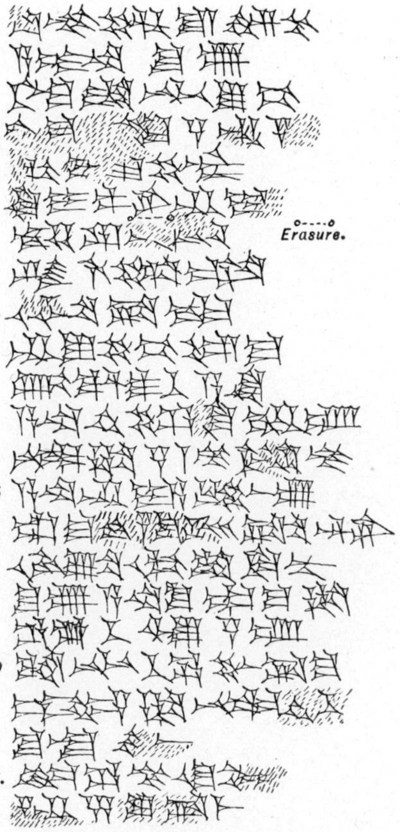

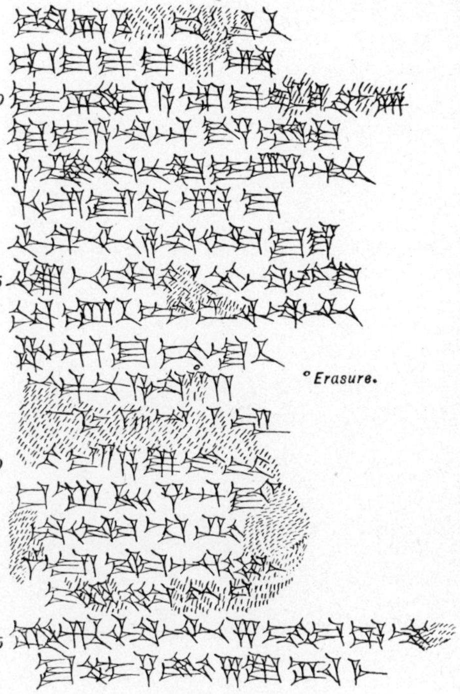

52

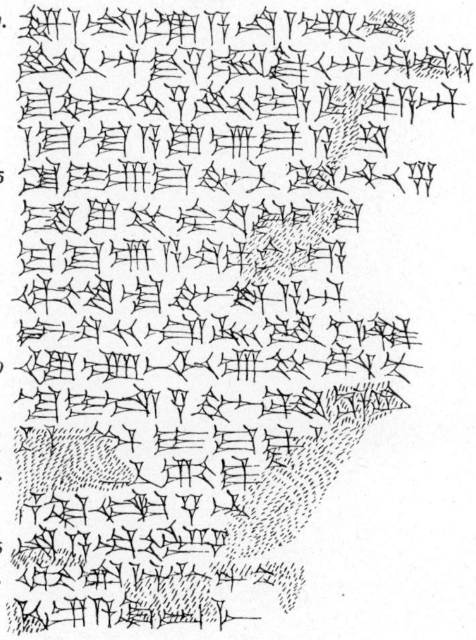

53

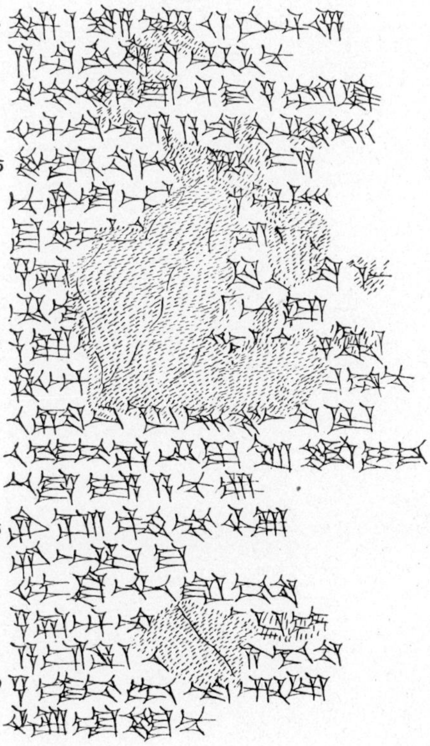

U.E.

L.E.

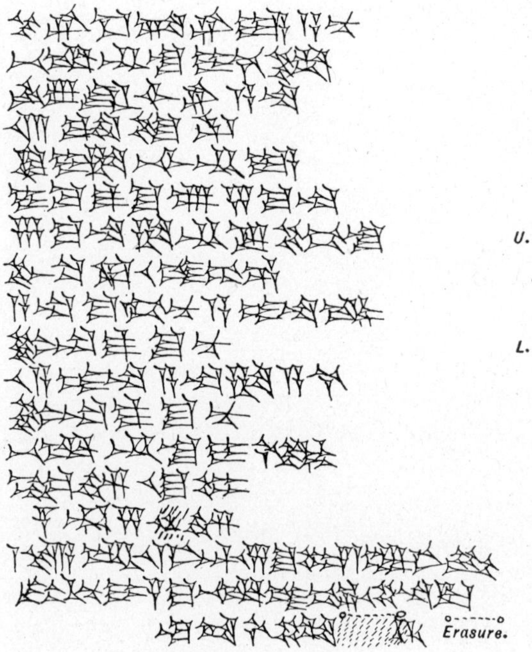

54

O.

Lo.E.

R.

U.E.

L.E.

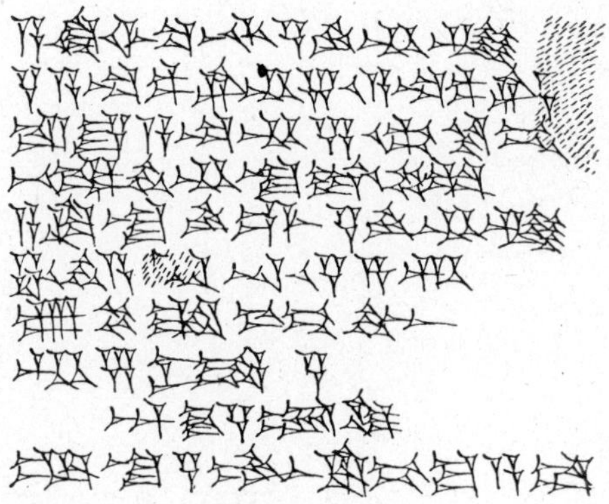

55

O.

Lo.E.

R.

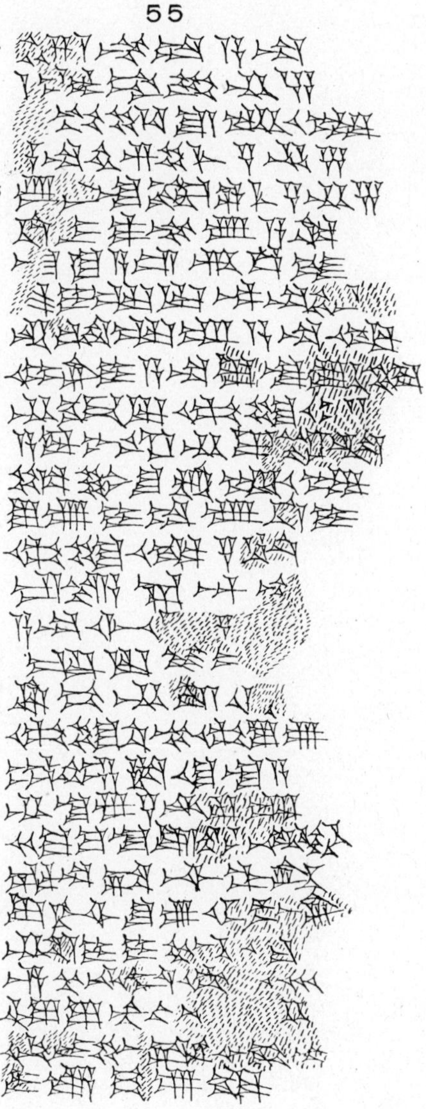

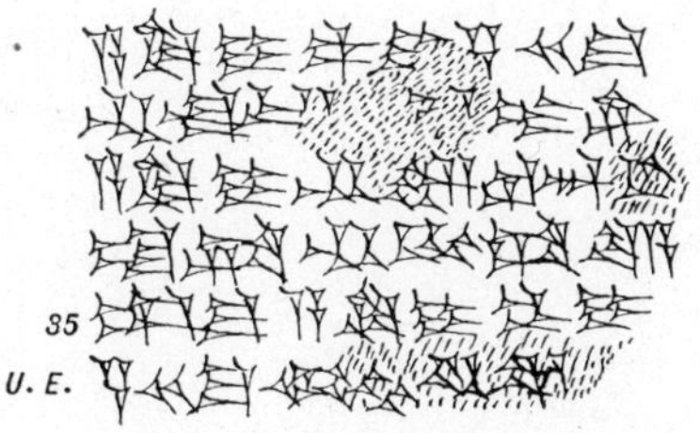

56

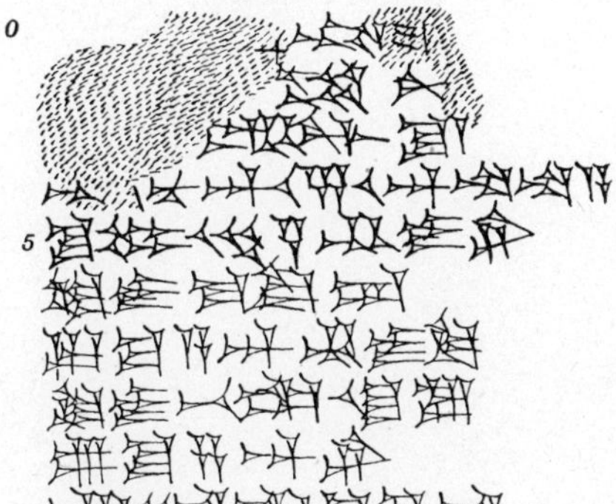

57

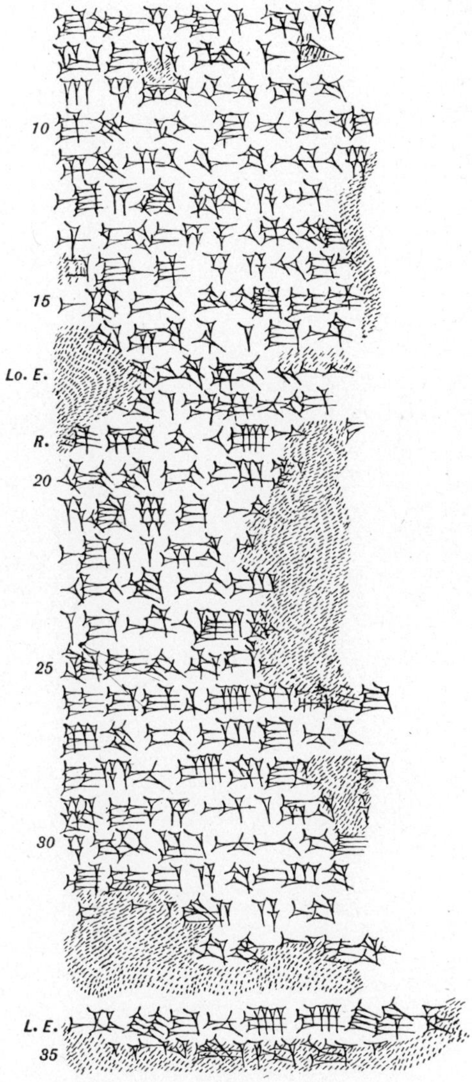

58

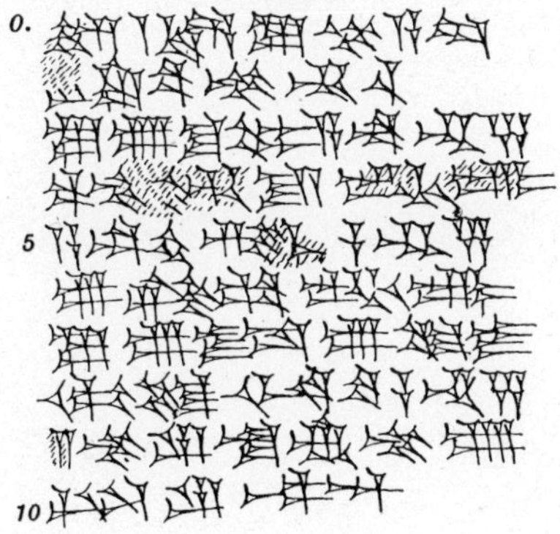

Lo. E.
R.
U. E.

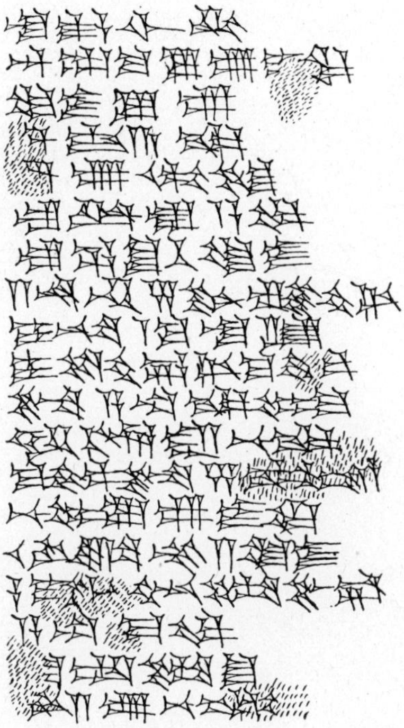

59

O.
Lo. E.
R.

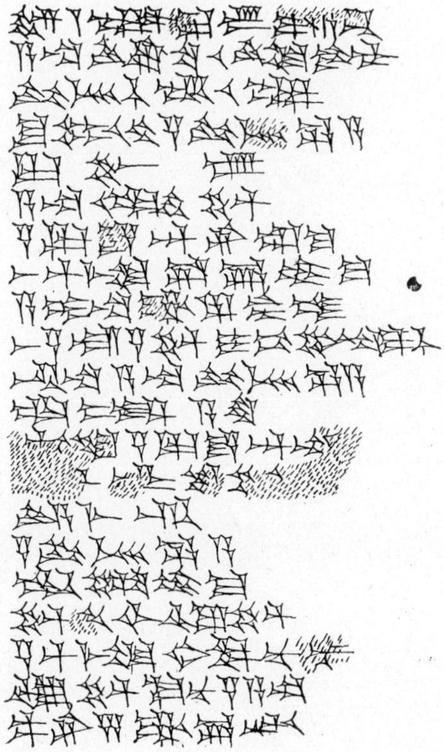

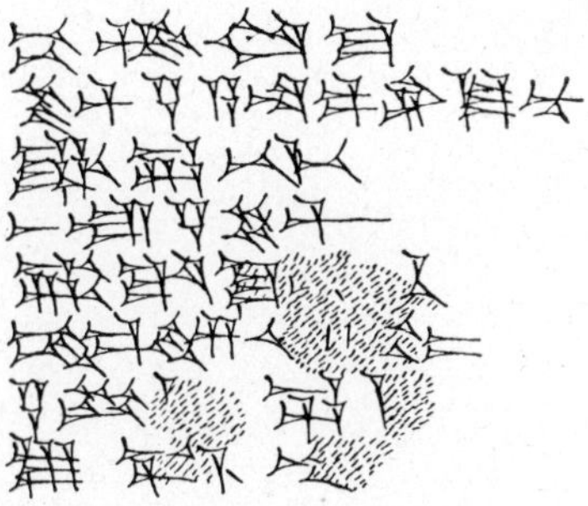

60

O.
Lo. E.
R.

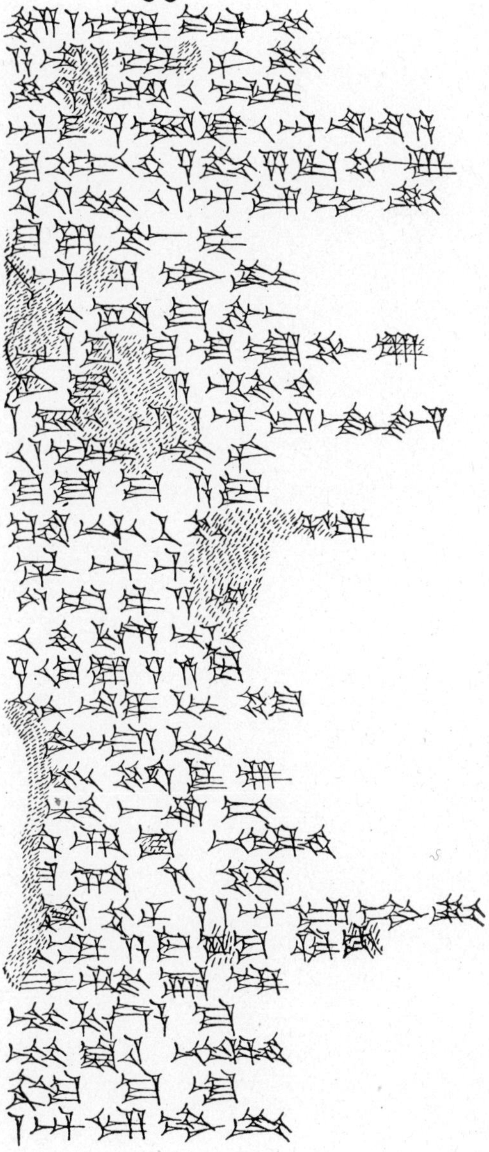

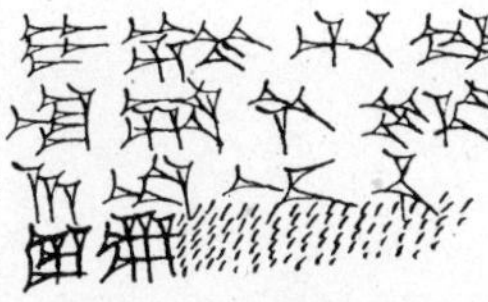

61

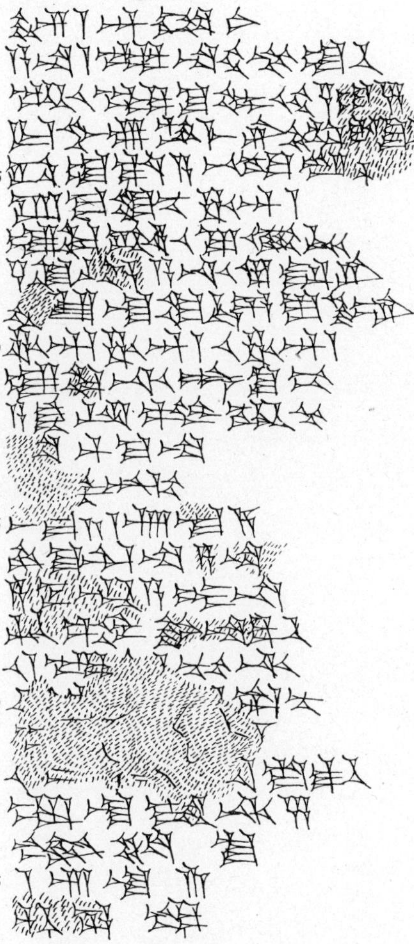

62

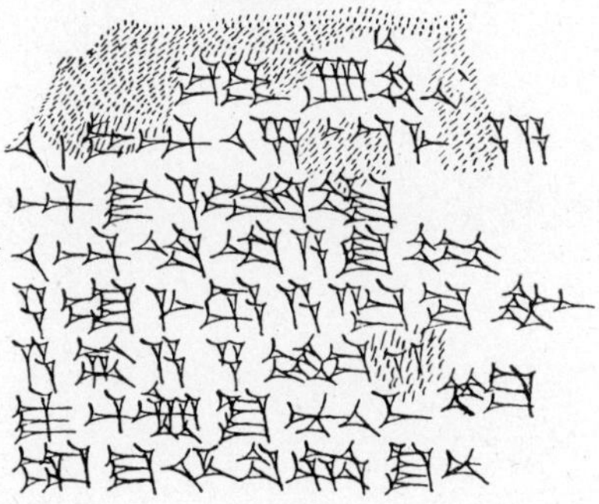

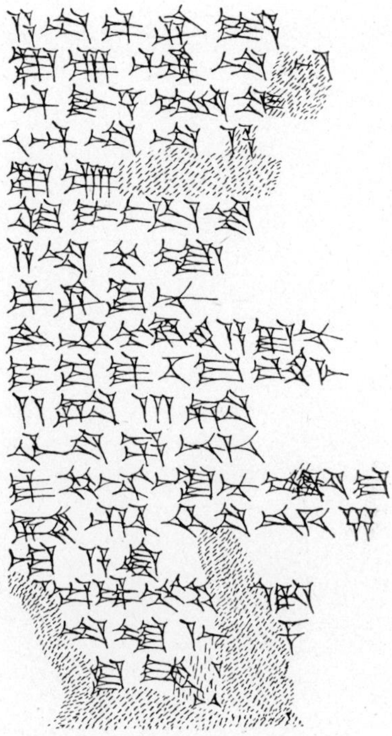

63

64

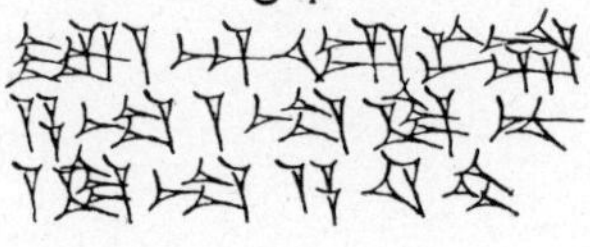

R.

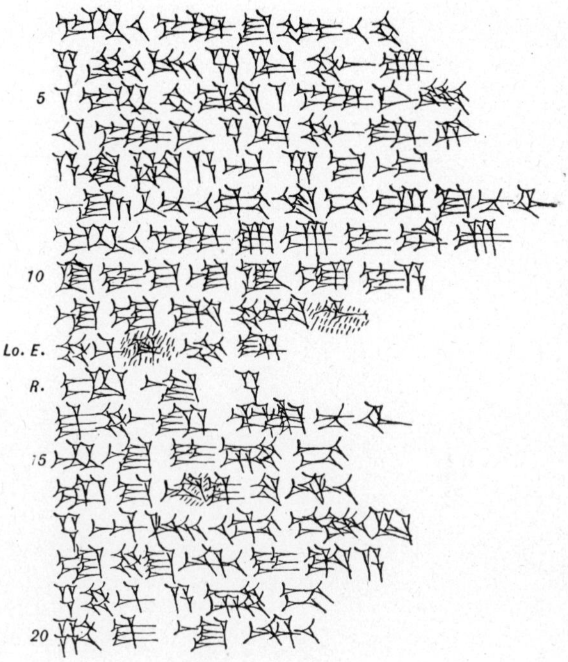
Lo. E.
R.

65

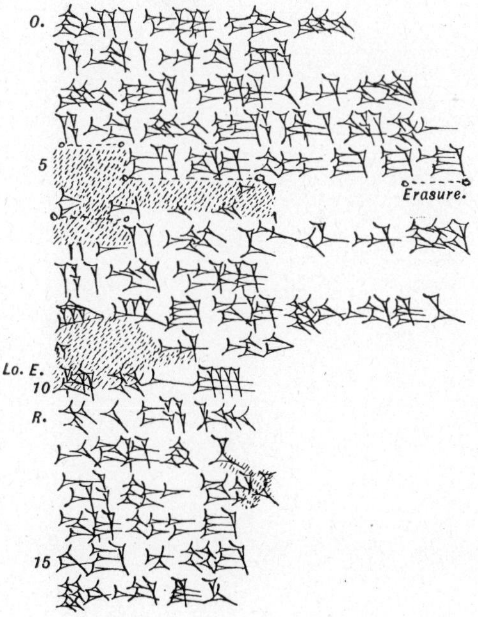
O.
Erasure.
Lo. E.
R.

66

O.

67

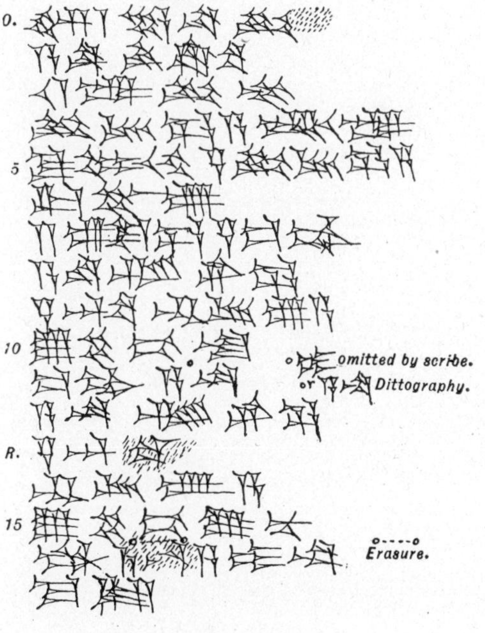
O.
omitted by scribe.
or Dittography.
R.
Erasure.

68

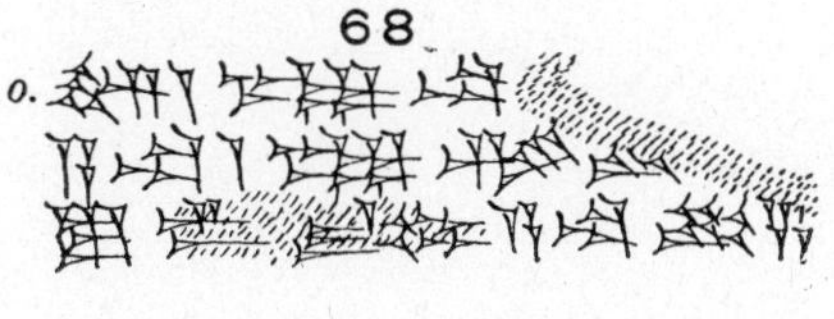
O.

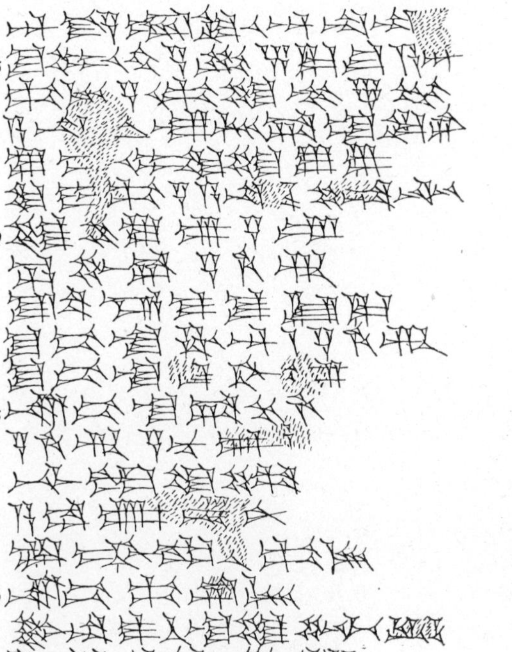
Lo. E.
R.
U. E.
L. E.
° rest erasure.

69

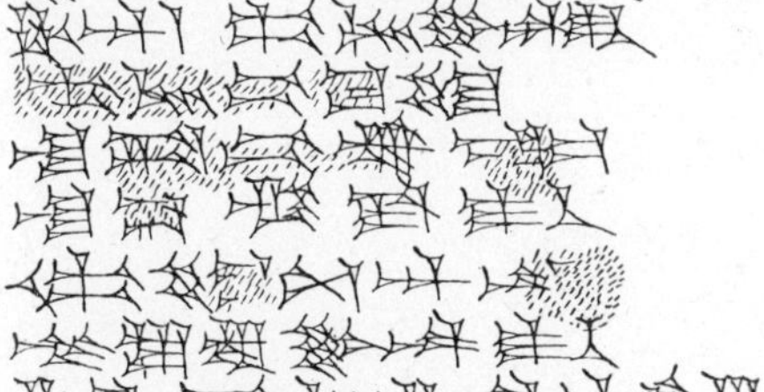
O.

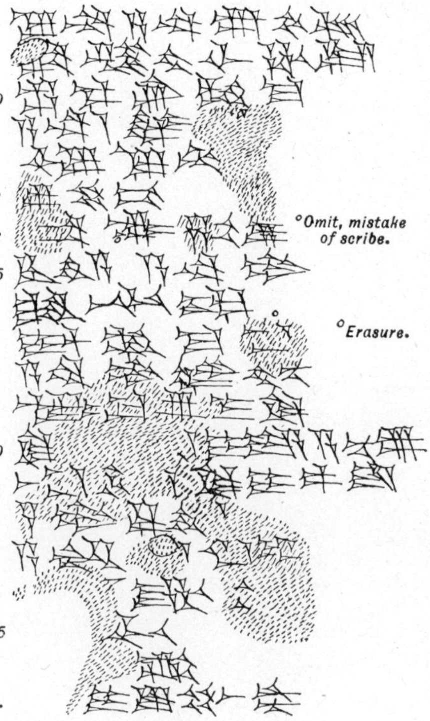
Lo. E.
R.
°Omit, mistake of scribe.
°Erasure.
U. E.

70

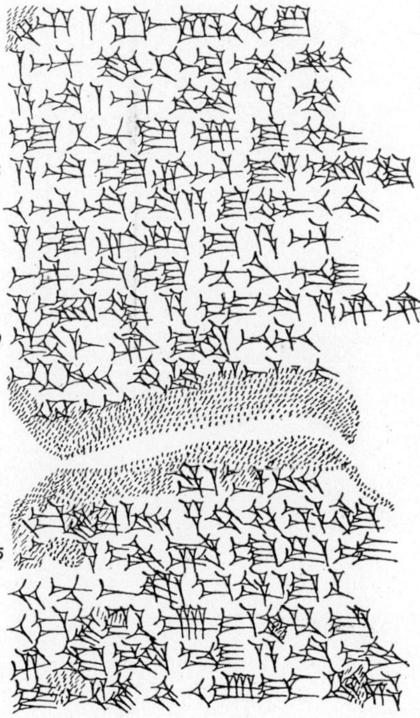
O.
R.

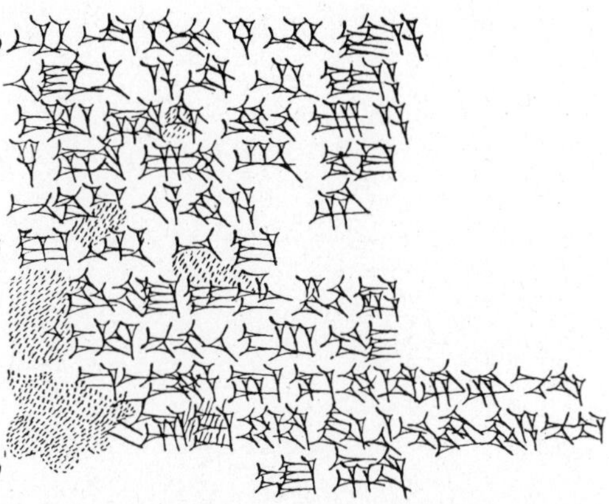

71

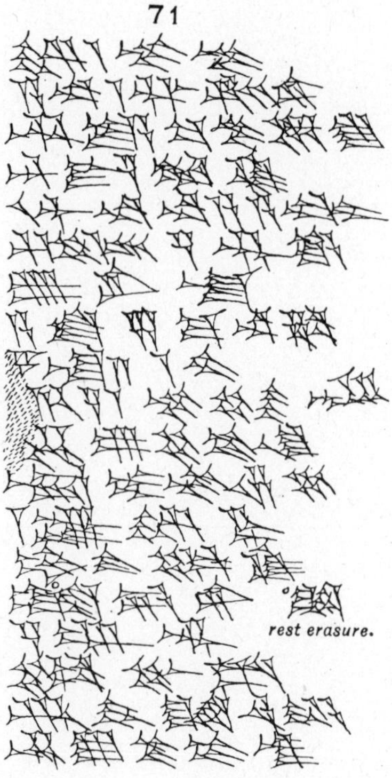

72

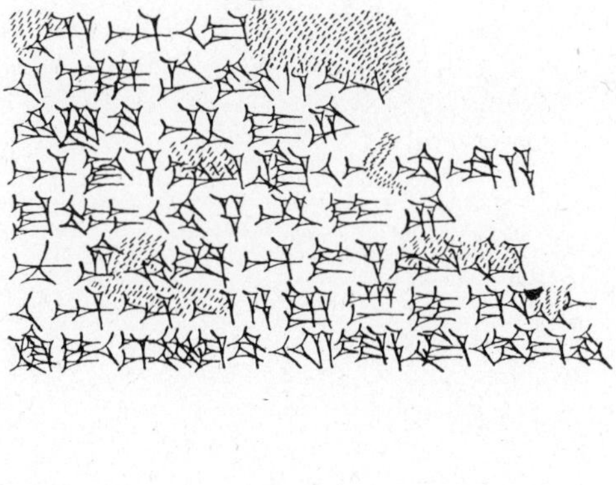

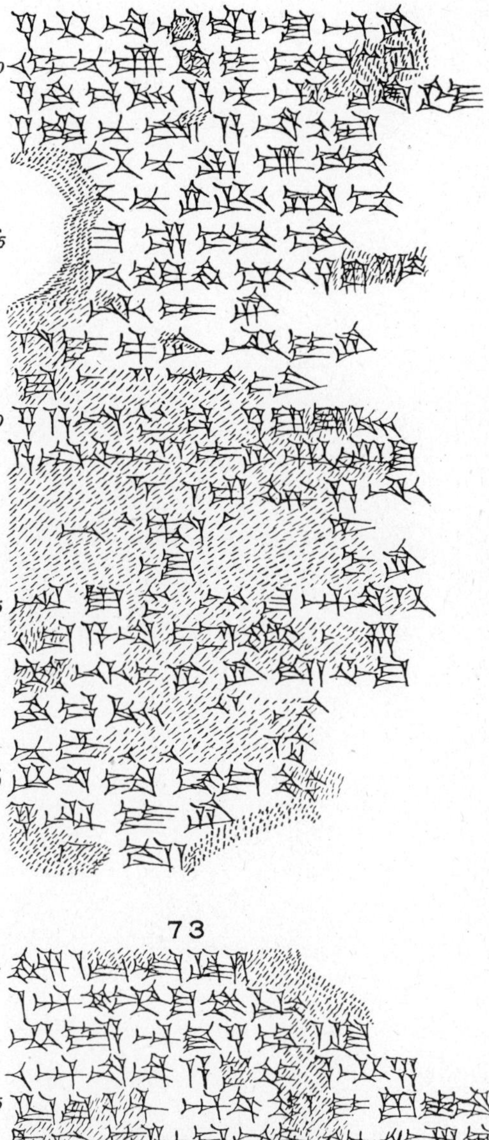

73

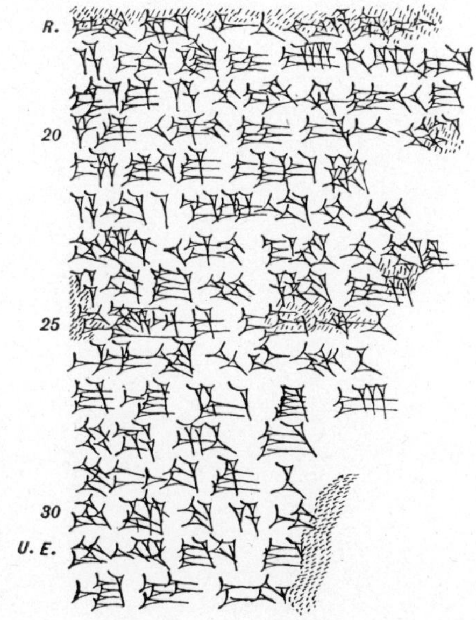

74

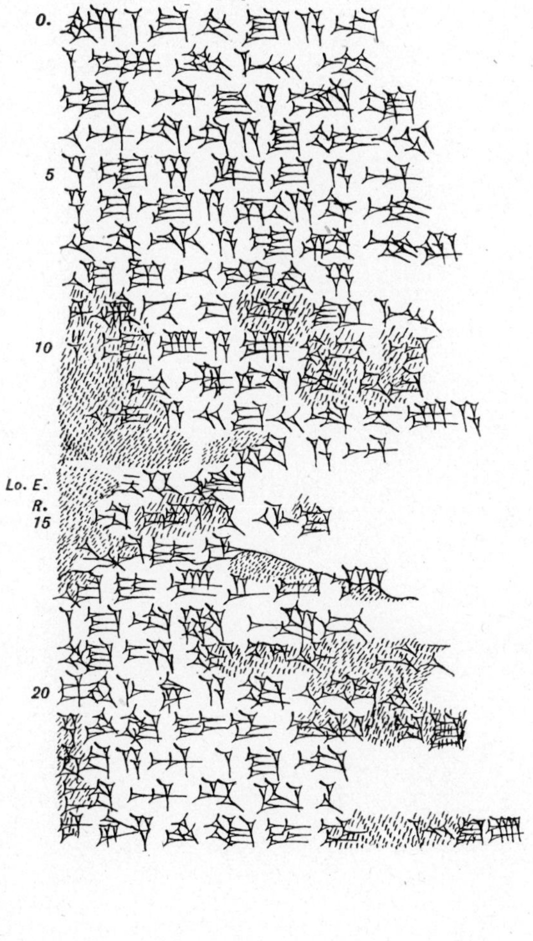

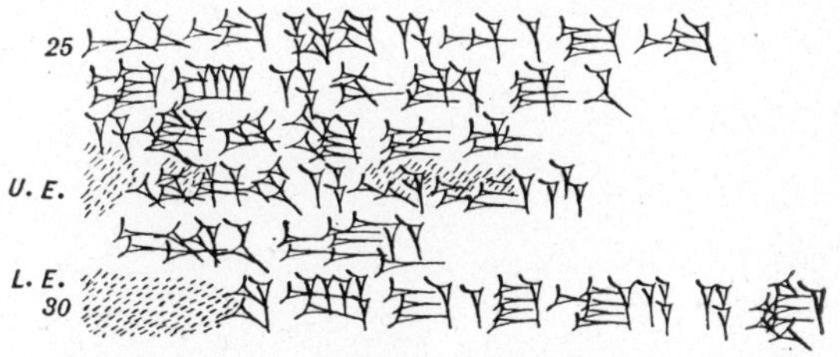

75

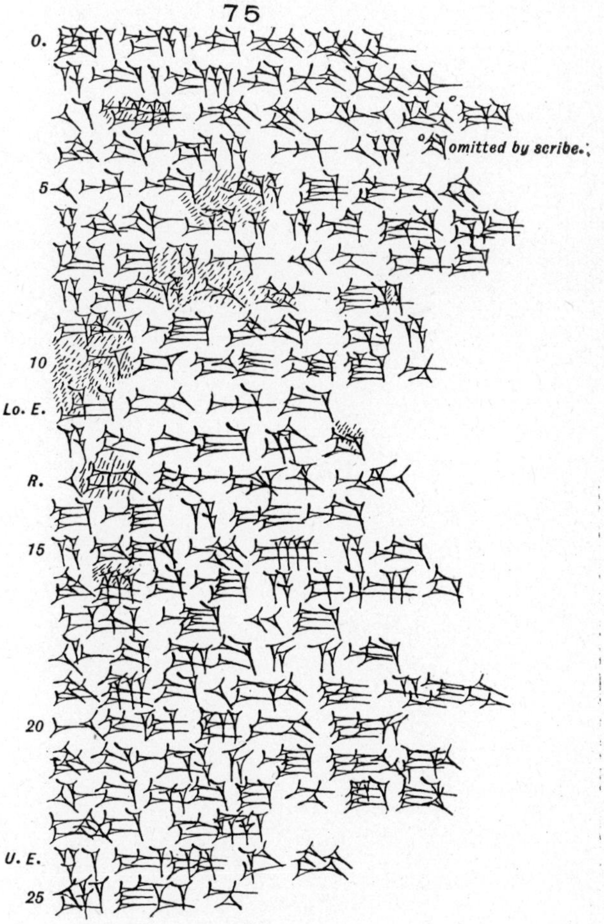

76

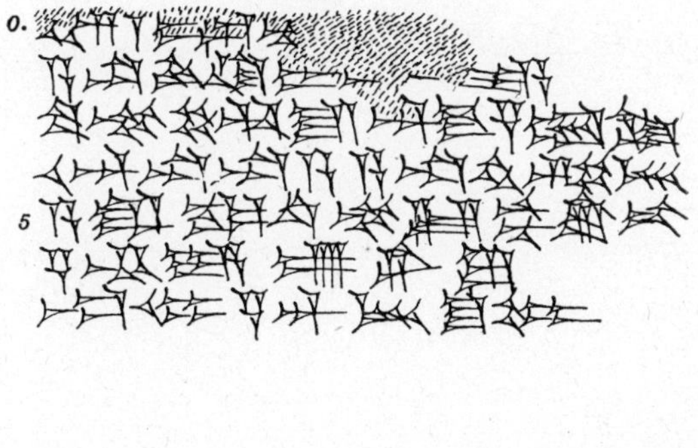

Lo. E. R. U. E. L. E.

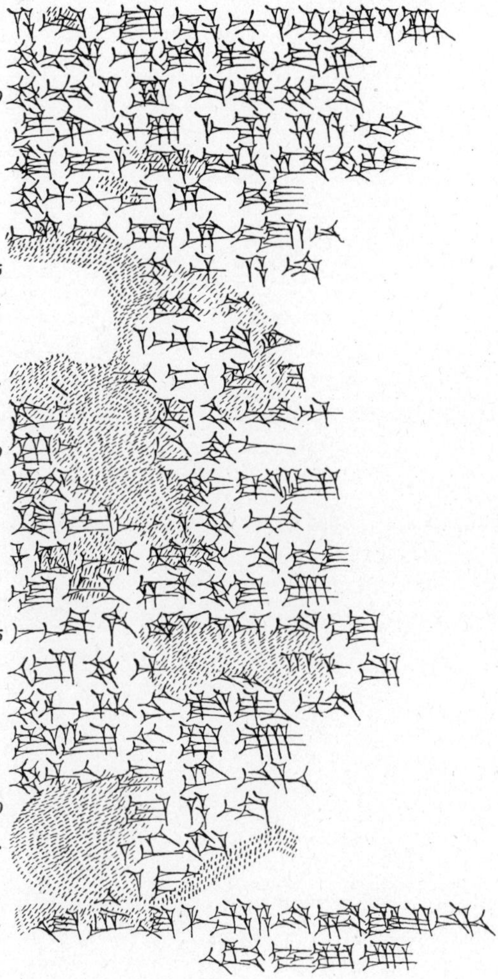

R. U. E.

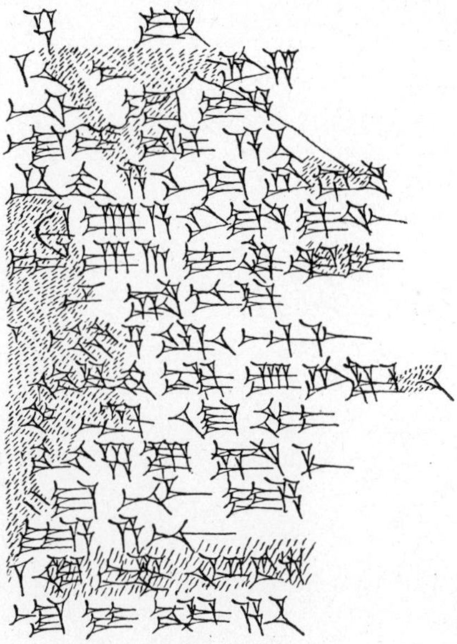

77

O.

78

O. Lo. E. R.

79

O.

Lo. E.

R.

U. E.

L. E.

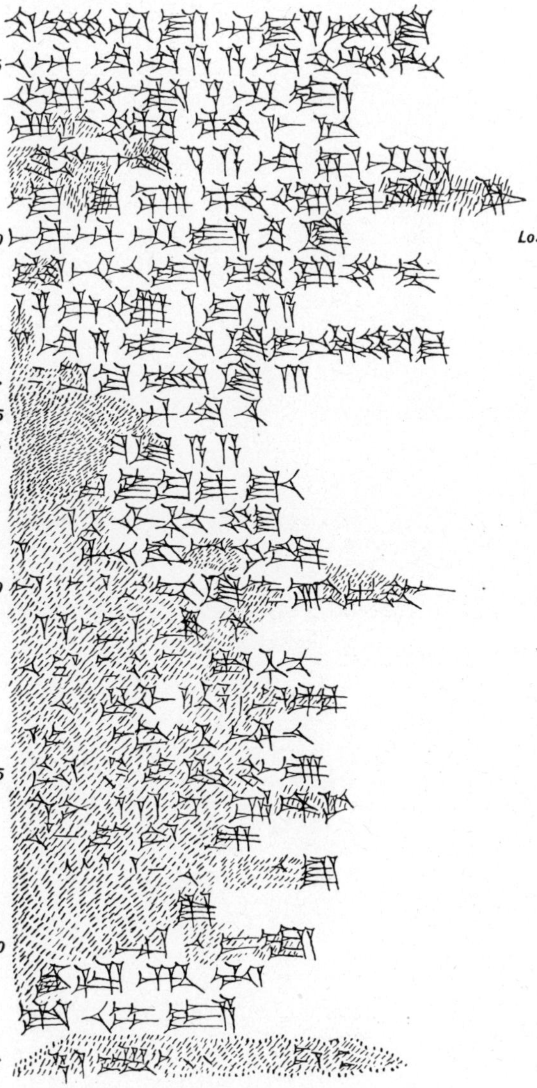

80

O.

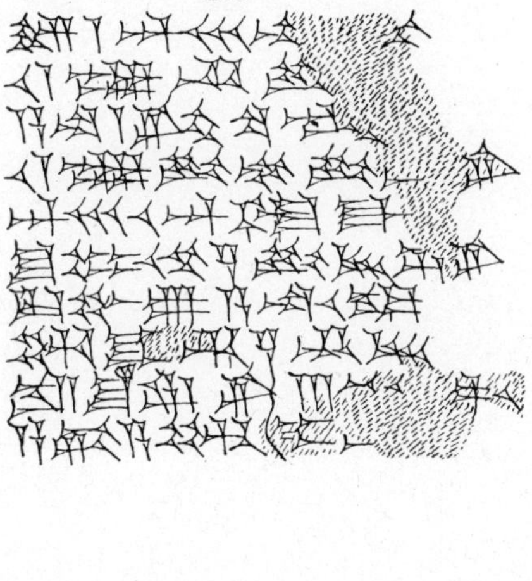

Lo. E.

R.

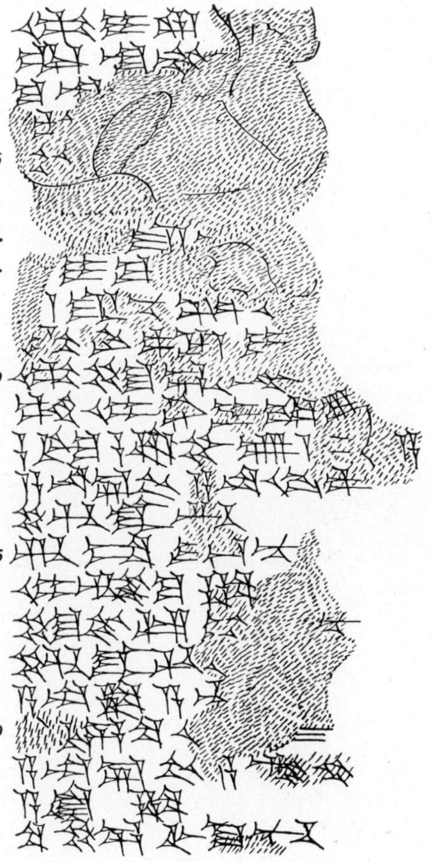

81

O.

Lo. E.

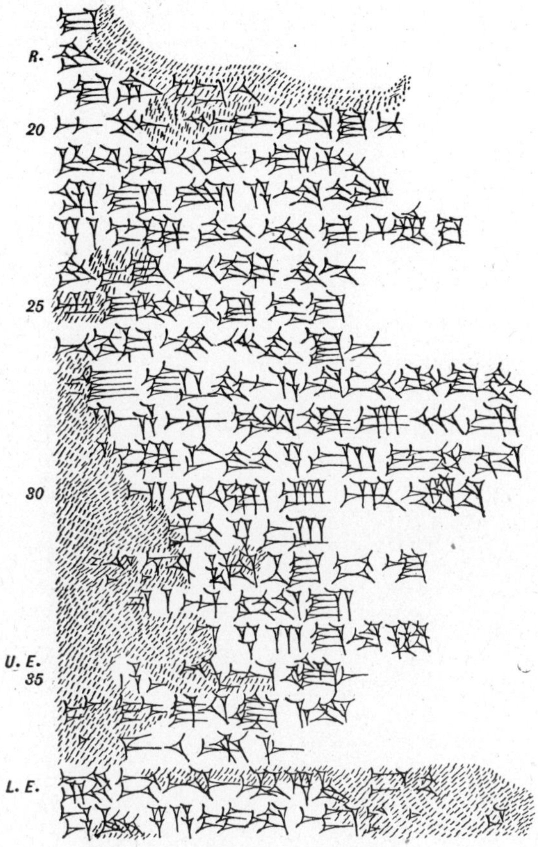

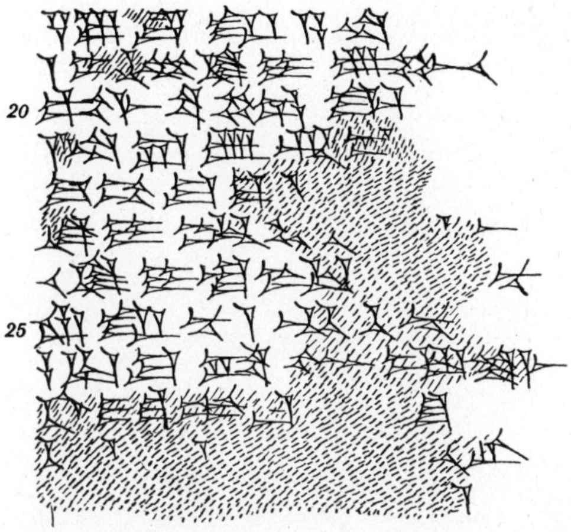

82

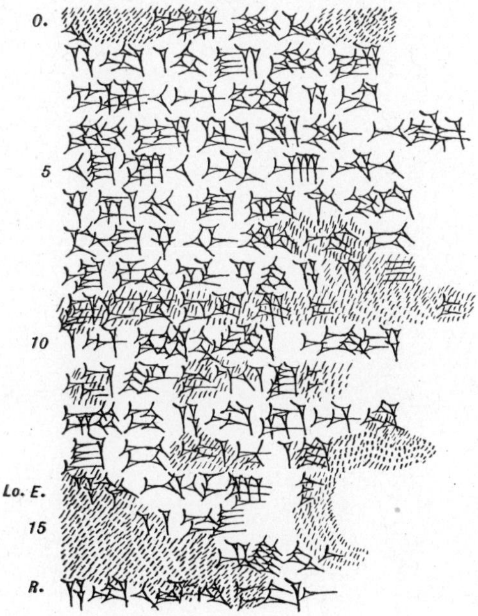

83

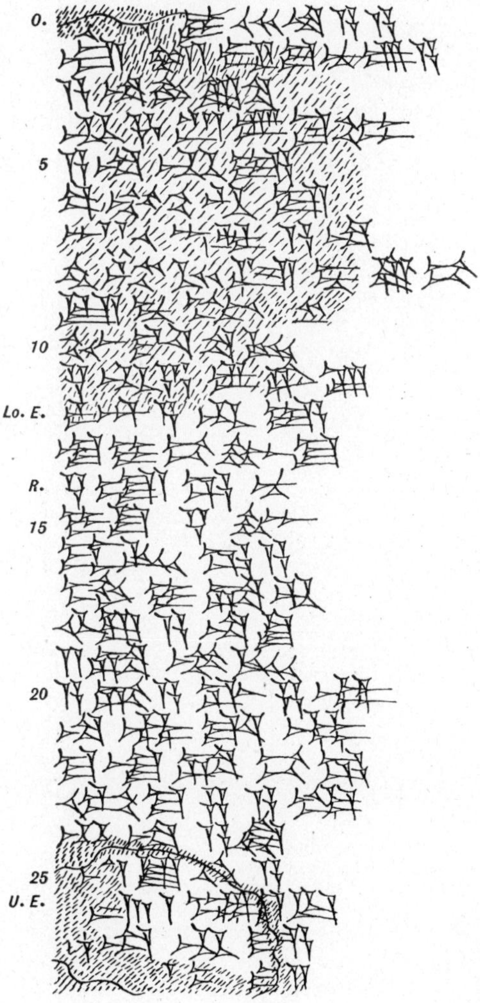

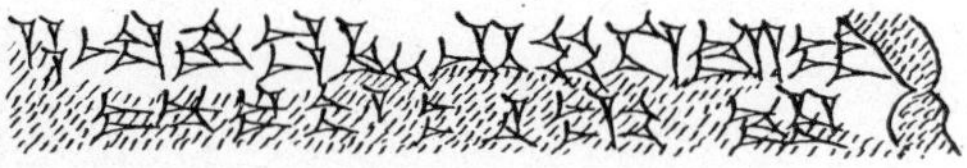

84

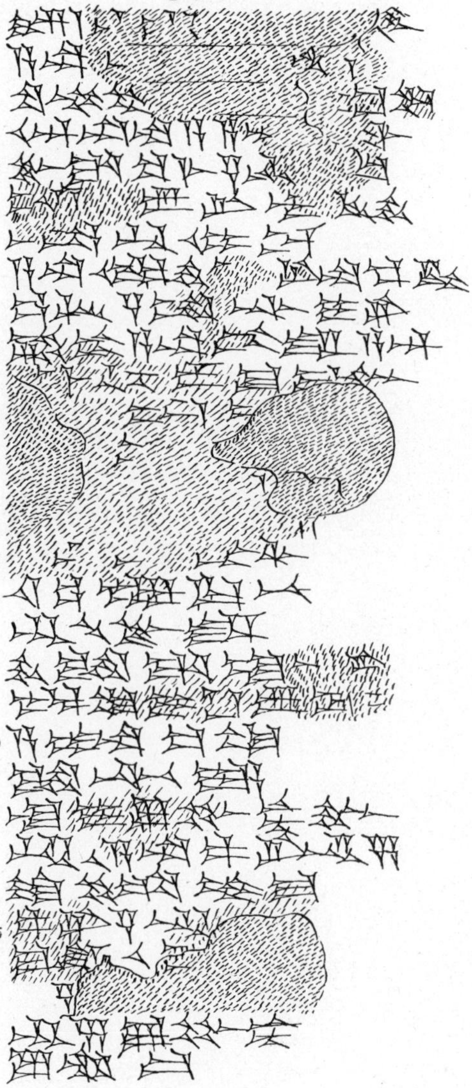

85

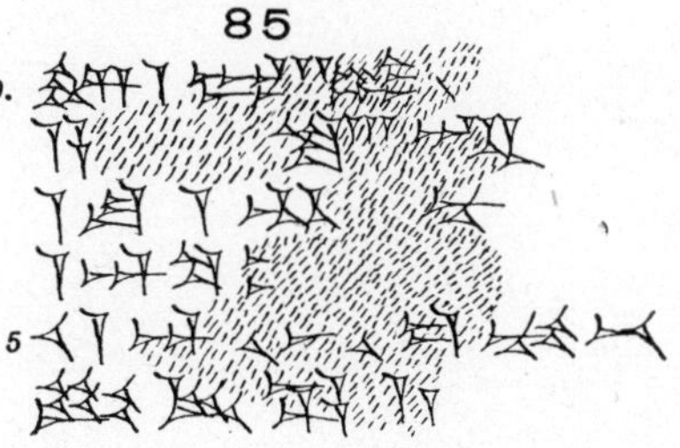

86

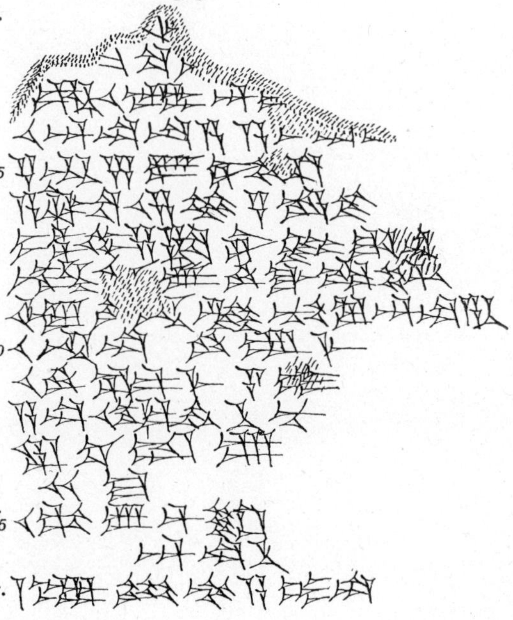

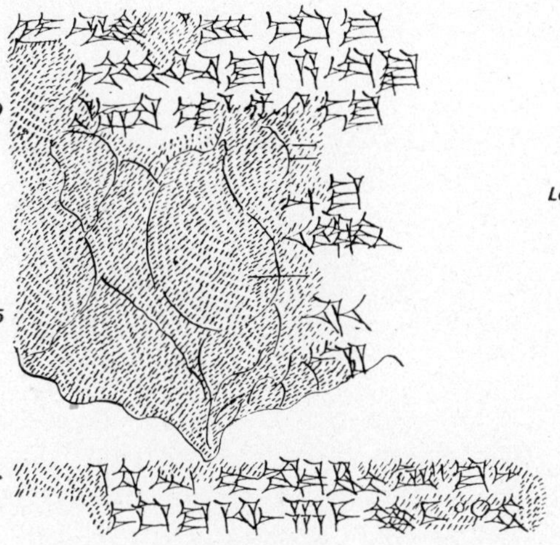

87

88

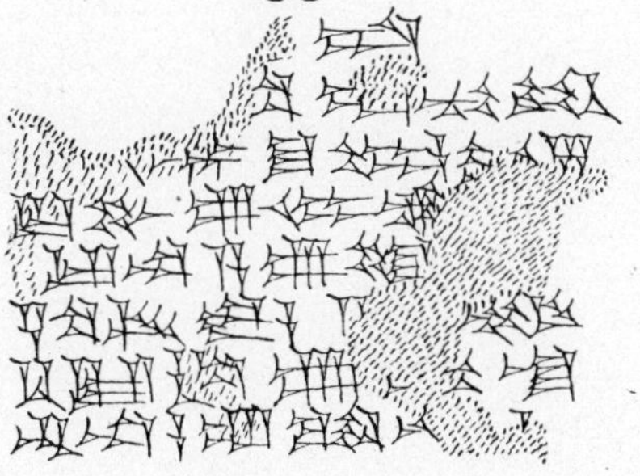

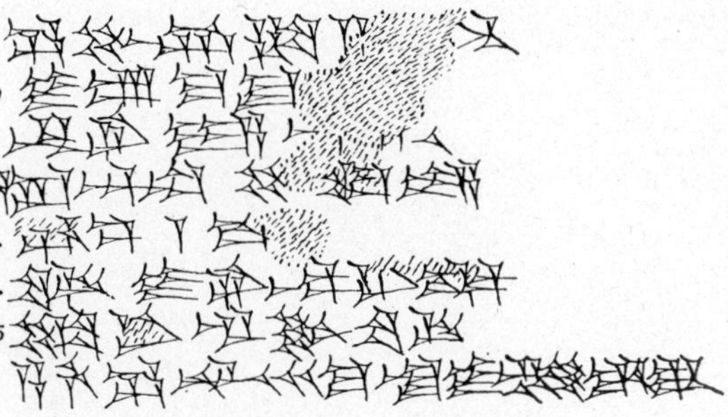

89

90

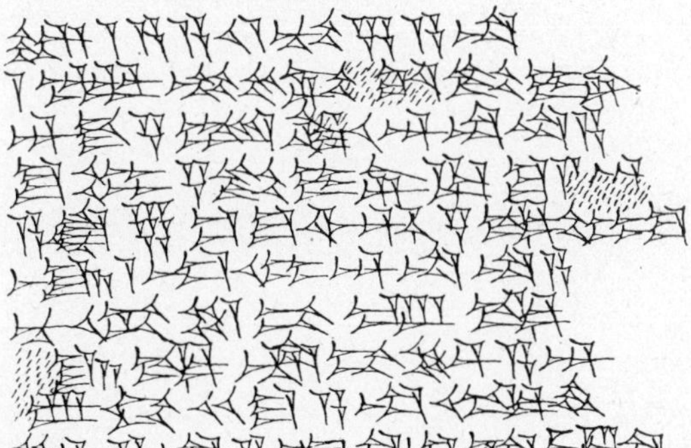

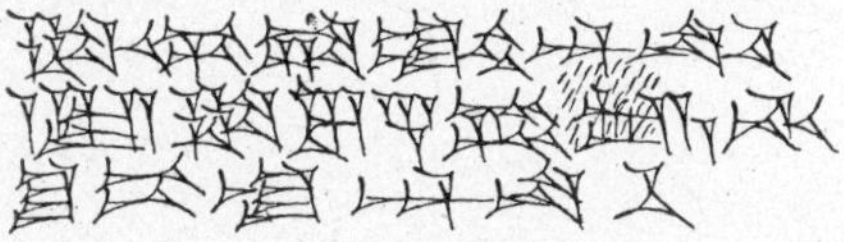

91

92

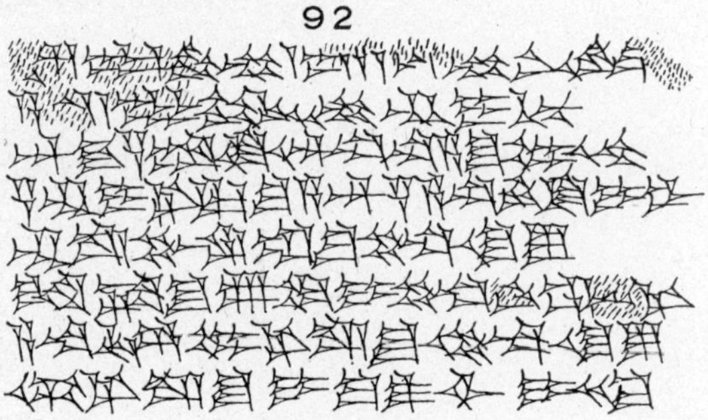

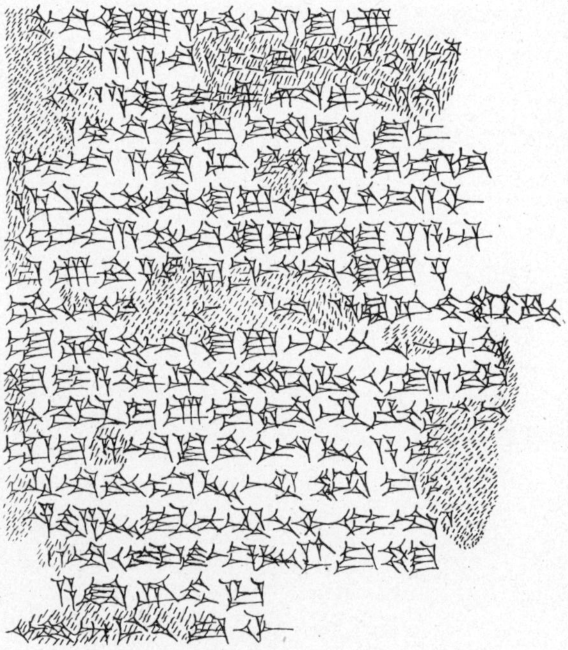

93

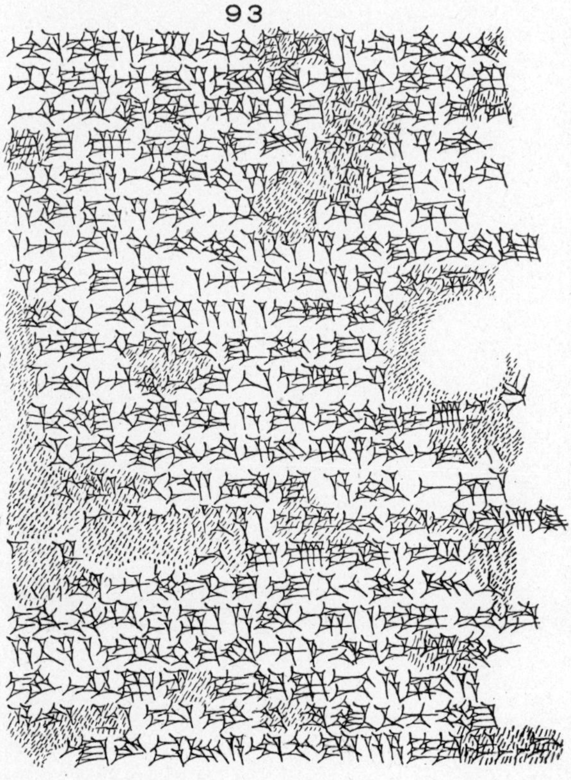

94

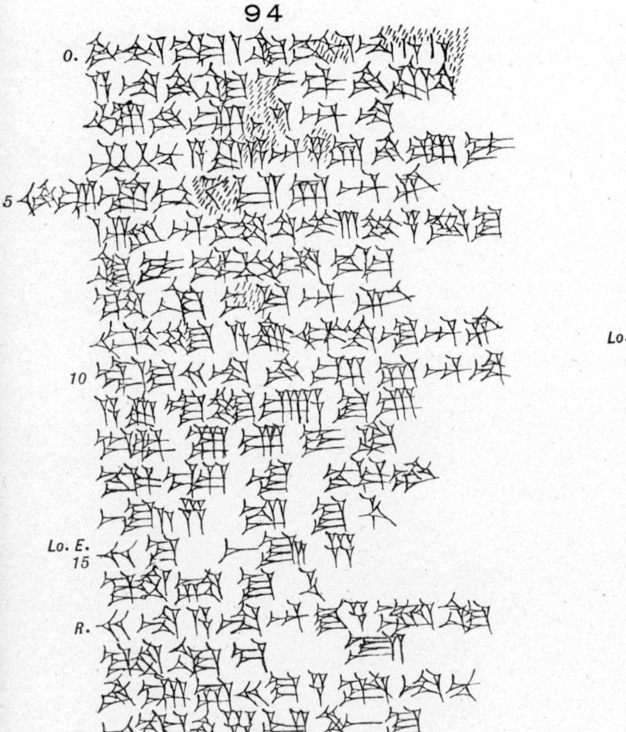

95

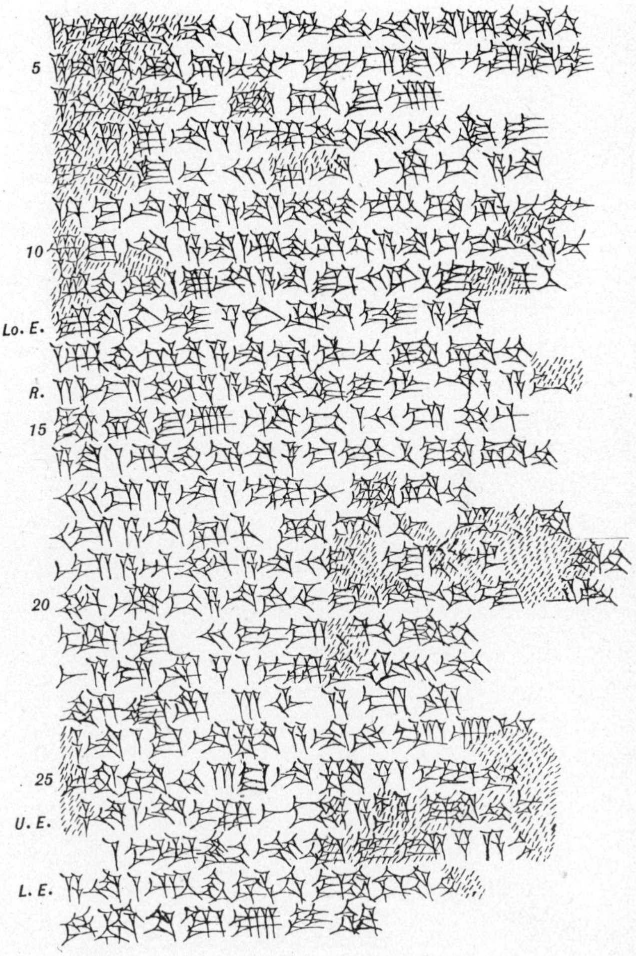

96

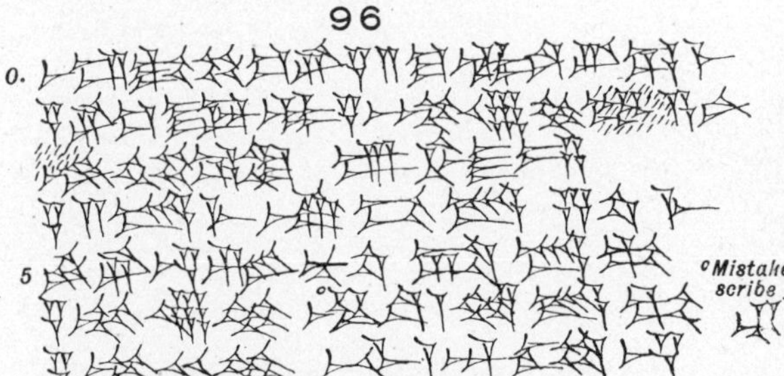

c Mistake of scribe for

97

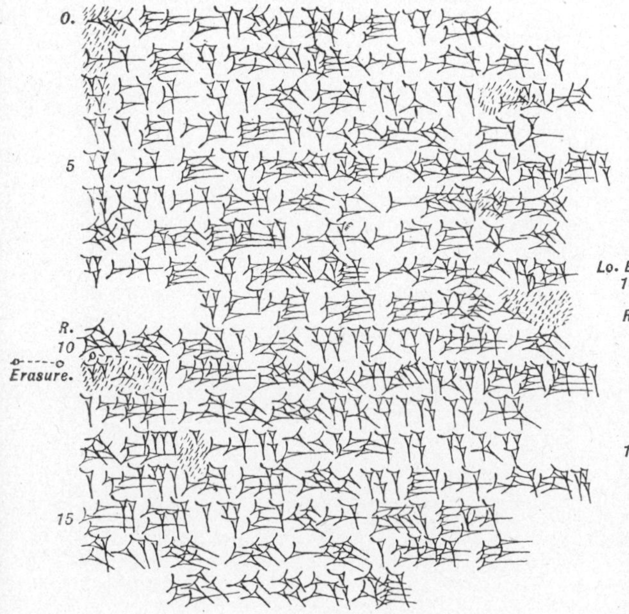

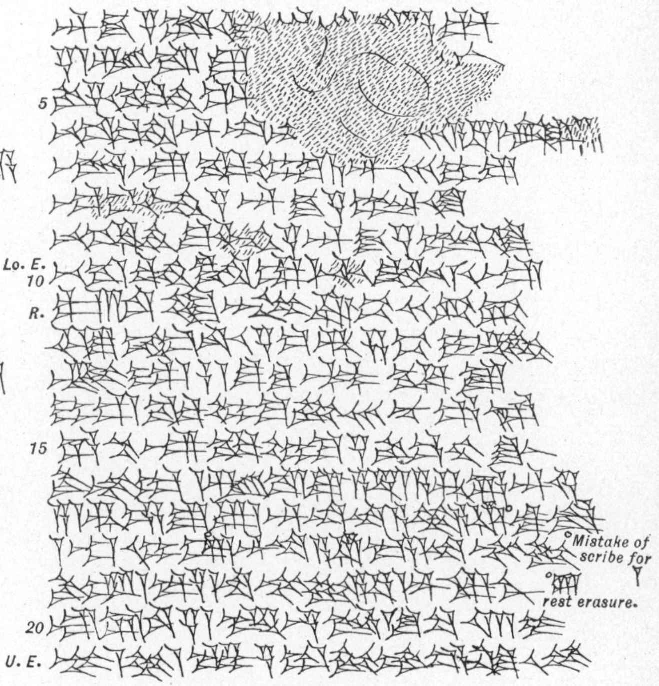

98

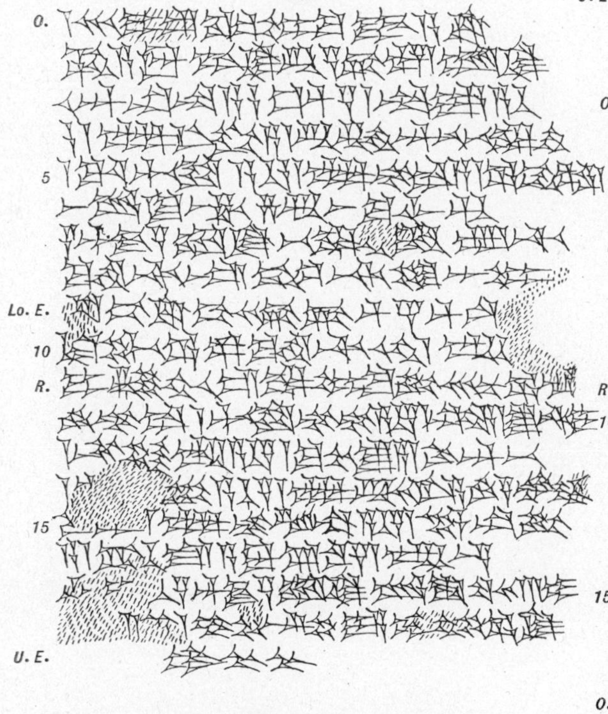

99

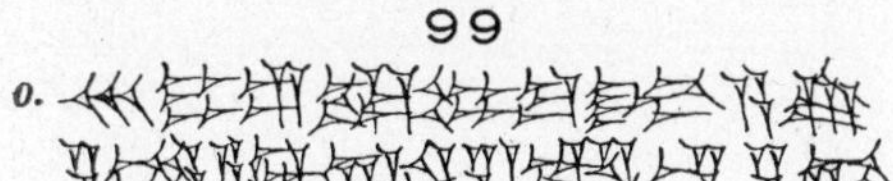

100

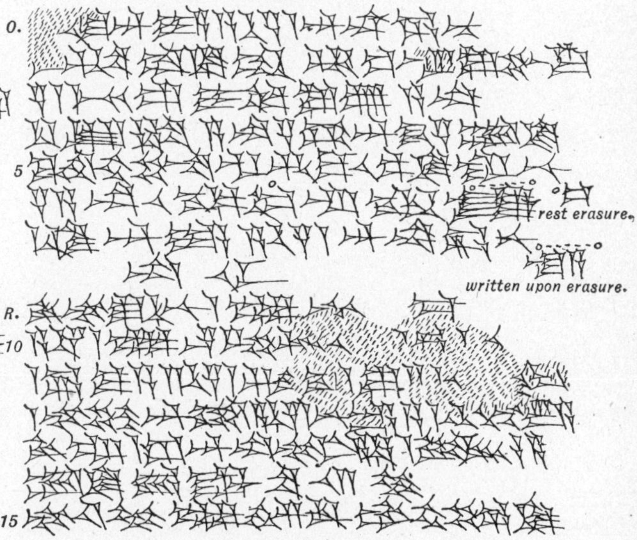

101

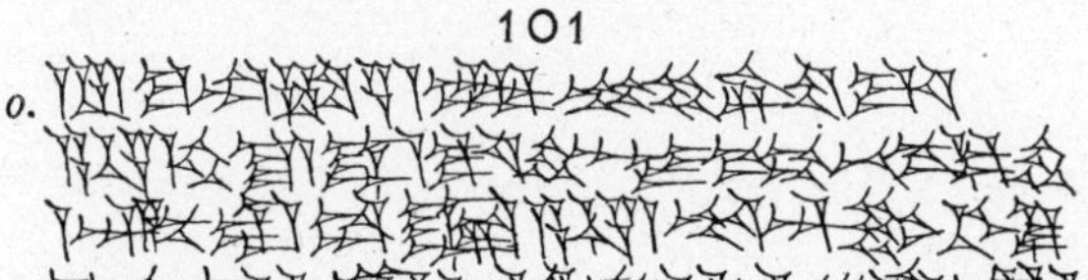

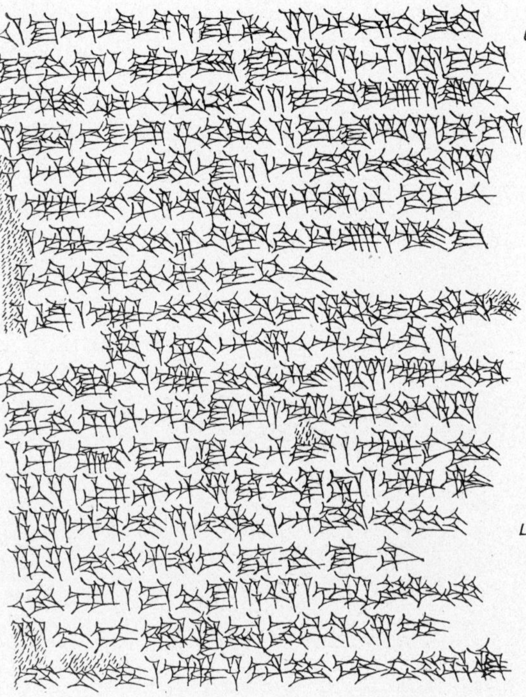

102

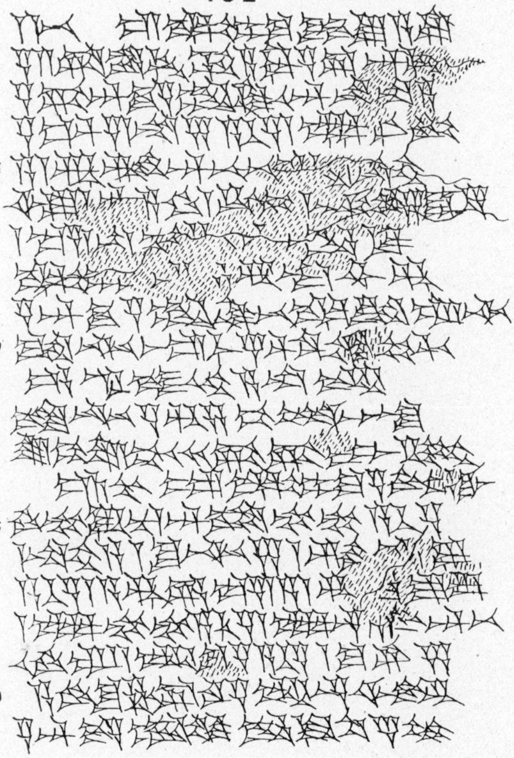

103

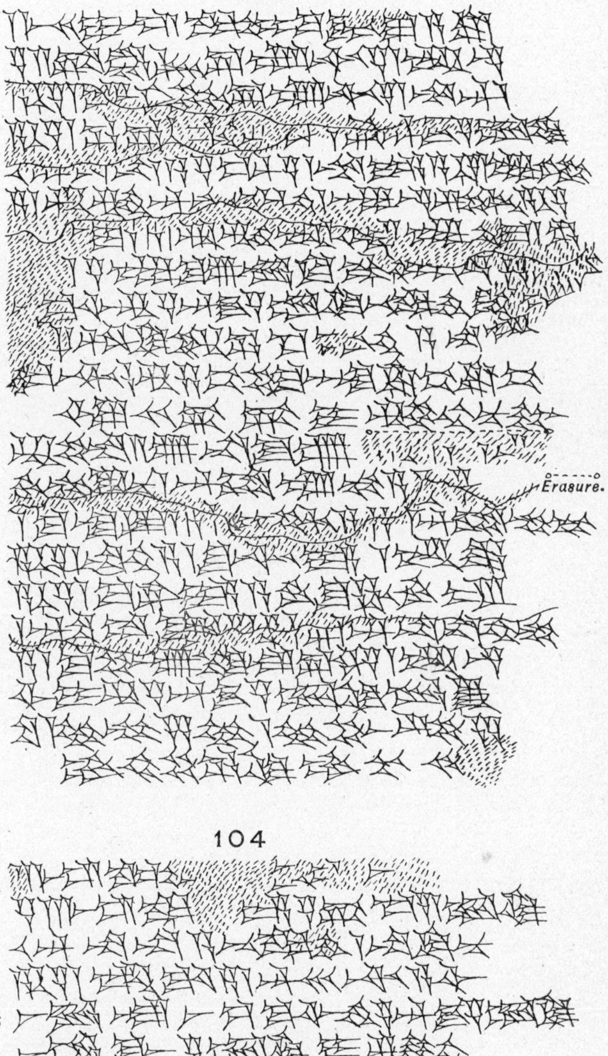

104

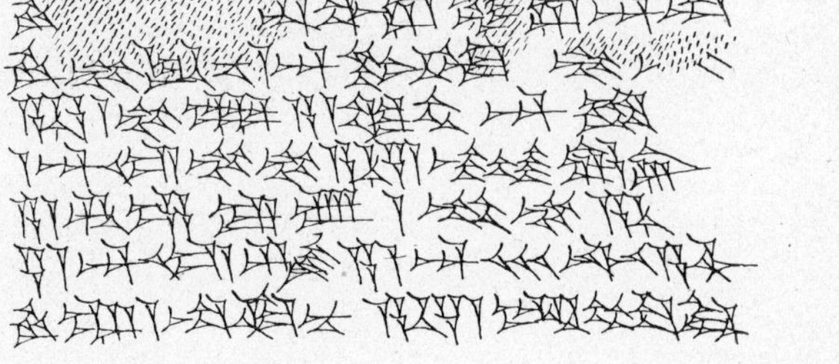

U. E.

105

O. Lo. E. R. U. E.

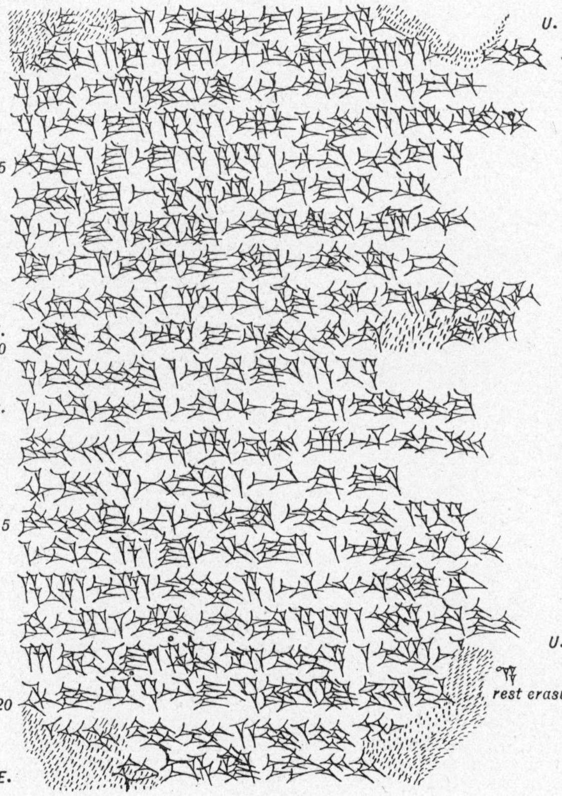

rest erasure.

106

O. Lo. E. R.

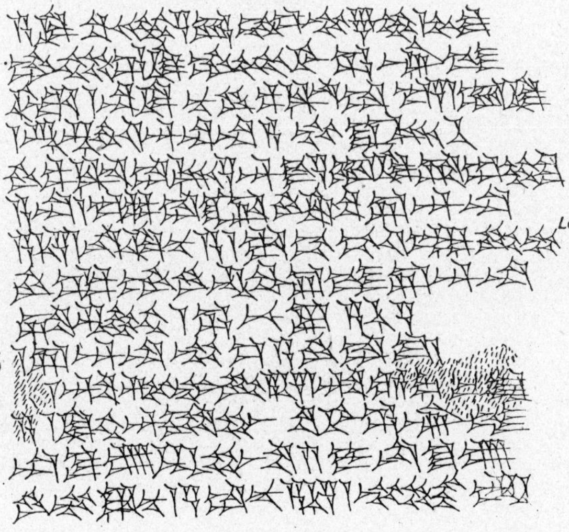

U. E.

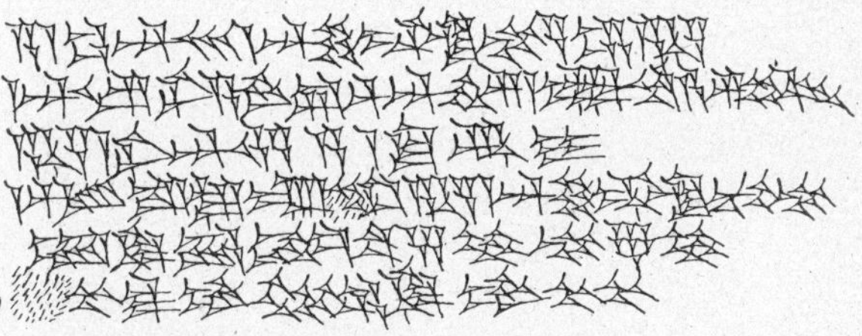

107

O. R. U. E.

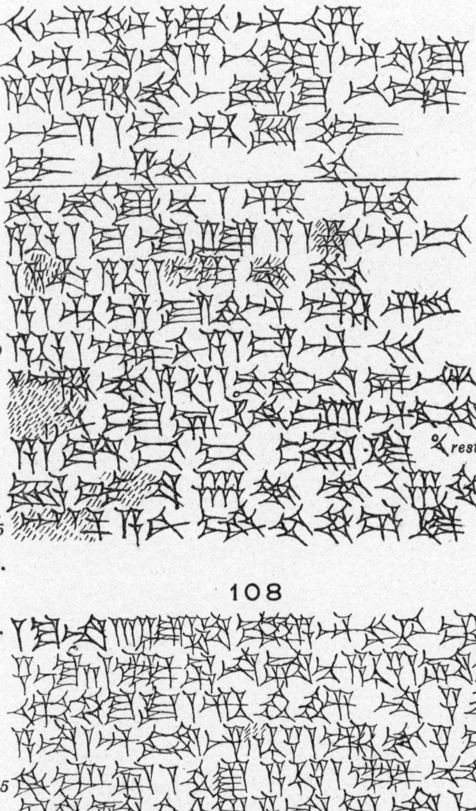

rest erasure.

108

O. Lo. E. R.

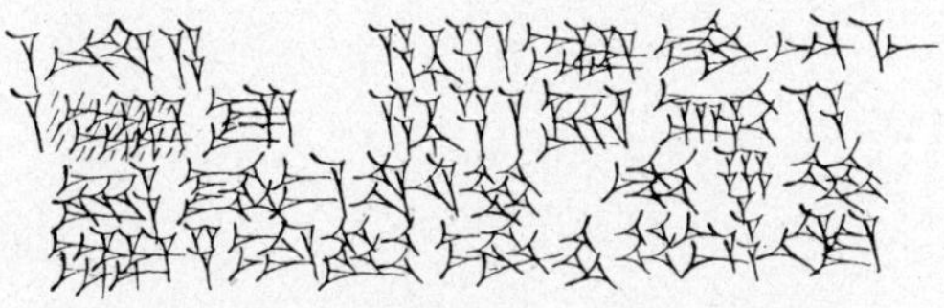

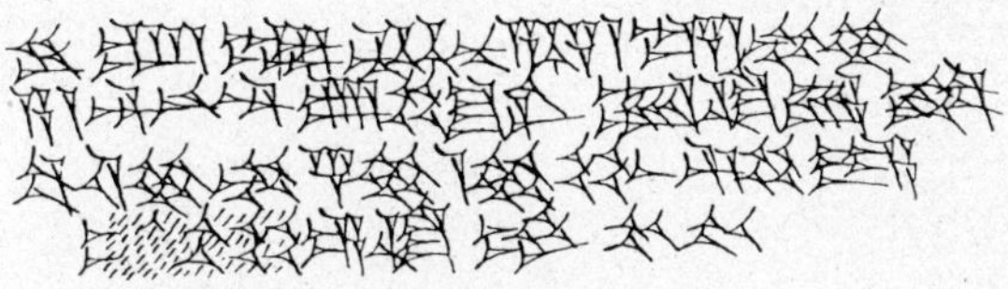

109

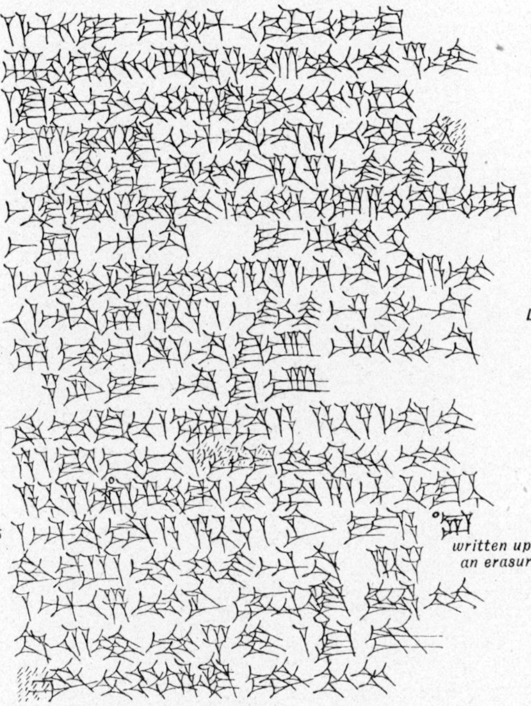

111

110

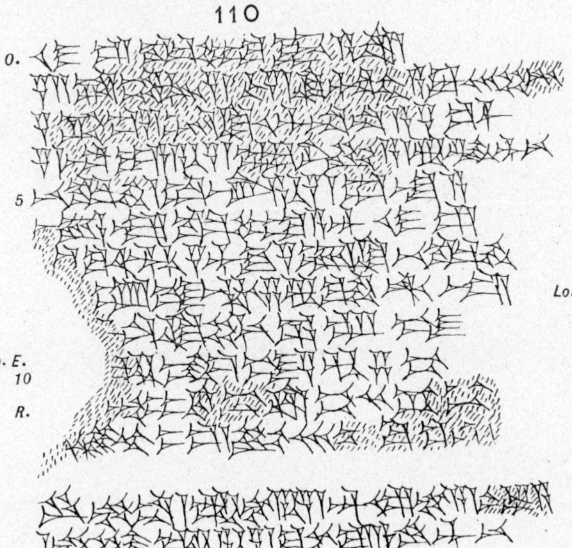

112

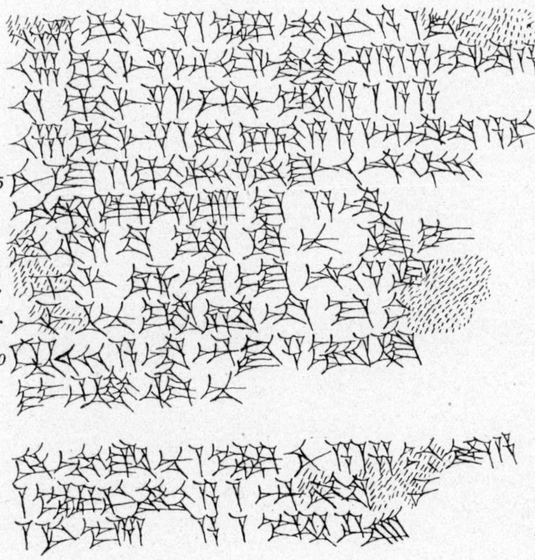

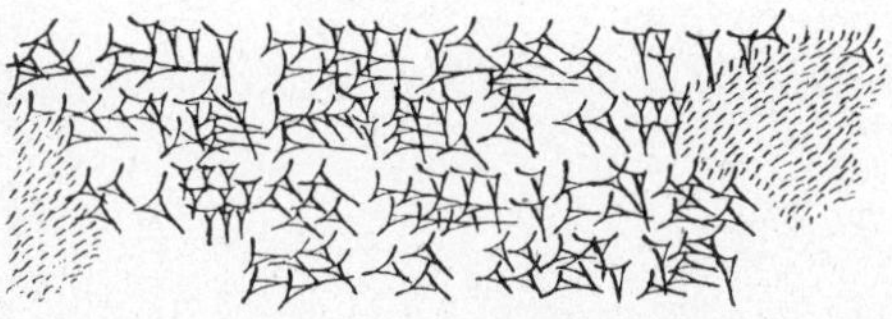

113

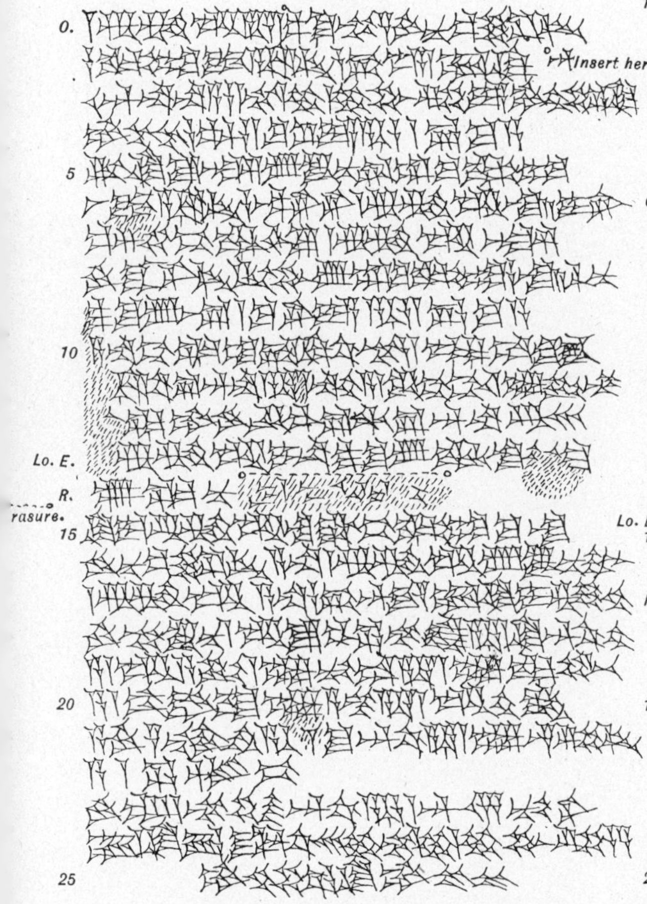

114

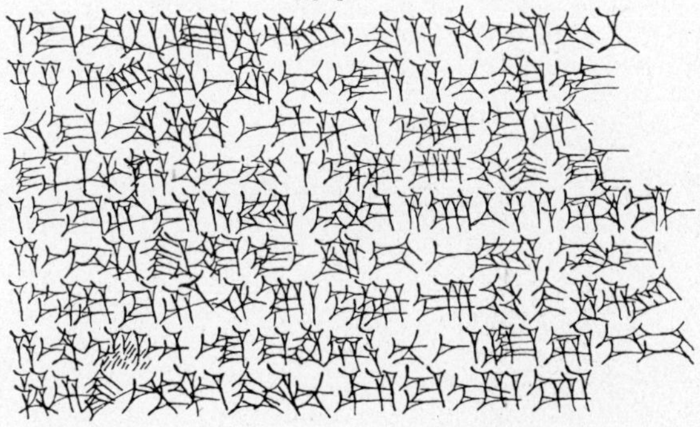

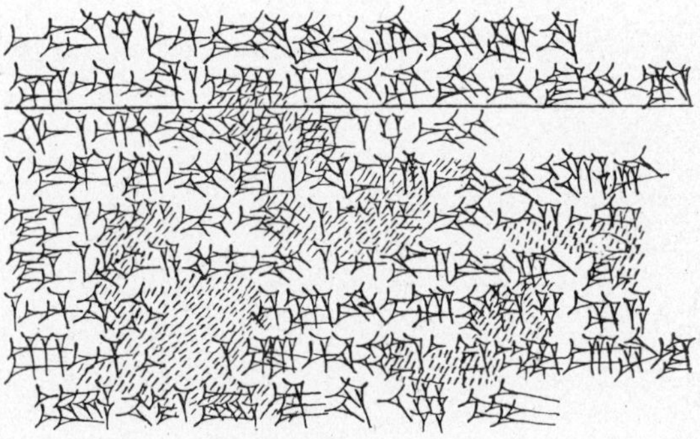

115

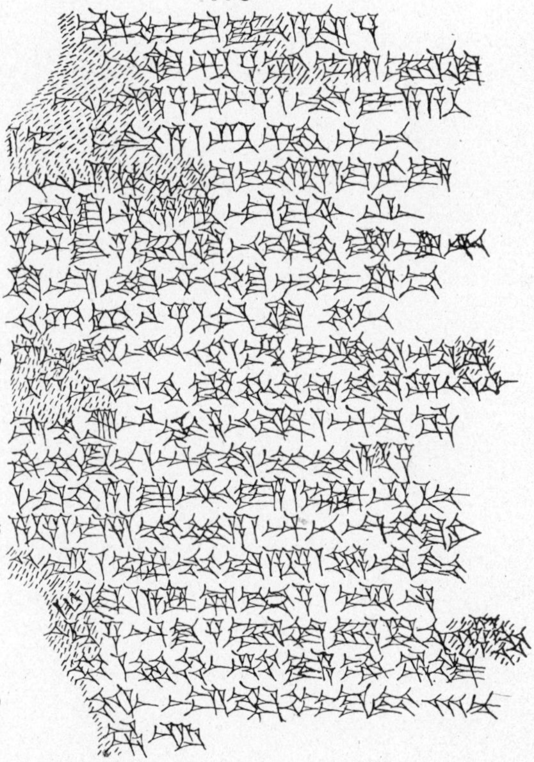

116

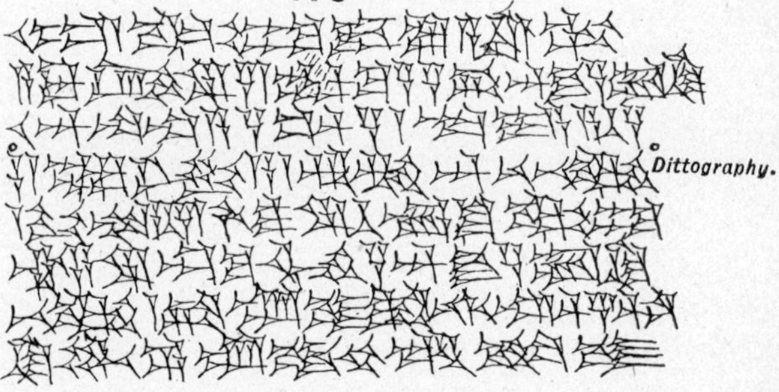

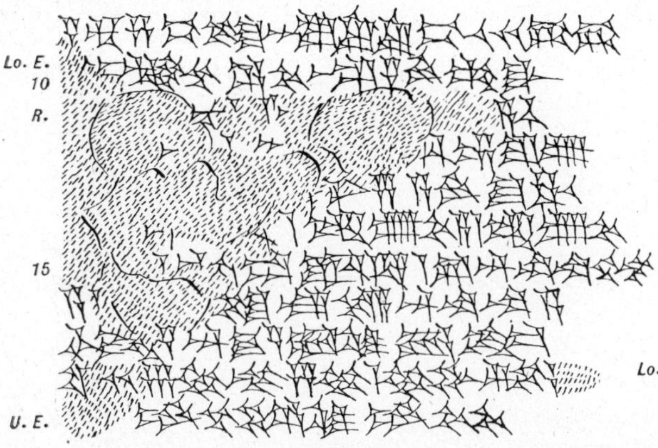

117

°Y omitted by scribe.

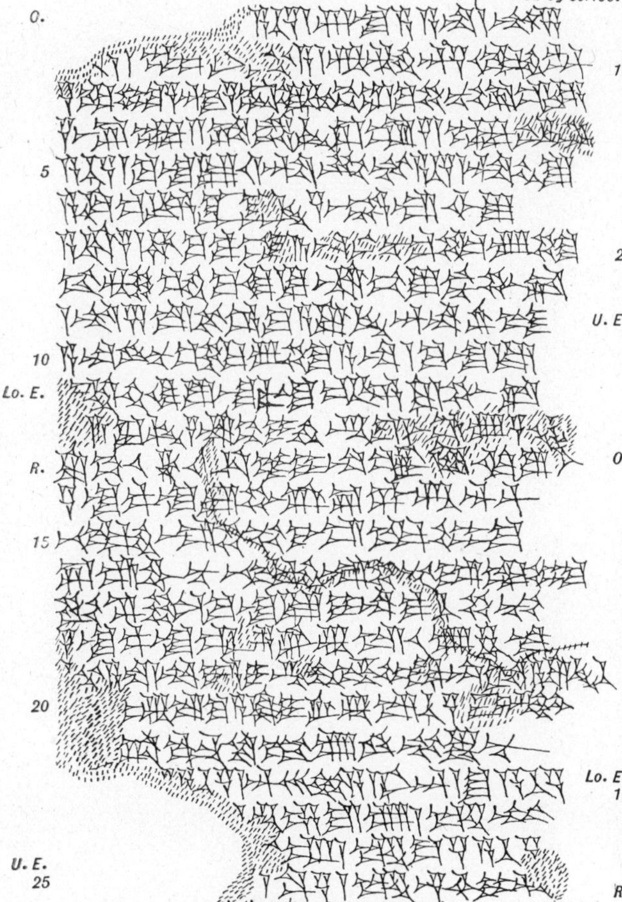

118

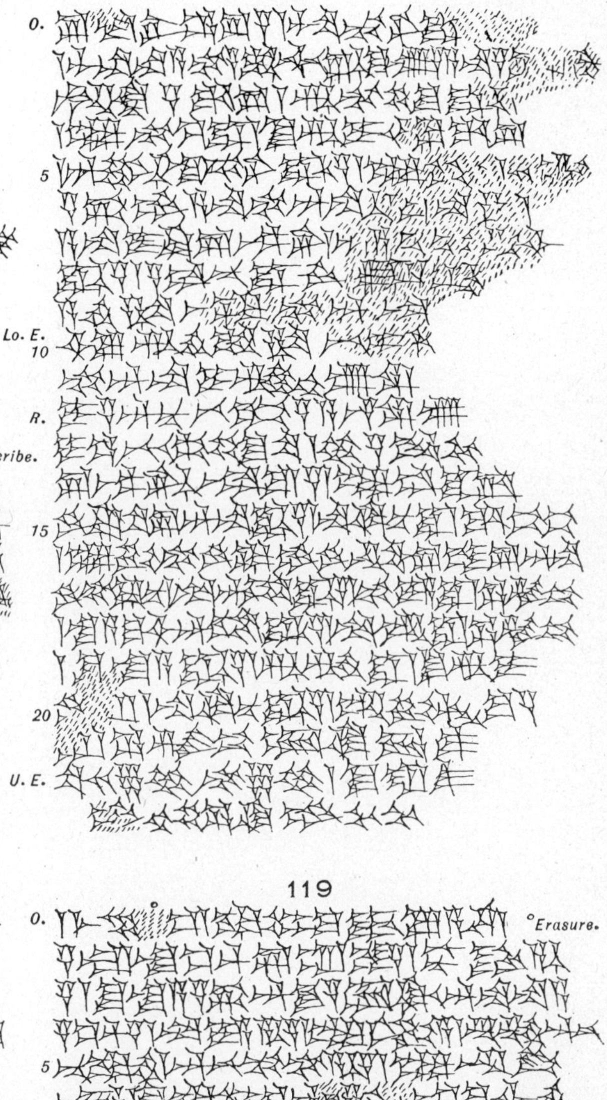

119

°Erasure.

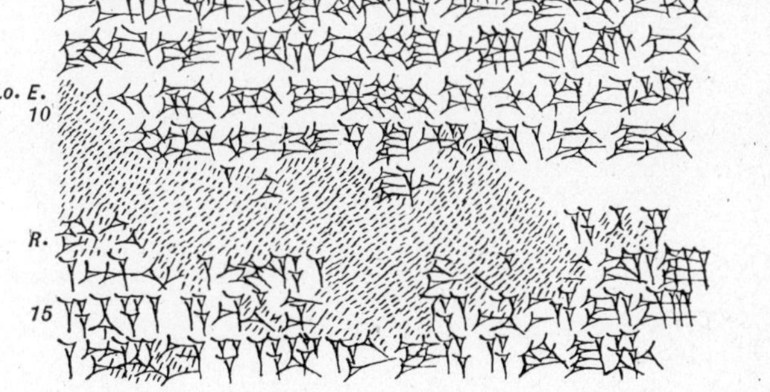

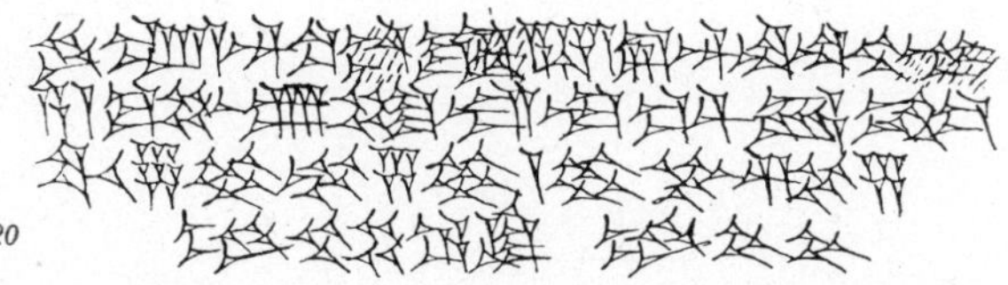

120

O. Lo. E. R.

121

O.

Lo. E. R.

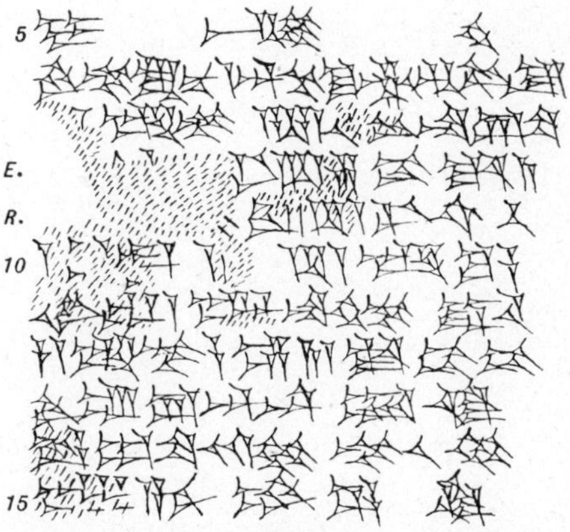

122

O. Lo. E. R. U. E.

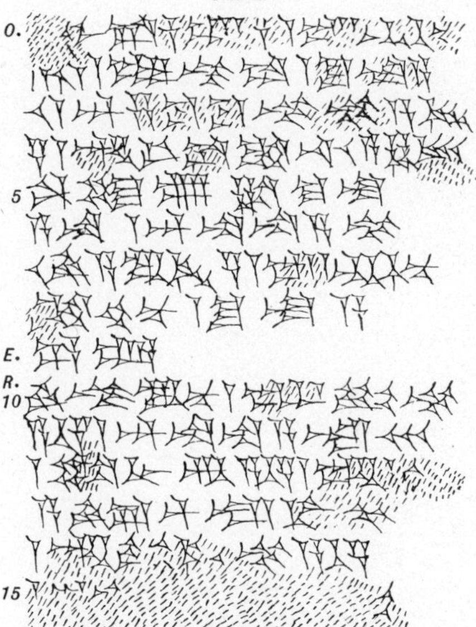

123

O. Lo. E.

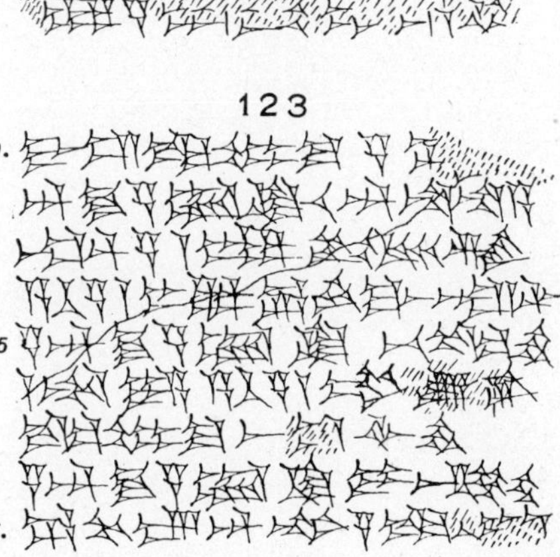

[illegible]

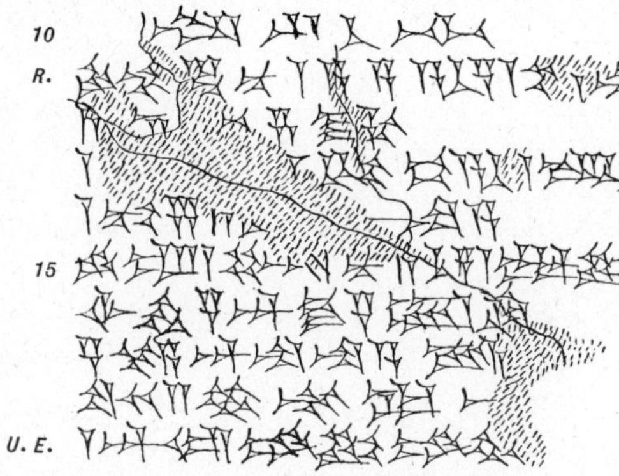
R.
U. E.

124

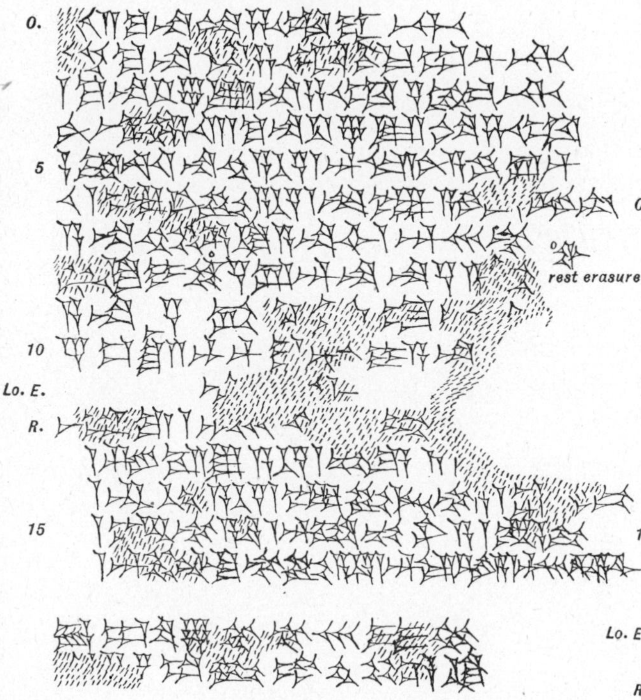
O.
Lo. E.
R.
rest erasure.

125

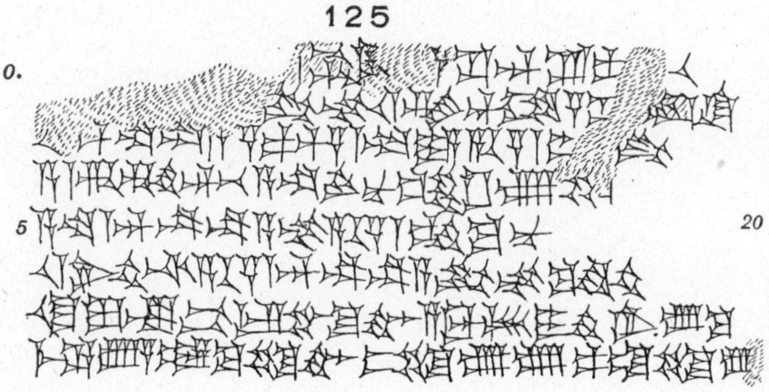
O.

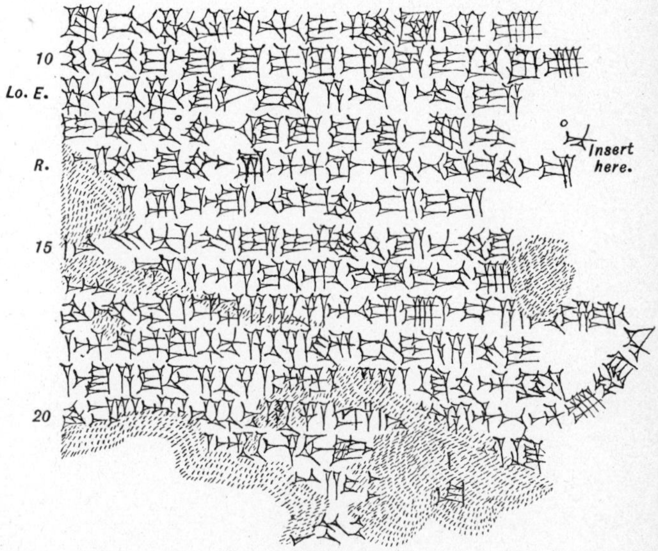
Lo. E.
R.
Insert here.

126

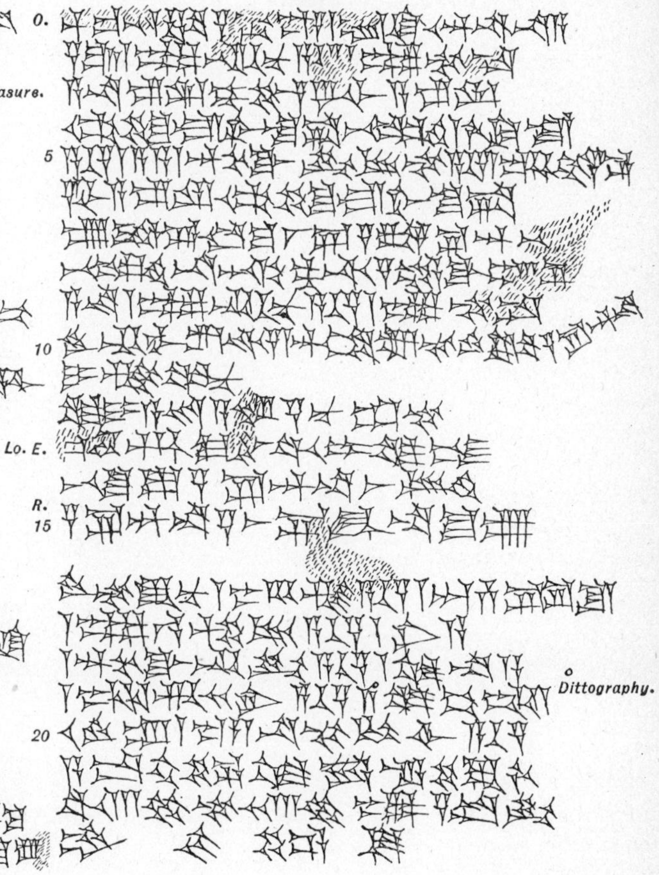
O.
Lo. E.
R.
Dittography.

127

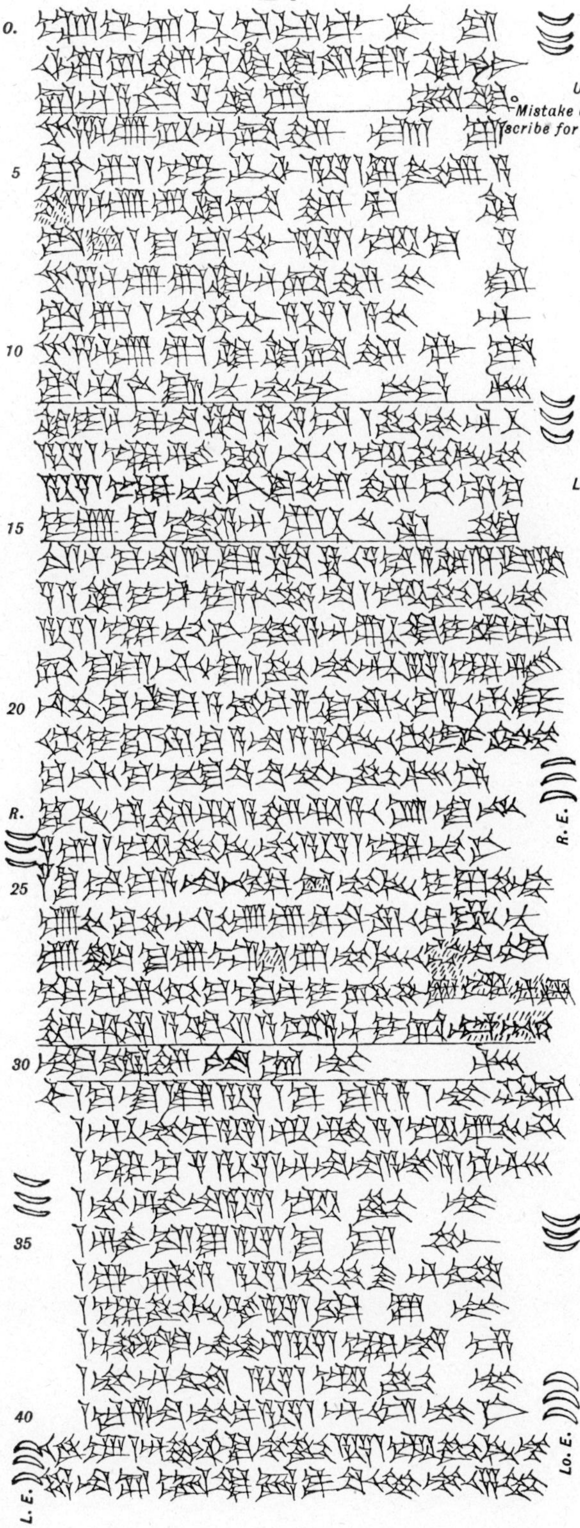
O.
Mistake of scribe for
R.
R. E.
Lo. E.
L. E.

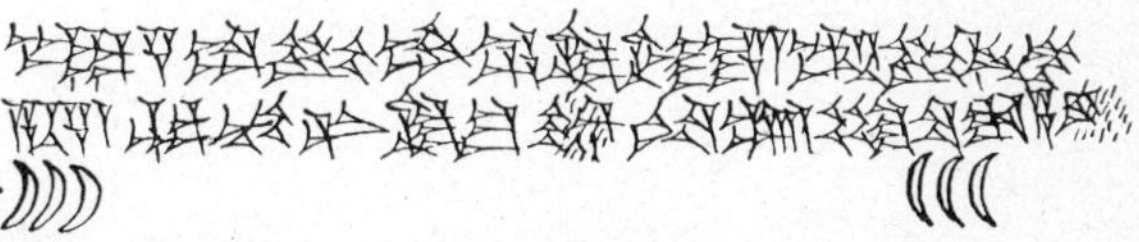
U. E.

128

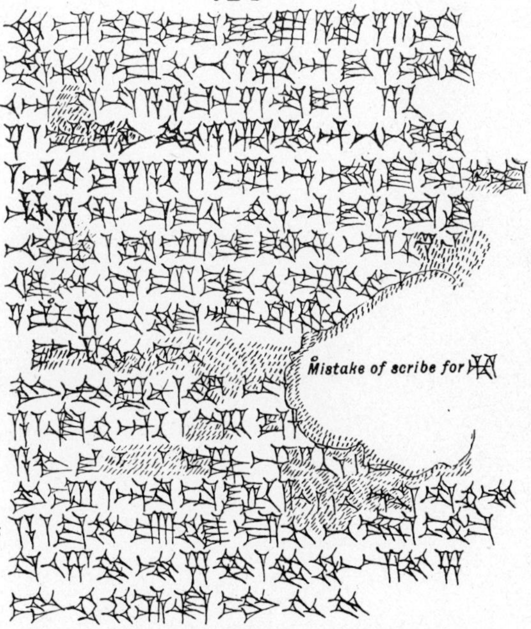
O.
Lo. E.
R.
Mistake of scribe for

129

O.
R.

130

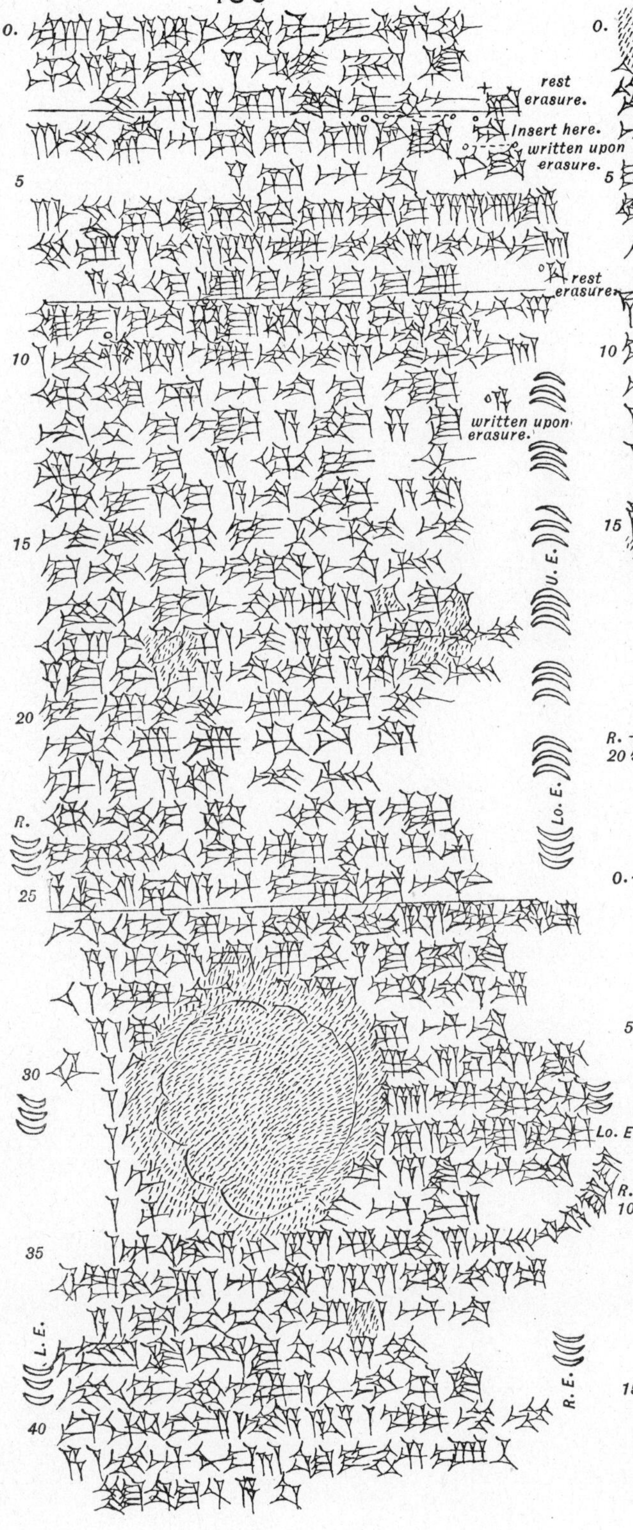
rest erasure.
Insert here.
written upon erasure.
rest erasure.
written upon erasure.
U. E.
Lo. E.
R.
L. E.
R. E.

131

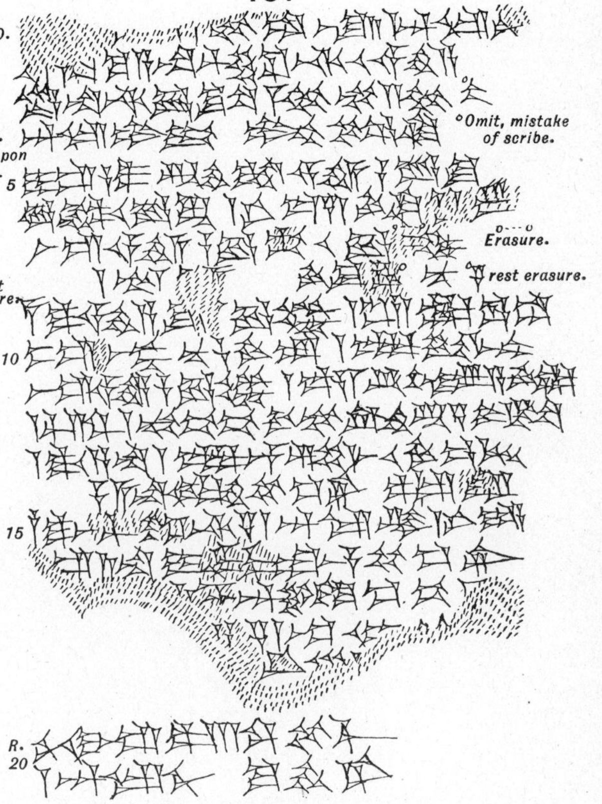
Omit, mistake of scribe.
Erasure.
rest erasure.
R.

132

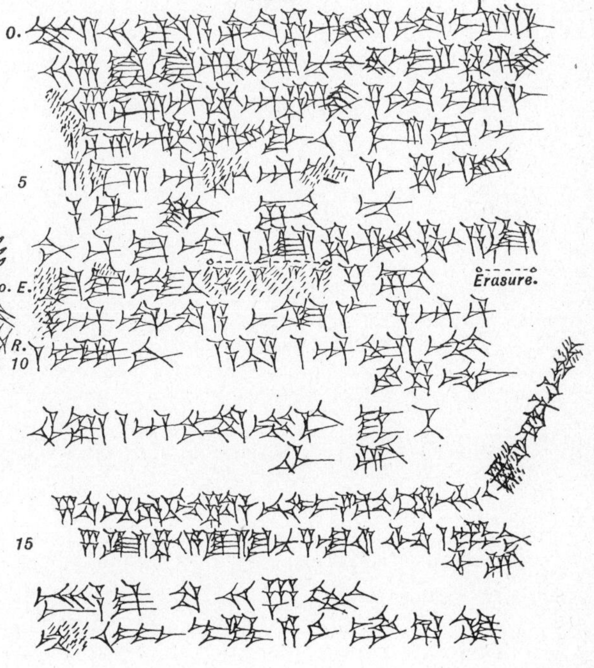
Erasure.
Lo. E.
R.

133

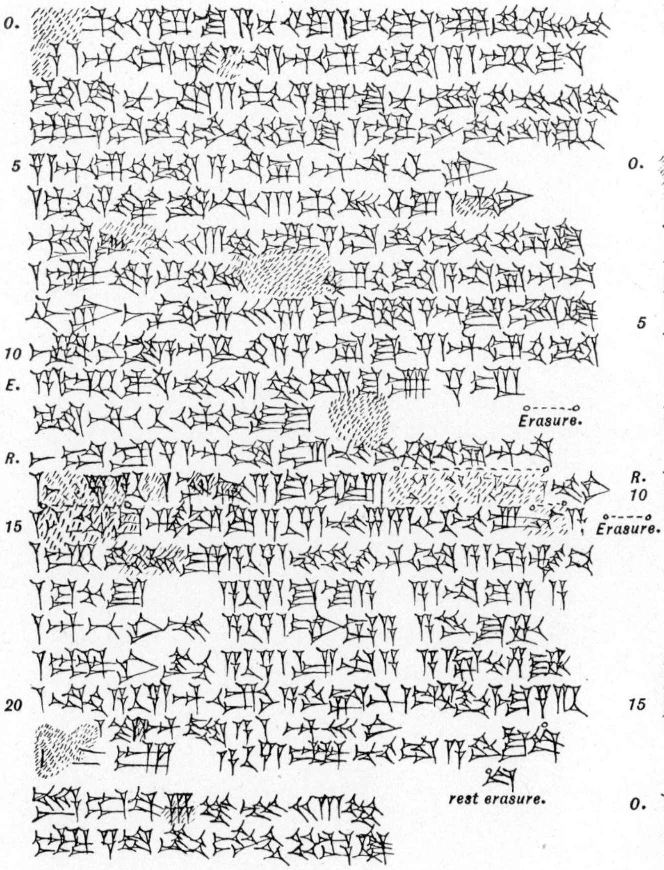

134

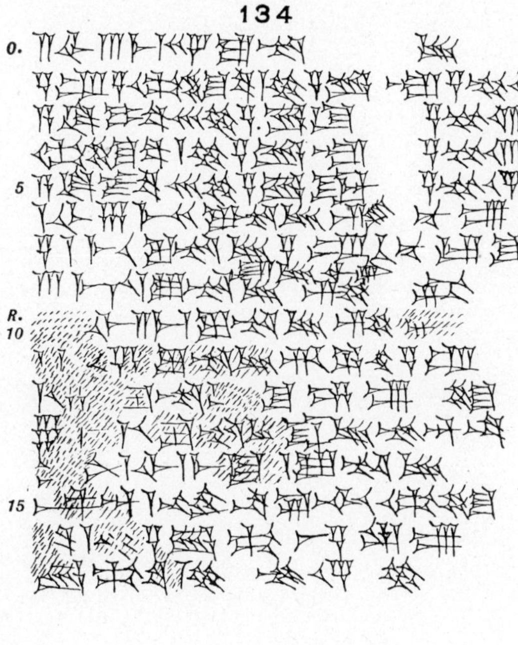

135

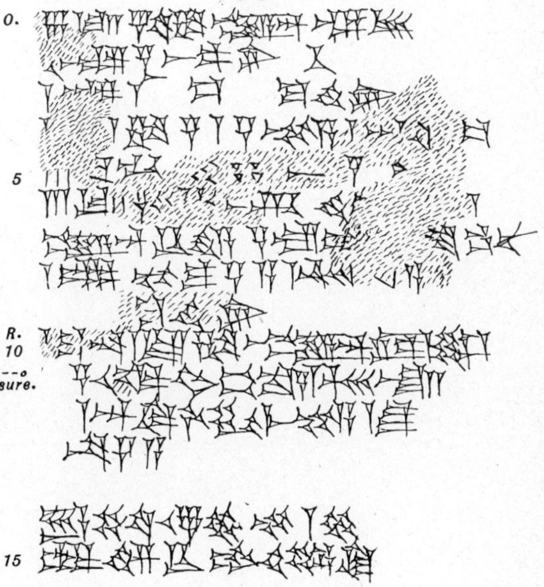

136

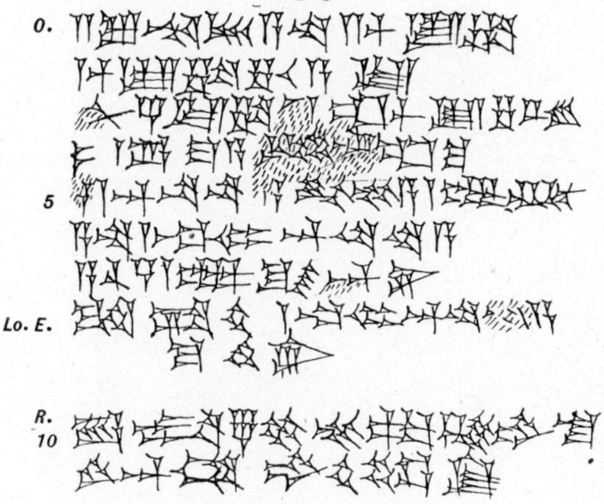

137

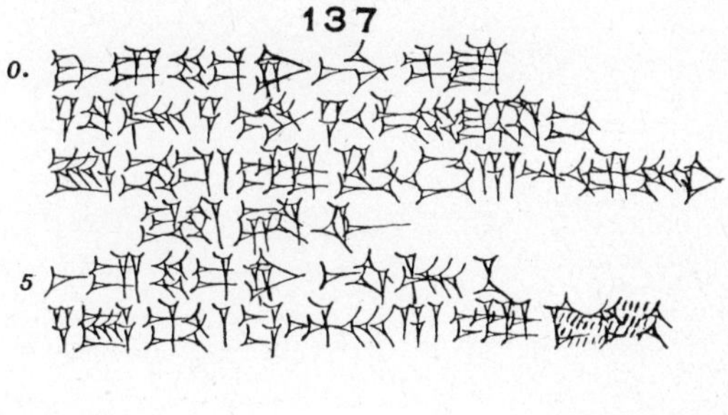

R.

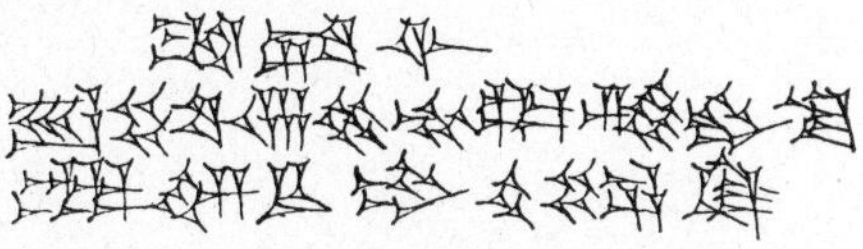

138

O. R.

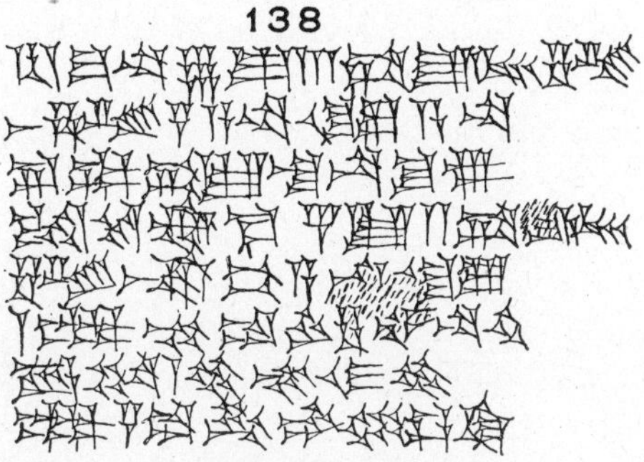

139

O. Lo. E. R.

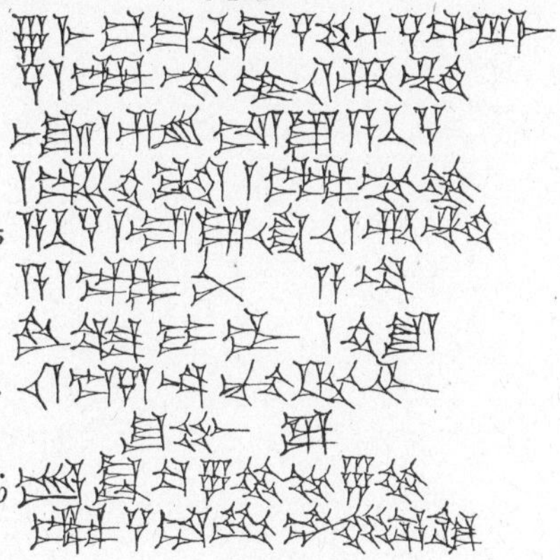

140

O. Lo. E. R.

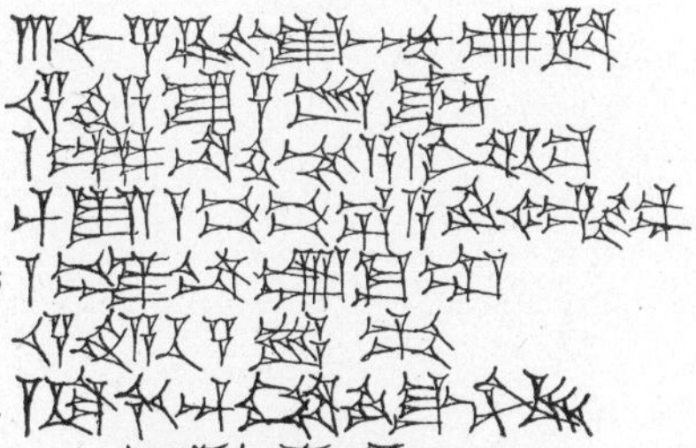

141

O. Lo. E. R. U. E. L. E.

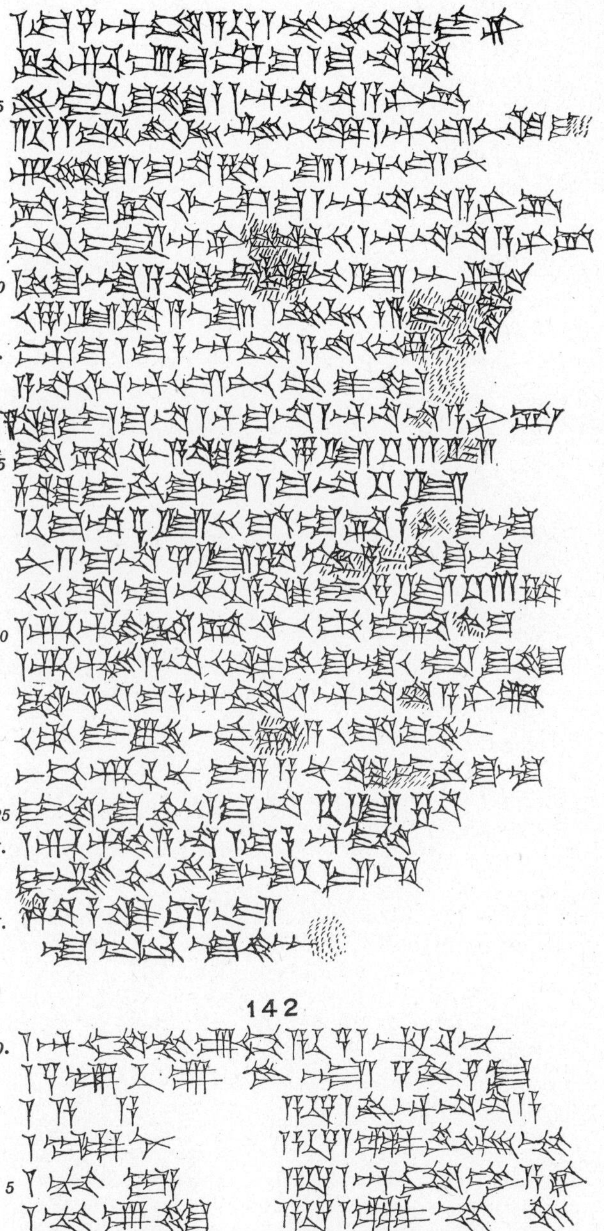

142

O. Lo. E. R.

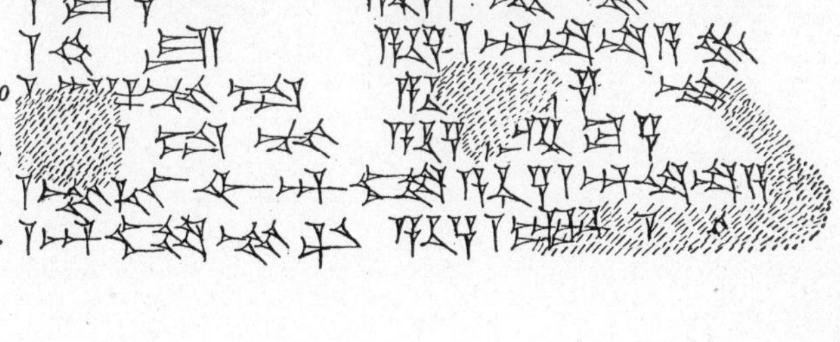

143

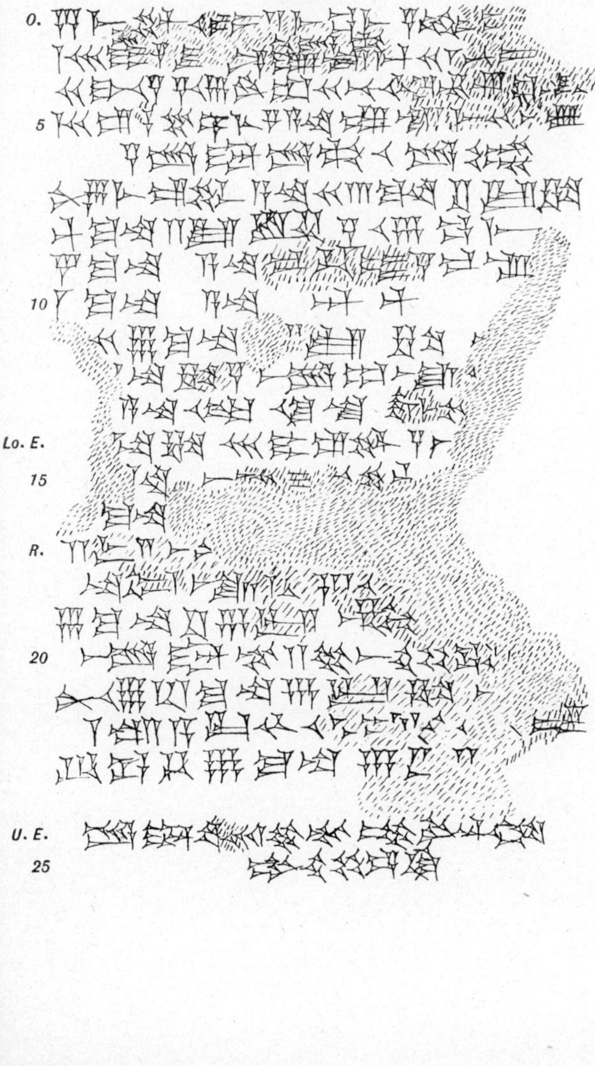

144

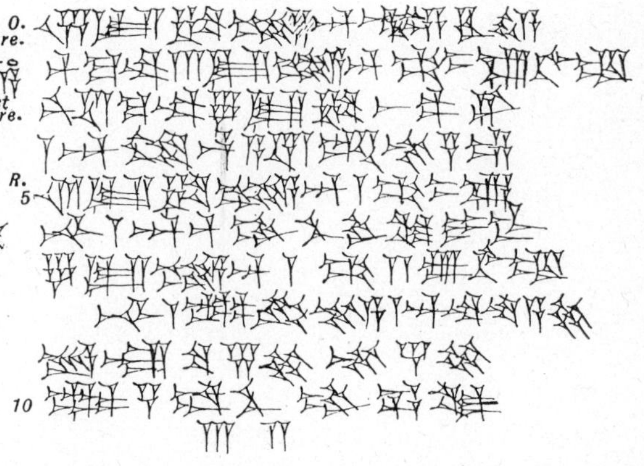

145

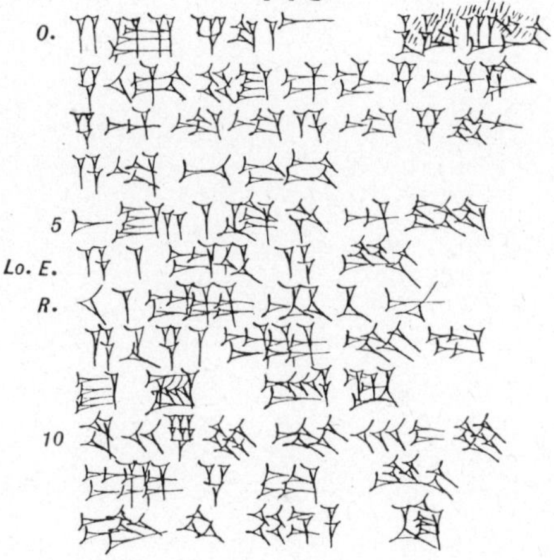

146

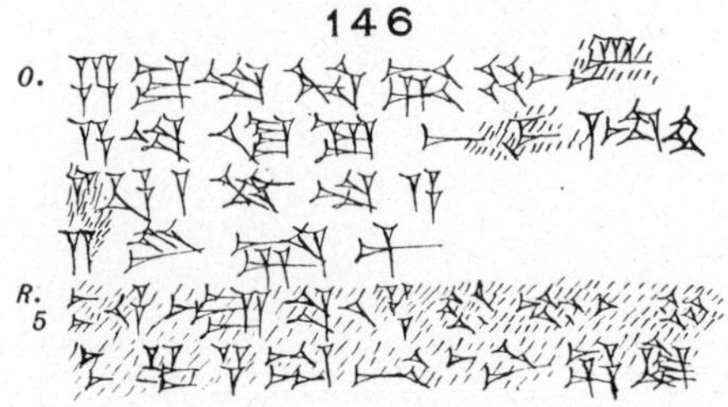

147

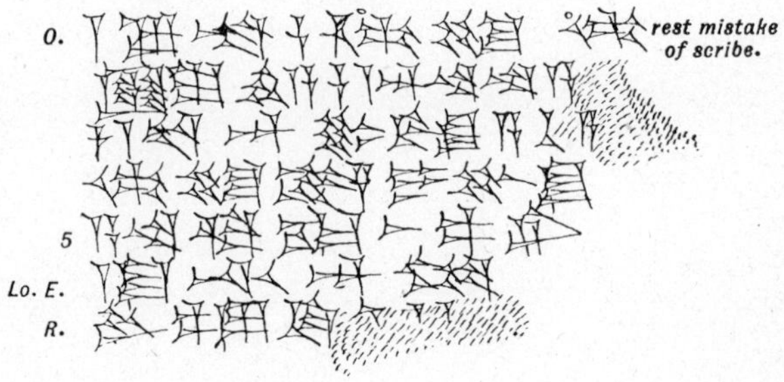

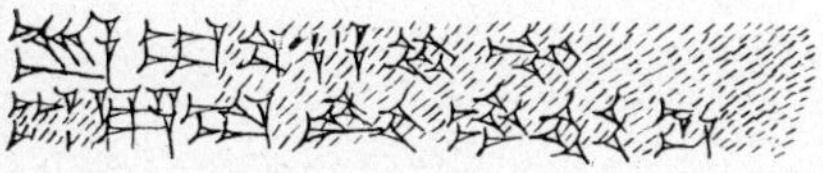

148

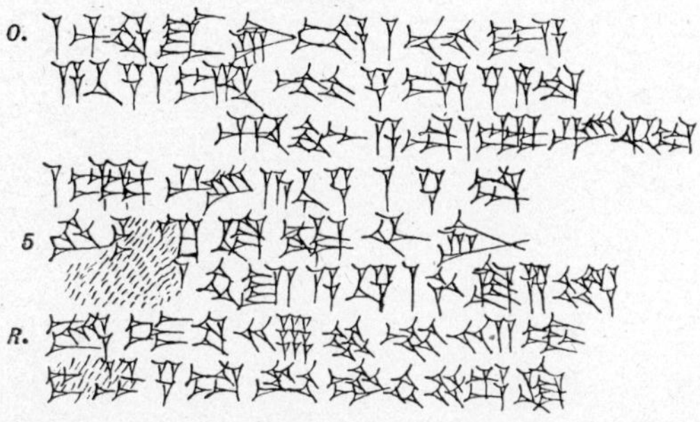

149

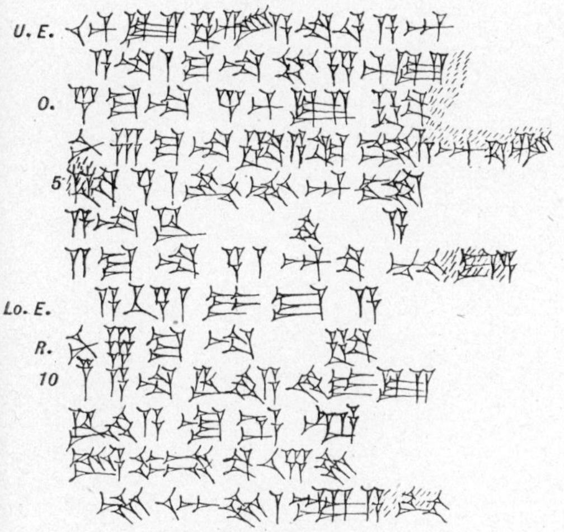

150

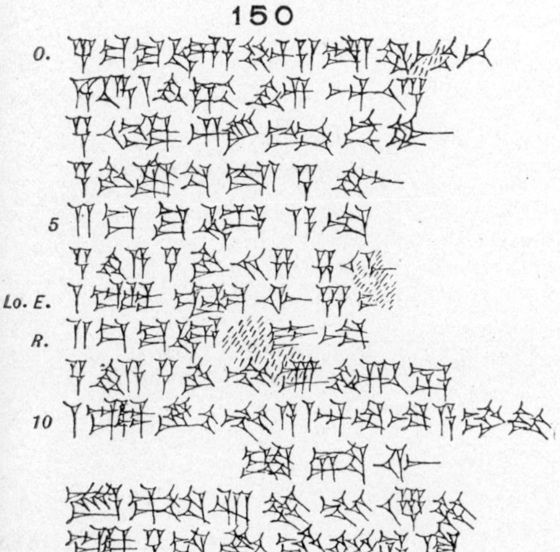

151

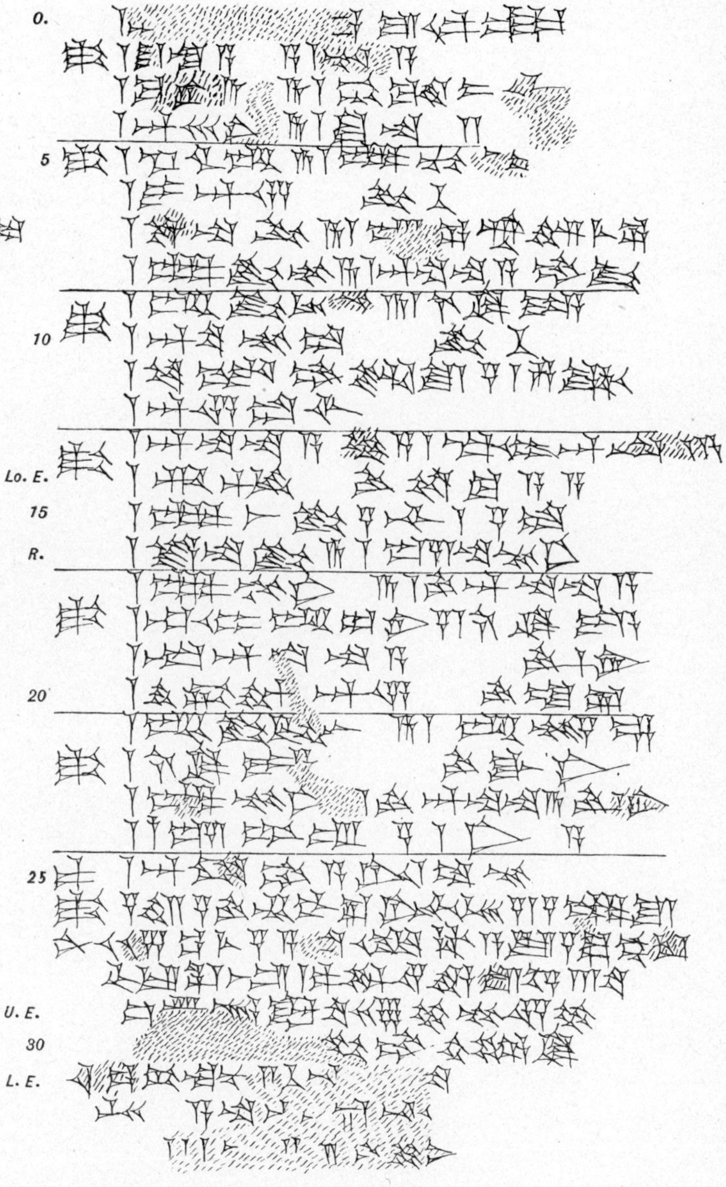

152

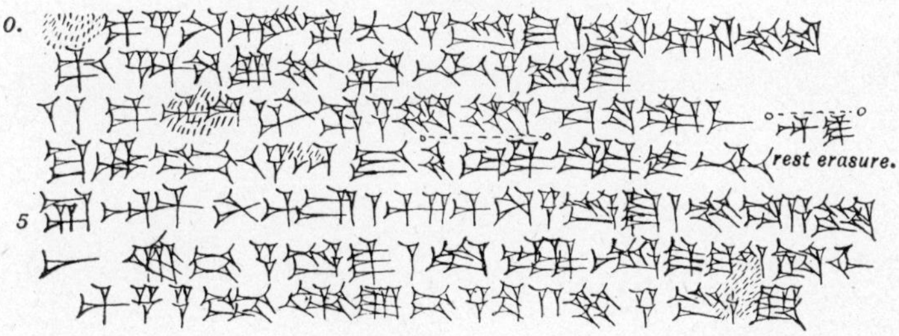

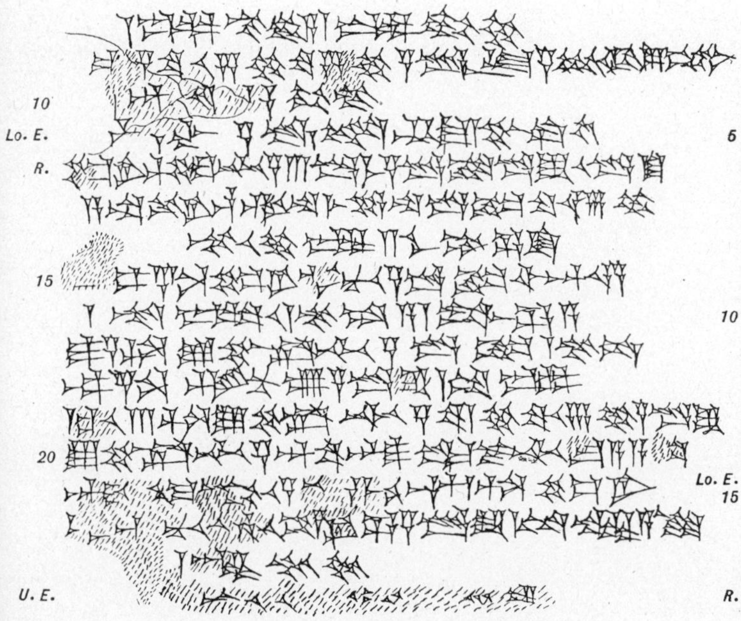

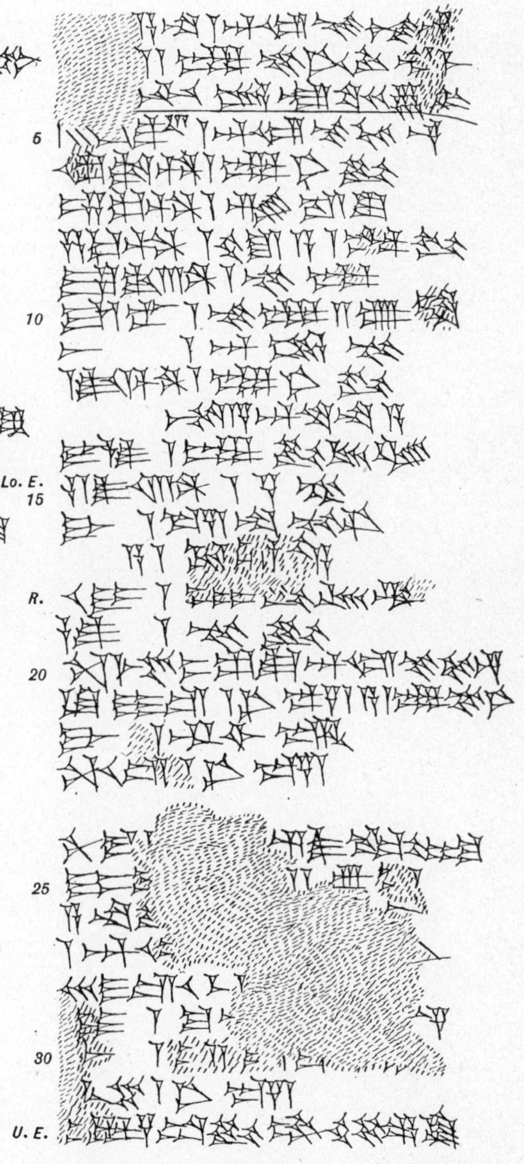

153

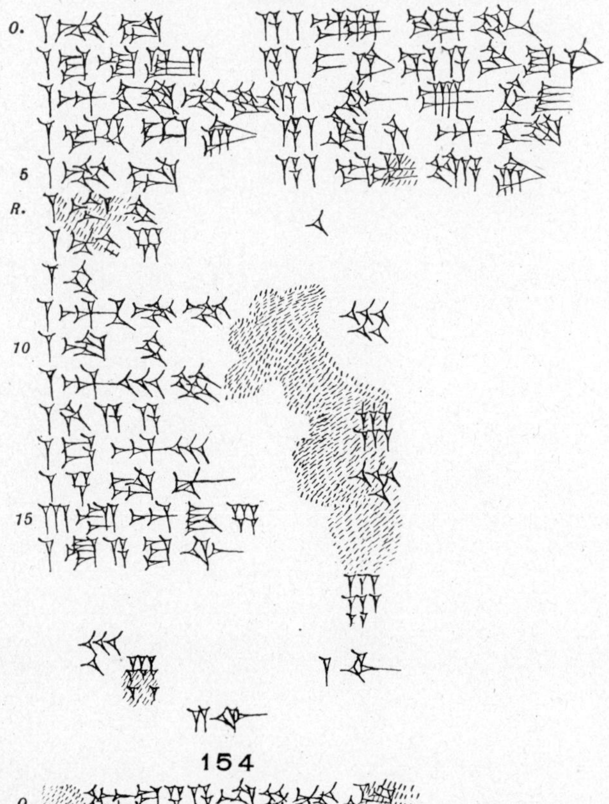

154

155

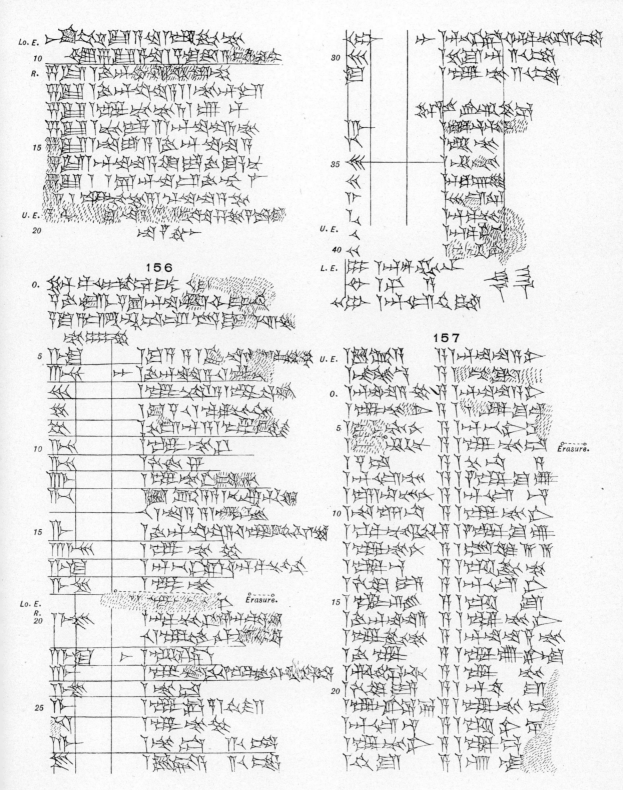

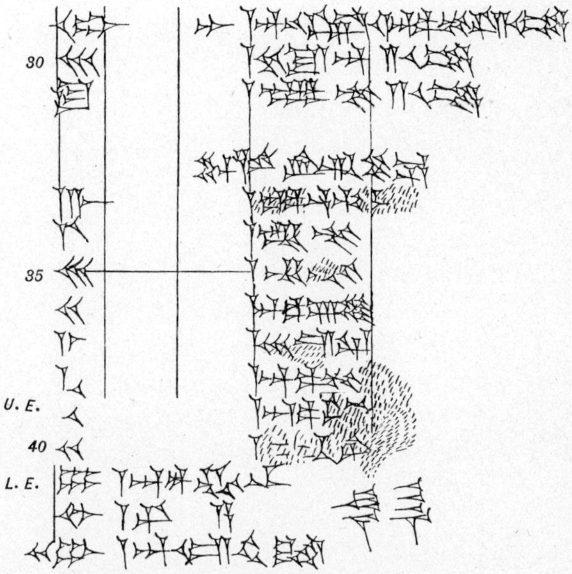

156

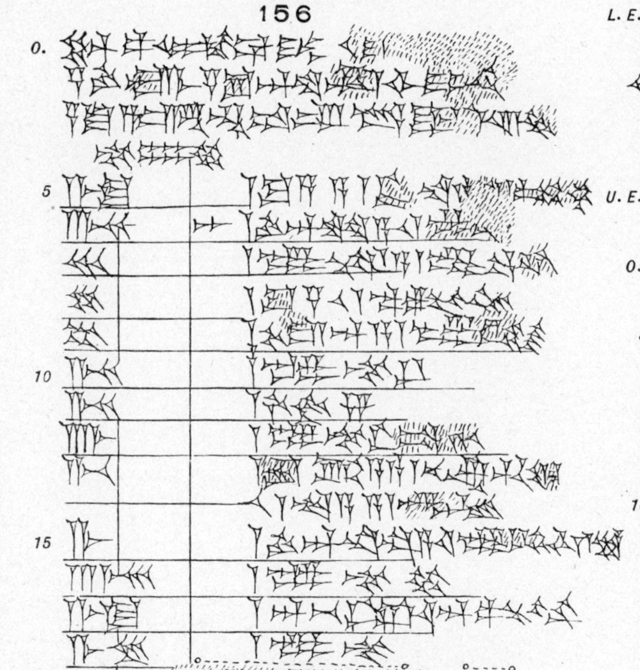

157

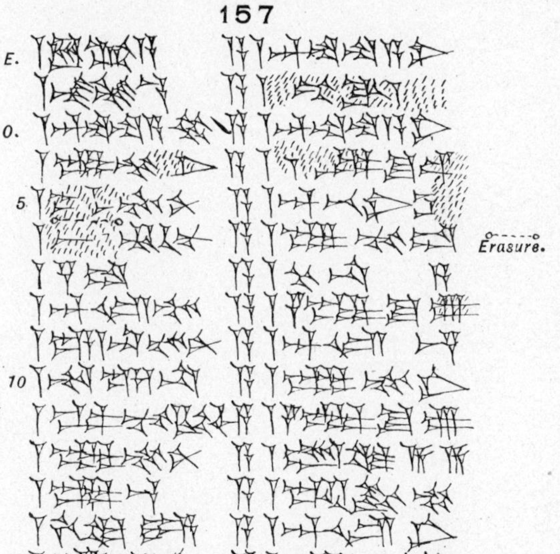

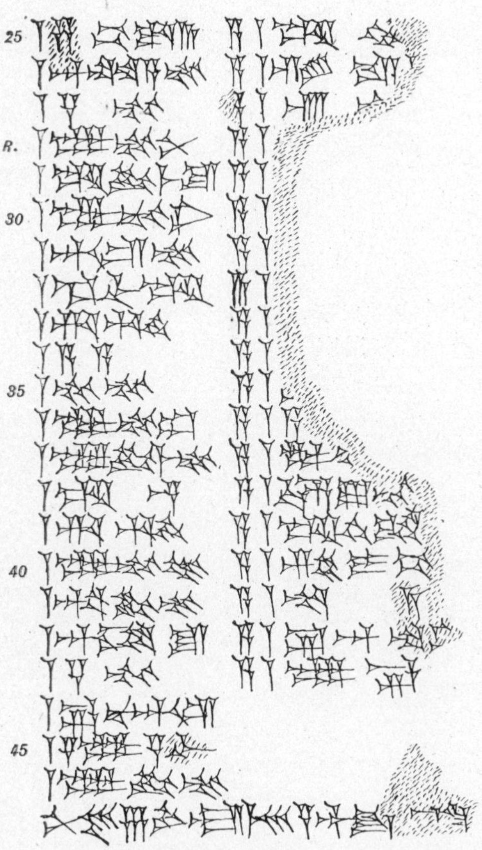

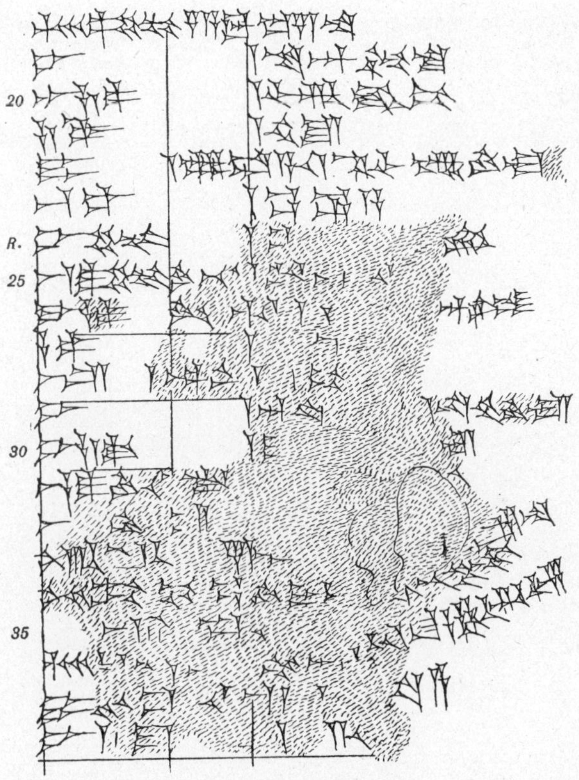

158

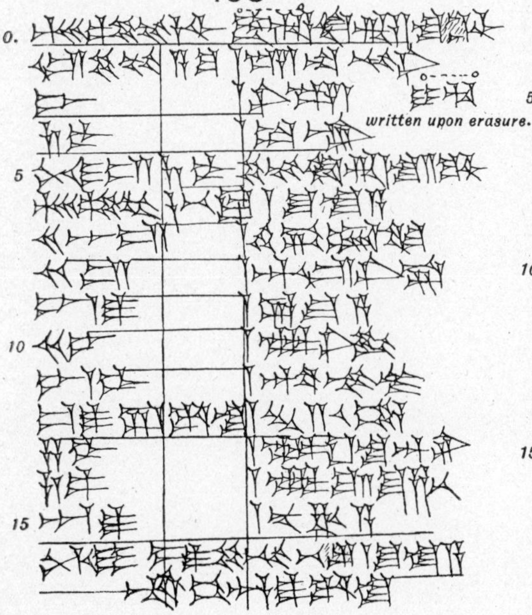

159

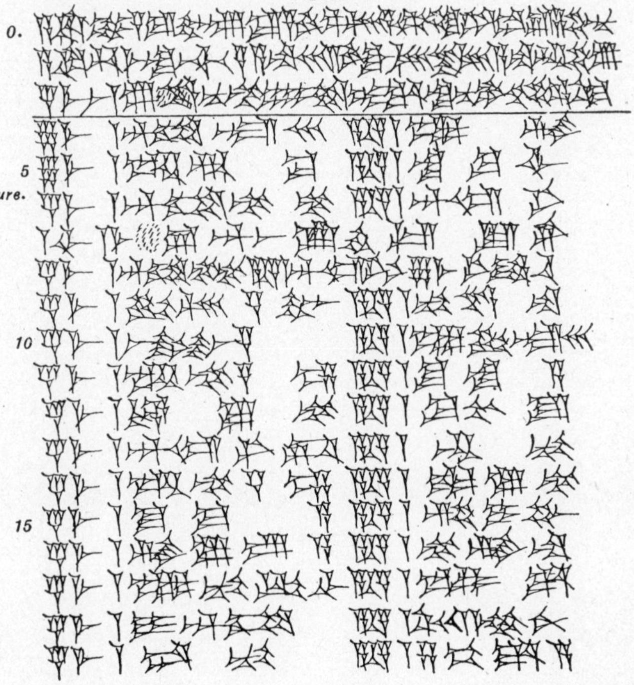

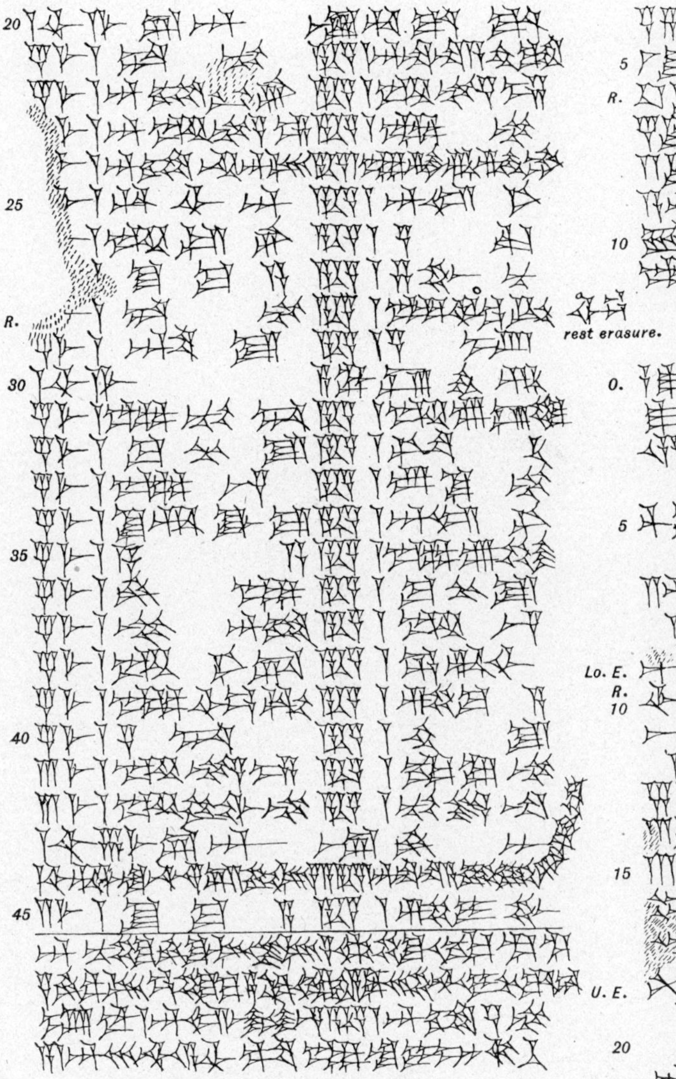

160

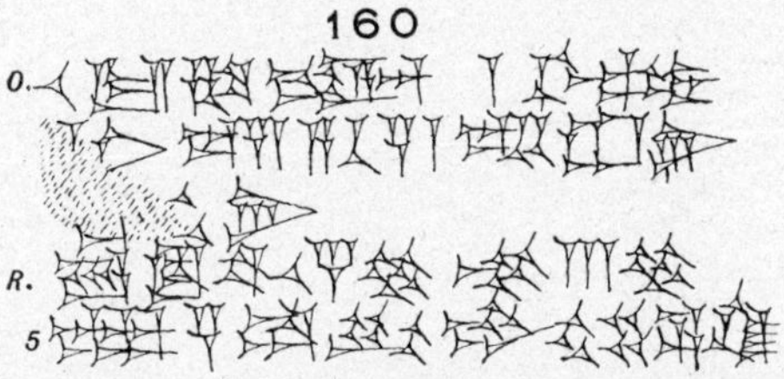

161

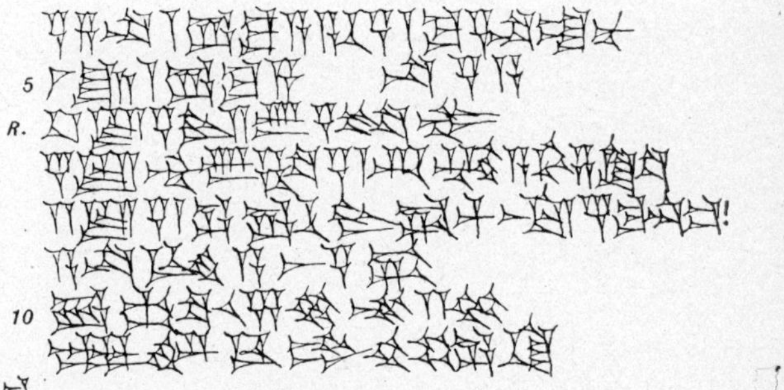

162

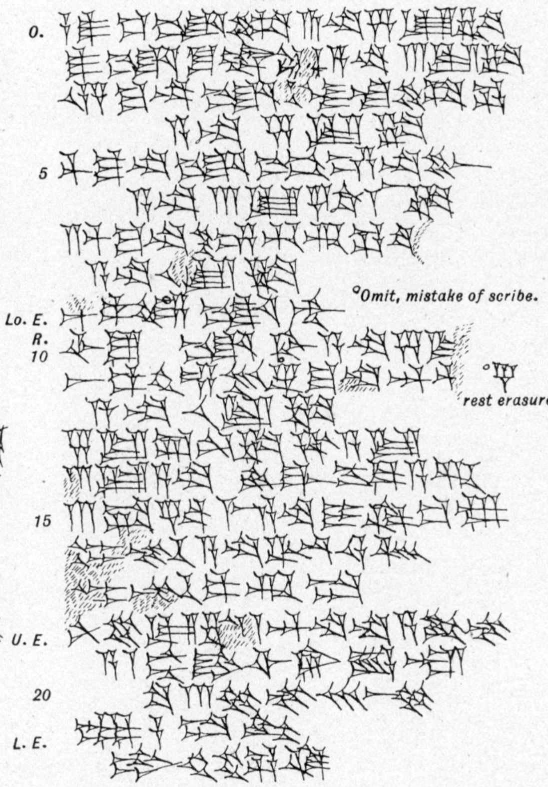

163

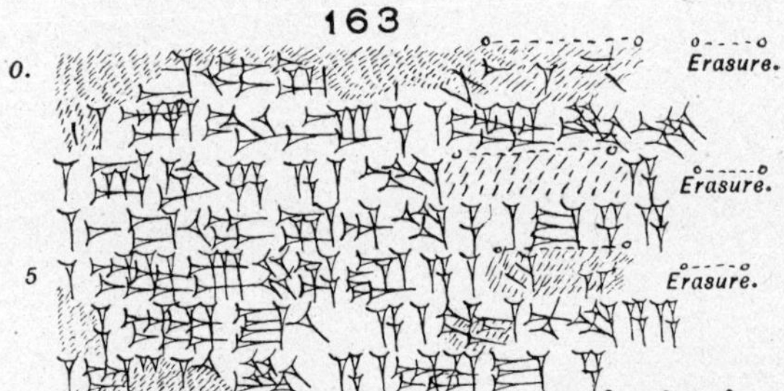

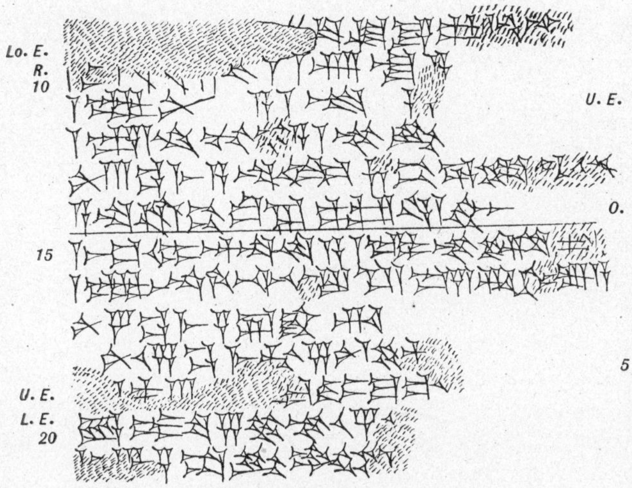

164

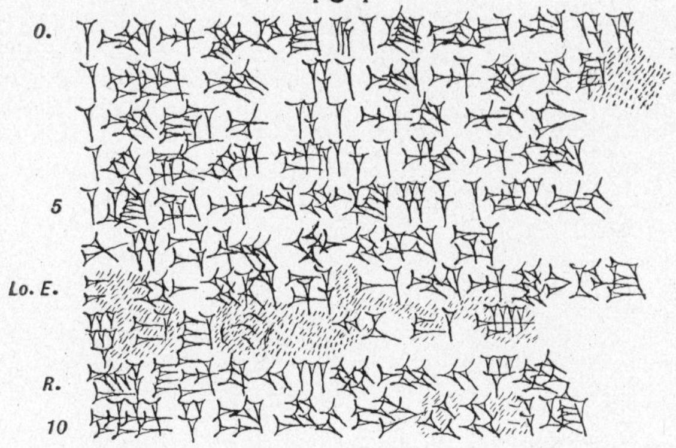

165

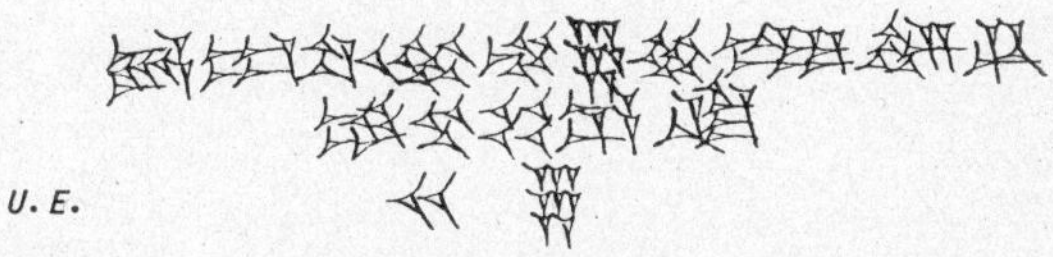

166

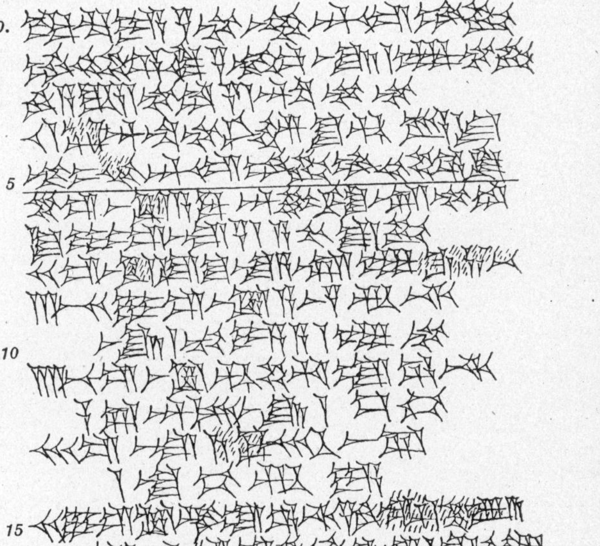

167

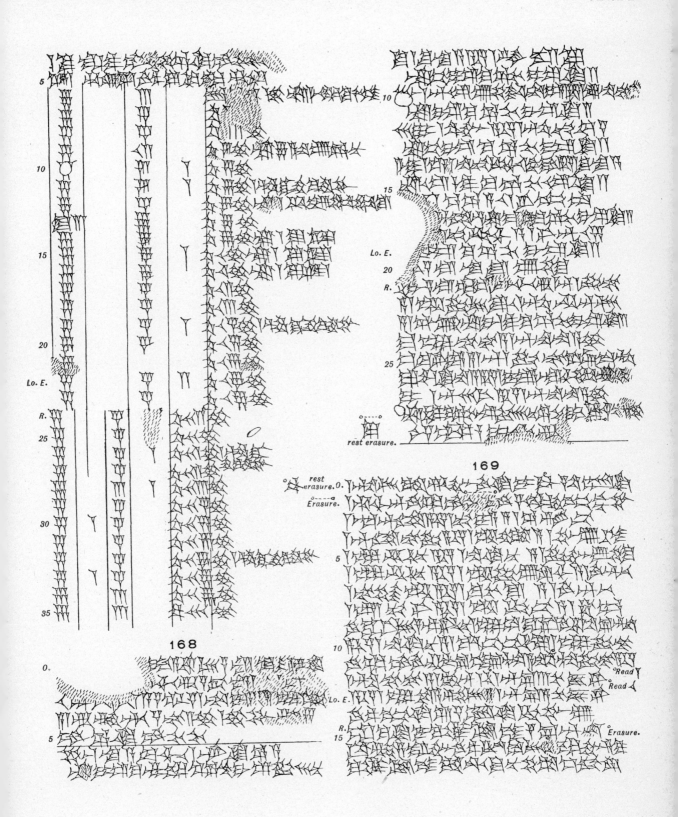

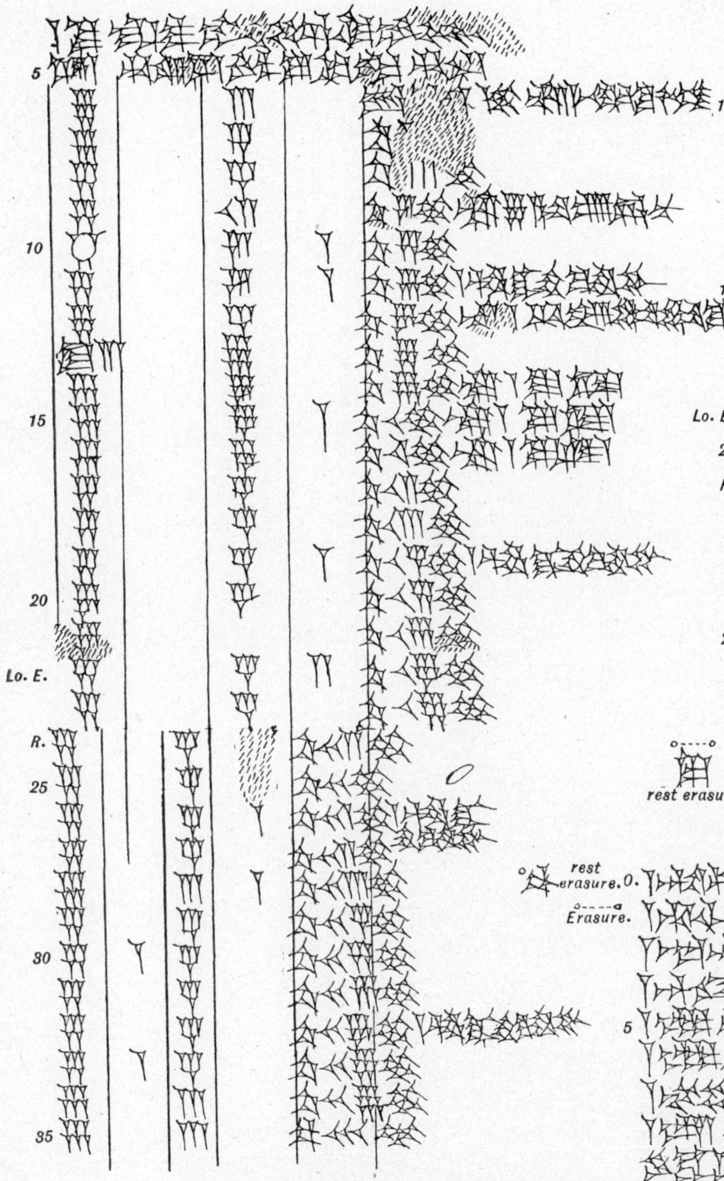
Lo. E.
R.

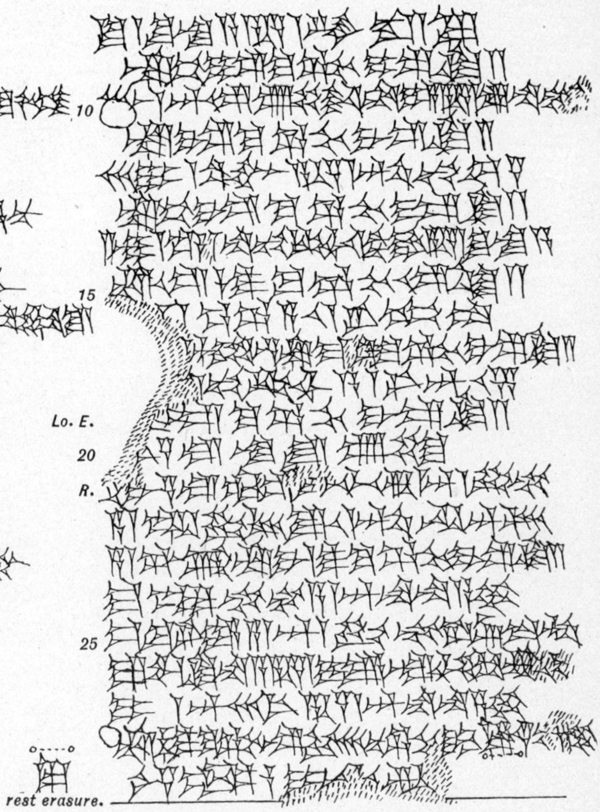
Lo. E.
R.
rest erasure.

168

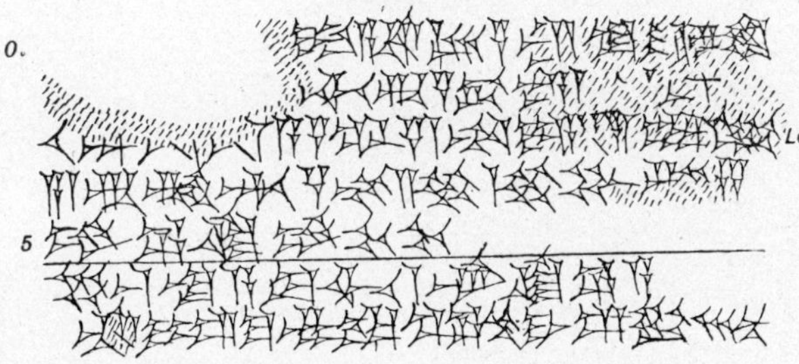
O.

169

rest erasure.
O.
Erasure.
Read
Read
Lo. E.
R.
Erasure.

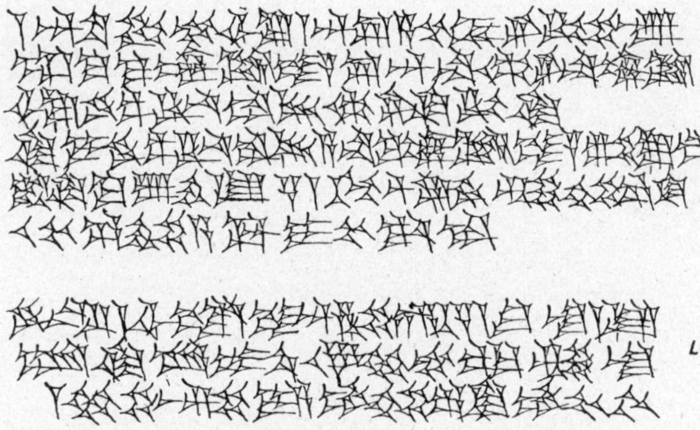

170

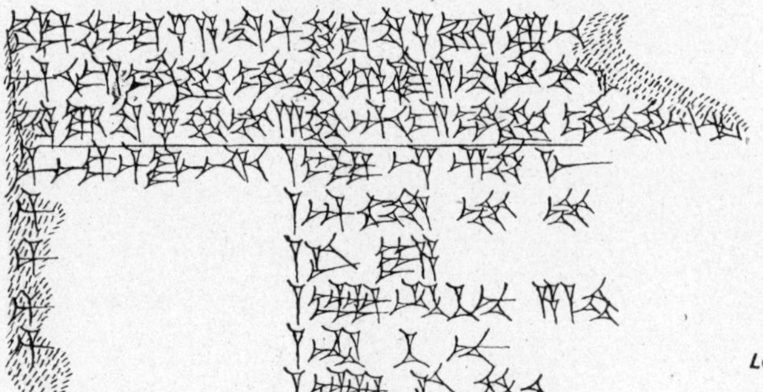

171

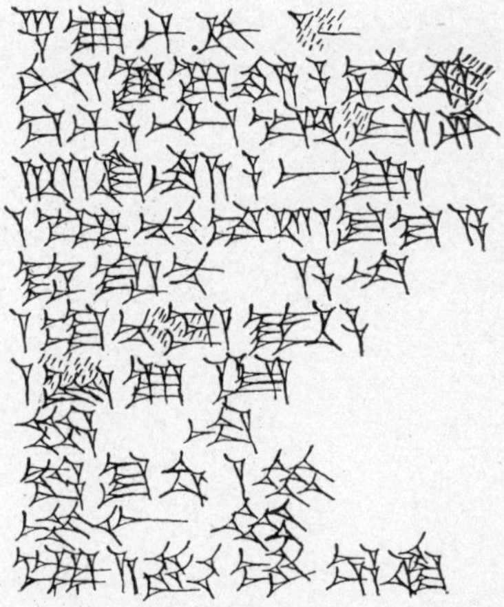

172

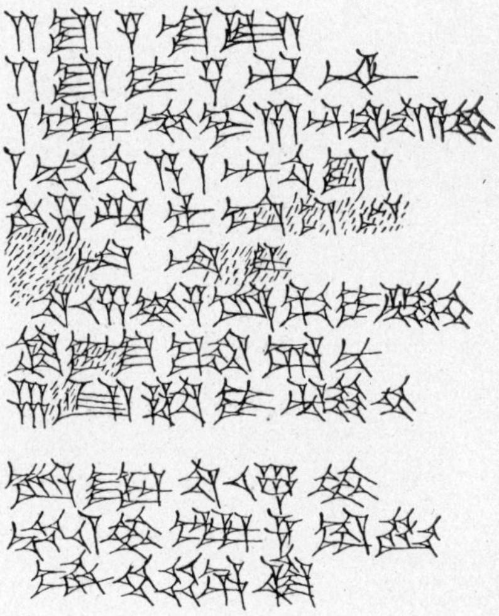

173

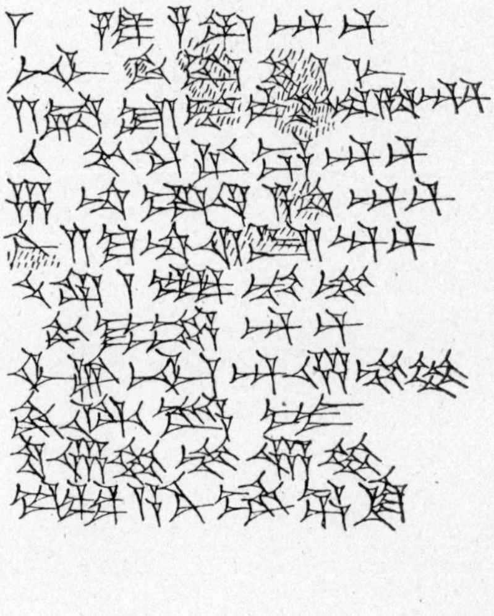

174

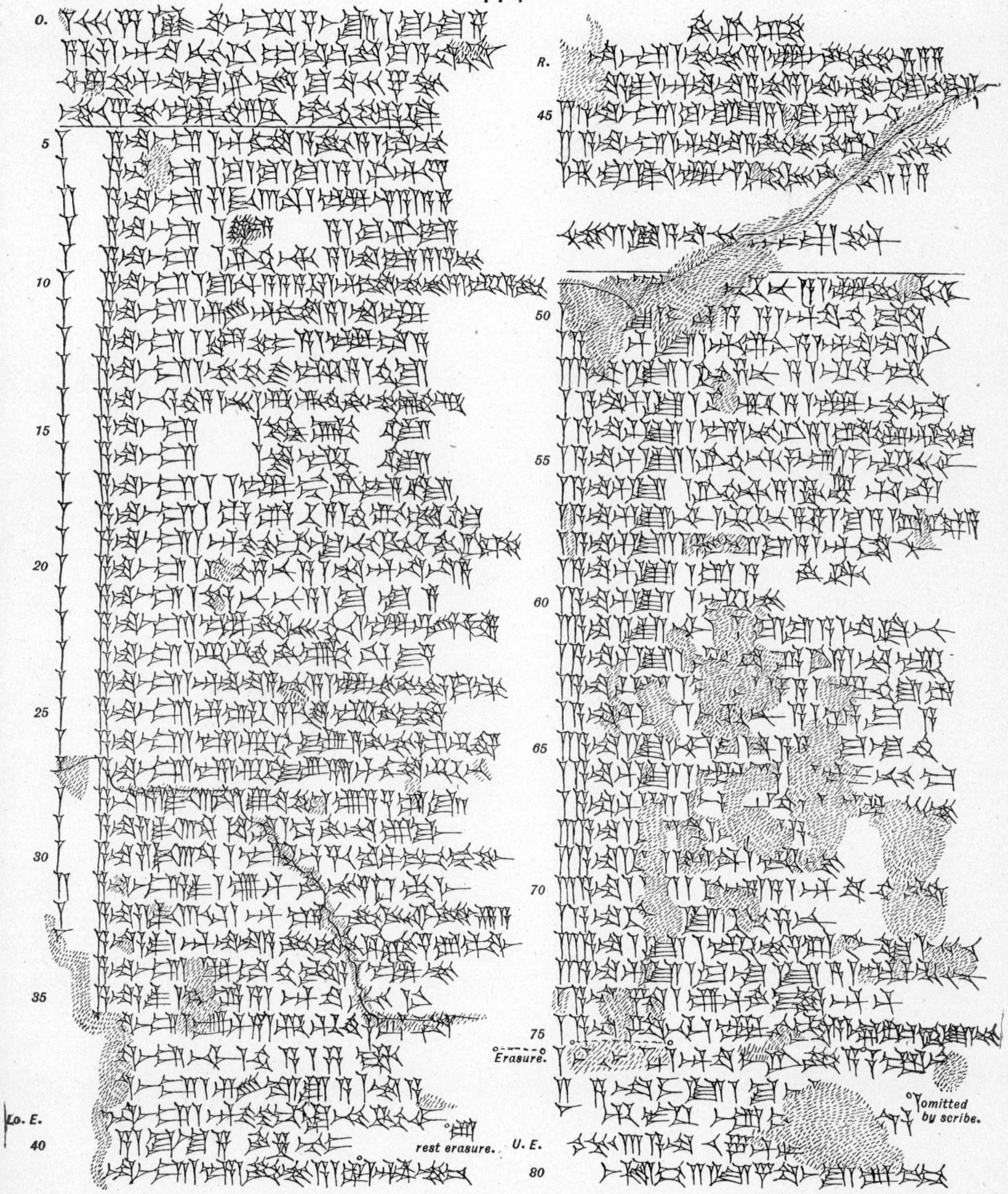

175

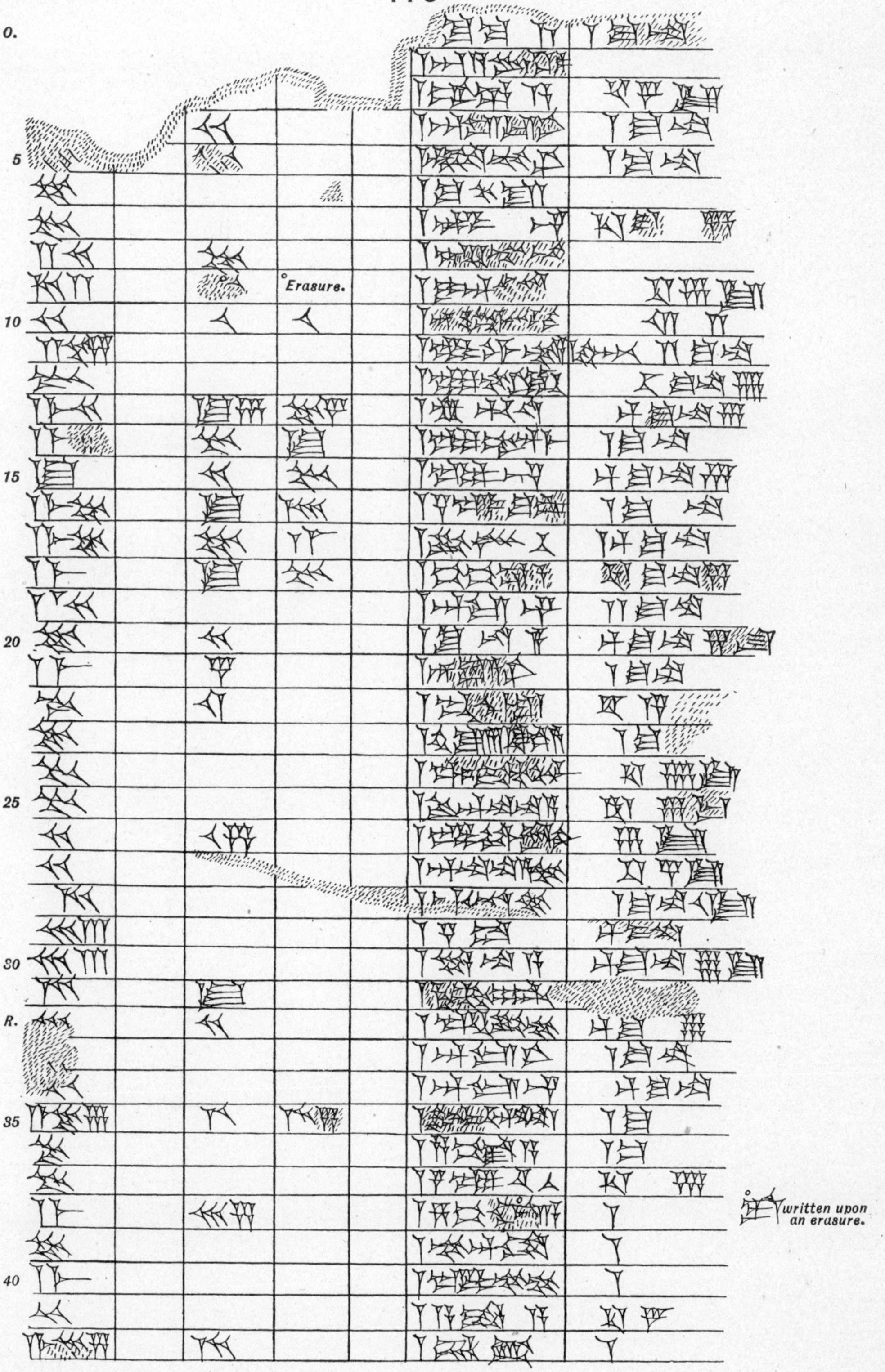

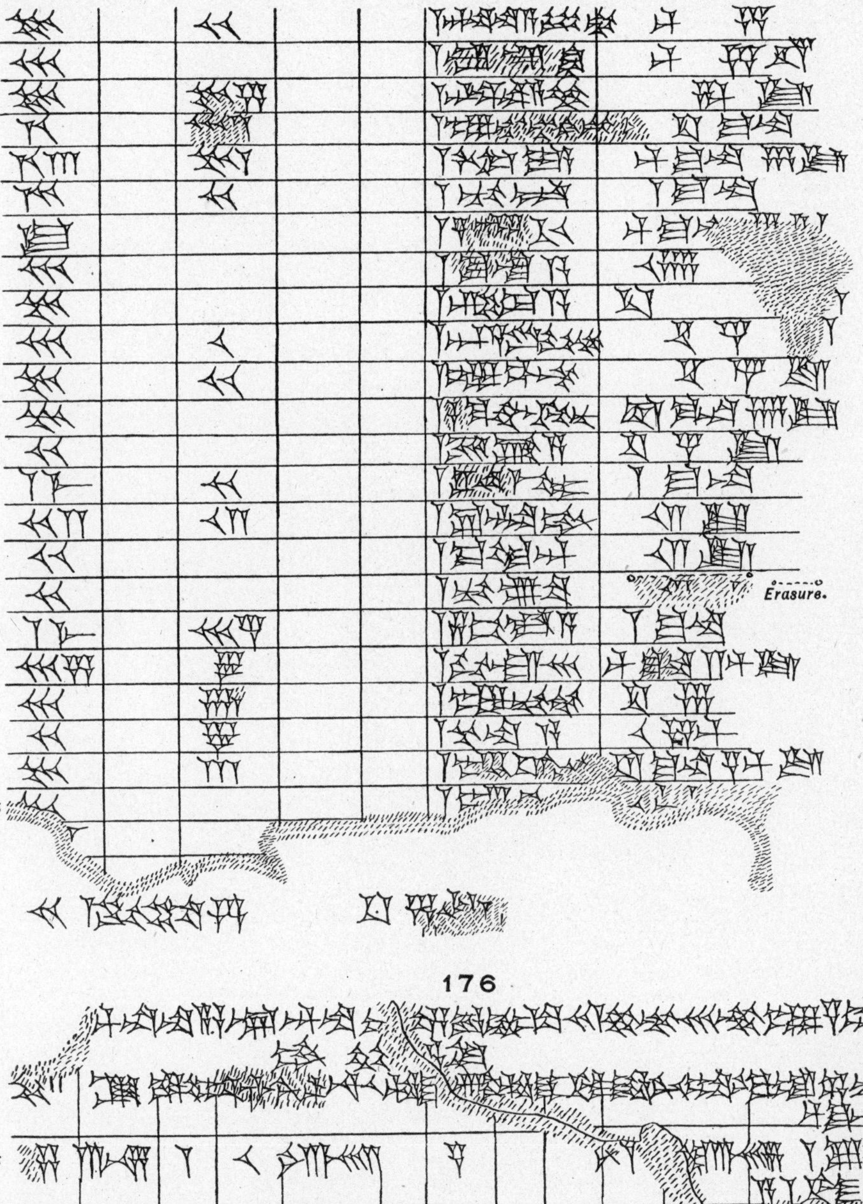

176

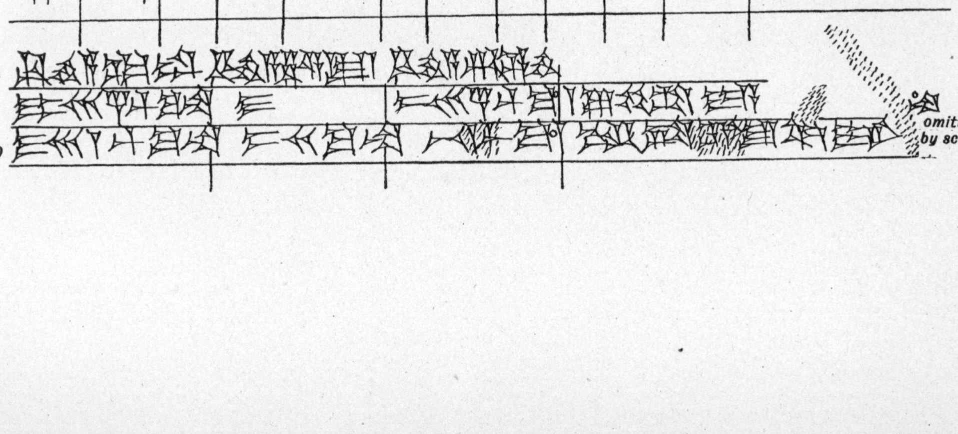

177

O.

Lo. E.

R.

U. E.

L. E.

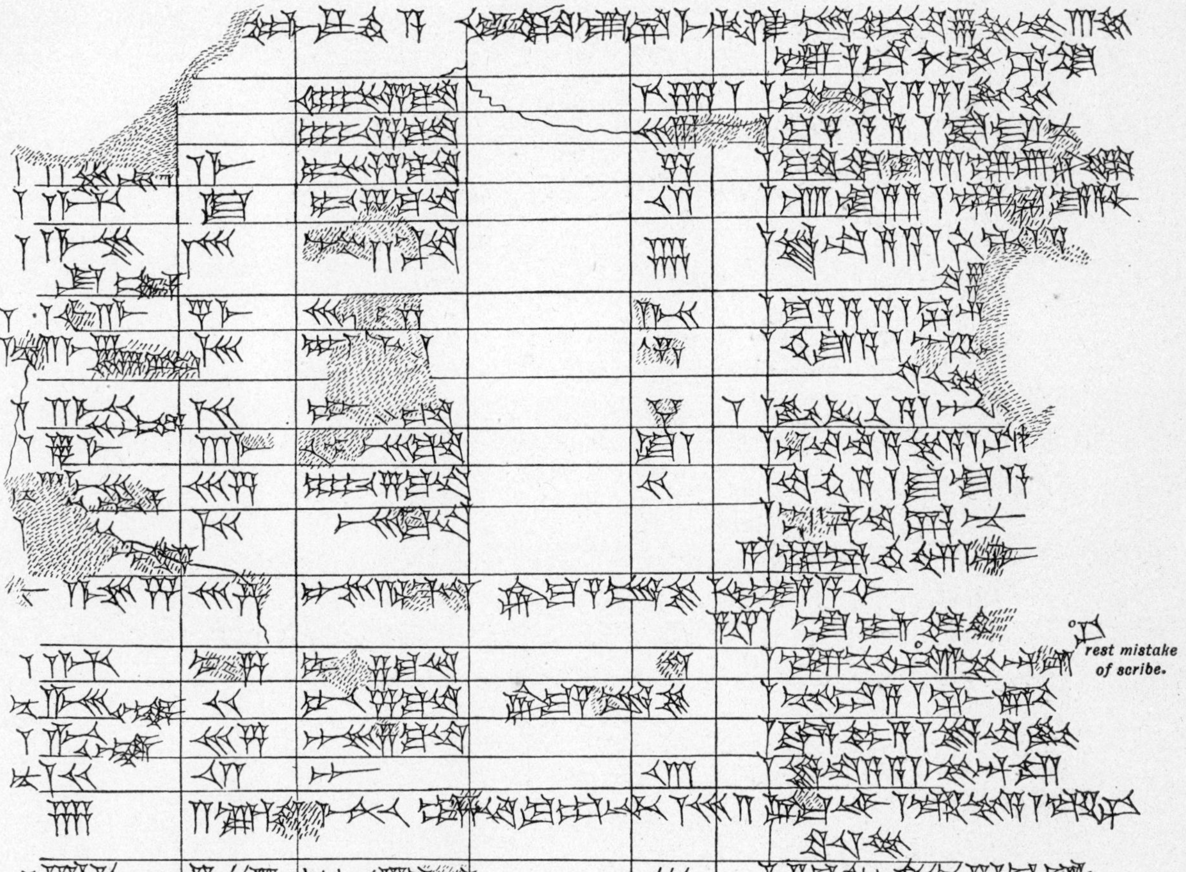